European Social Movements and the Transnationalization of Public Spheres

Many contemporary social movements observe, copy, learn from, coordinate and cooperate with other movements abroad, and some mobilise to influence processes of global governance. Can these transnational dimensions of mobilization transform the territorial scale of political debate on issues of common concern in public spheres? In contrast to many existing studies, which focus on the media as carriers of public sphere transnationalization, this book presents a theoretical and empirical exploration of the role of social movements in such processes. As 'arenas' or subaltern counterpublics in themselves, social movements may provide a setting in which activists come to frame claims in a comparative manner, interact with activists from other countries, frame problems as matters of transnational concerns or consider themselves members of transnational communities. As 'actors' social movements may contribute to the transnational transformation of public spheres by directing claims to political authorities beyond the state, claiming to represent transnational constituencies, and focus on similar issues and use similar frames of reference as movements abroad. The book's case studies addressing efforts to build transnational social movements and transnational dimensions of anti-austerity and prodemocracy movements in Spain, Portugal, Greece, Turkey and Ireland provide contemporary empirical illustrations of such processes at work.

The chapters in this book were originally published in a special issue of the *Journal of Civil Society*.

Angela Bourne is Associate Professor at the Department of Social Science and Business, Roskilde University, Roskilde, Denmark.

European Social Movements and the Transnationalization of Public Spheres

Anti-austerity and Pro-democracy Mobilisation from the National to the Global

Edited by
Angela Bourne

LONDON AND NEW YORK

First published 2018
by Routledge
2 Park Square, Milton Park, Abingdon, Oxon, OX14 4RN, UK

and by Routledge
711 Third Avenue, New York, NY 10017, USA

Routledge is an imprint of the Taylor & Francis Group, an informa business

© 2018 Taylor & Francis

All rights reserved. No part of this book may be reprinted or reproduced or utilised in any form or by any electronic, mechanical, or other means, now known or hereafter invented, including photocopying and recording, or in any information storage or retrieval system, without permission in writing from the publishers.

Trademark notice: Product or corporate names may be trademarks or registered trademarks, and are used only for identification and explanation without intent to infringe.

British Library Cataloguing in Publication Data
A catalogue record for this book is available from the British Library

ISBN 13: 978-1-138-49514-2

Typeset in Minion Pro
by diacriTech, Chennai

Publisher's Note
The publisher accepts responsibility for any inconsistencies that may have arisen during the conversion of this book from journal articles to book chapters, namely the possible inclusion of journal terminology.

Disclaimer
Every effort has been made to contact copyright holders for their permission to reprint material in this book. The publishers would be grateful to hear from any copyright holder who is not here acknowledged and will undertake to rectify any errors or omissions in future editions of this book.

Contents

Citation Information	vii
Notes on Contributors	ix

Introduction: Social Movements as 'Arenas' and 'Actors' in
Transnationalizing Public Spheres   1
Angela Bourne

1. Social Movements and the Transnational Transformation of
Public Spheres   9
Angela Bourne

2. More than a Copy Paste: The Spread of Spanish Frames and
Events to Portugal   25
Britta Baumgarten and Rubén Díez García

3. Beyond Nationalism? The Anti-Austerity Social Movement in Ireland:
Between Domestic Constraints and Lessons from Abroad   45
Richard Dunphy

4. National Anti-austerity Protests in a European Crisis: Comparing
the Europeanizing Impact of Protest in Greece and Germany
During the Eurozone Crisis   62
Jochen Roose, Kostas Kanellopoulos and Moritz Sommer

5. The Gezi Protests and the Europeanization of the Turkish Public Sphere   85
Isabel David and Gabriela Anouck Côrte-Real Pinto

6. European Counterpublics? DiEM25, Plan B and the Agonistic
European Public Sphere   101
Óscar García Agustín

CONTENTS

7 Essay: Rethinking Global Civil Society and the Public Sphere in the Age of Pro-democracy Movements   115
Ramón A. Feenstra

Conclusion: Social Activism Against Austerity – The Conditions for Participatory and Deliberative Forms of Democracy   127
Thomas P. Boje

Index   135

Citation Information

The chapters in this book were originally published in the *Journal of Civil Society*, volume 13, issue 3 (September 2017). When citing this material, please use the original page numbering for each article, as follows:

Introduction
Social Movements as 'Arenas' and 'Actors' in Transnationalizing Public Spheres
Angela Bourne
Journal of Civil Society, volume 13, issue 3 (September 2017) pp. 223–230

Chapter 1
Social Movements and the Transnational Transformation of Public Spheres
Angela Bourne
Journal of Civil Society, volume 13, issue 3 (September 2017) pp. 231–246

Chapter 2
More than a Copy Paste: The Spread of Spanish Frames and Events to Portugal
Britta Baumgarten and Rubén Díez García
Journal of Civil Society, volume 13, issue 3 (September 2017) pp. 247–266

Chapter 3
Beyond Nationalism? The Anti-Austerity Social Movement in Ireland: Between Domestic Constraints and Lessons from Abroad
Richard Dunphy
Journal of Civil Society, volume 13, issue 3 (September 2017) pp. 267–283

Chapter 4
National Anti-austerity Protests in a European Crisis: Comparing the Europeanizing Impact of Protest in Greece and Germany During the Eurozone Crisis
Jochen Roose, Kostas Kanellopoulos and Moritz Sommer
Journal of Civil Society, volume 13, issue 3 (September 2017) pp. 284–306

Chapter 5
The Gezi Protests and the Europeanization of the Turkish Public Sphere
Isabel David and Gabriela Anouck Côrte-Real Pinto
Journal of Civil Society, volume 13, issue 3 (September 2017) pp. 307–322

CITATION INFORMATION

Chapter 6
European Counterpublics? DiEM25, Plan B and the Agonistic European Public Sphere
Óscar García Agustín
Journal of Civil Society, volume 13, issue 3 (September 2017) pp. 323–336

Chapter 7
Essay: Rethinking Global Civil Society and the Public Sphere in the Age of Pro-democracy Movements
Ramón A. Feenstra
Journal of Civil Society, volume 13, issue 3 (September 2017) pp. 337–348

Conclusion
Social Activism Against Austerity – The Conditions for Participatory and Deliberative Forms of Democracy
Thomas P. Boje
Journal of Civil Society, volume 13, issue 3 (September 2017) pp. 349–356

For any permission-related enquiries please visit:
http://www.tandfonline.com/page/help/permissions

Notes on Contributors

Óscar García Agustín is Associate Professor at the Department of Culture and Global Studies, Aalborg University, Aalborg, Denmark.

Britta Baumgarten is a Professor at the Centre for Research and Studies in Sociology, University Institute of Lisbon, Lisbon, Portugal.

Thomas P. Boje is Reader in Social Science at the Department of Social Science and Business, Roskilde University, Roskilde, Denmark.

Angela Bourne is Associate Professor at the Department of Social Science and Business, Roskilde University, Roskilde, Denmark.

Gabriela Anouck Côrte-Real Pinto is based at the School of Environment, Education and Development, University of Manchester, Manchester, UK.

Isabel David is based at the Instituto do Oriente, Instituto Superior de Ciências Sociais e Políticas, Universidade de Lisboa, Lisbon, Portugal.

Richard Dunphy is based at the School of Social Sciences, University of Dundee, Dundee, Scotland.

Ramón A. Feenstra is based at the Department of Philosophy and Sociology, Faculty of Human and Social Sciences, Jaume I University, Castellón, Spain.

Rubén Díez García is Lecturer of Sociology at the Social Sciences Department, University Carlos III of Madrid and University Complutense of Madrid, Madrid, Spain.

Kostas Kanellopoulos is Senior Researcher at the Department of Sociology, University of Crete, Rethymnon, Greece.

Jochen Roose is Professor and Chair of Sociology at the Willy Brandt Center, University of Wroclaw, Wroclaw, Poland.

Moritz Sommer is a research assistant at the Department of Political & Social Science, Freie Universität Berlin, Berlin, Germany.

INTRODUCTION

Social Movements as 'Arenas' and 'Actors' in Transnationalizing Public Spheres

Angela Bourne

In July 2015, as Greeks voted in a referendum on the conditions of a third International Monetary Fund (IMF)-European Union (EU) bailout, many social movements around the world rallied, under the banner of the Greek 'No' campaign's 'Oxi' slogan, in protest against the introduction of further austerity measures in Greece and beyond. The international media, both old and new, covered the referendum in Greece extensively. Indeed in the latter, expressions of solidarity with Greece left a large footprint, with, for example, the hashtag #ThisIsACoup becoming the second top trending topic on Twitter worldwide (*The Guardian*, 2015). These were, of course, just a handful of the many thousands of acts of protest mobilized against austerity policies adopted by authorities at multiple territorial levels since the beginning of the financial crisis (Bourne & Chatzopoulou, 2015; Della Porta, 2015; Della Porta & Mattoni, 2014; Flesher Fominaya, 2014; Flesher Fominaya & Cox, 2013). As various scholars have observed, the recent global 'wave of contention', encompassing the Arab Spring and Occupy movements among many others, mostly aimed, as Flesher Fominaya put it, to 'reclaim the nation state as a locus and focus of action' (2014, p. 183; see also Della Porta & Mattoni, 2014, p. 6; Kaldor, Selchow, Deel, & Murray-Leach, 2013). Yet, as mobilization in solidarity with Greek 'no' voters in the Oxi campaigns showed, there is often a significant transnational dimension to contestation.

This special issue provides case studies examining Europeanization and transnationalization of social movements both from a bottom-up perspective, where domestic social movements adopt 'externalization' strategies, and as a form of 'transnational collective action', involving the building of horizontal linkages between activists in transnational arenas (Della Porta & Caiani, 2009; Della Porta & Tarrow, 2005; Imig & Tarrow Sidney, 2000). However, in addition to focusing on contemporary cases of transnational social movement activism in Europe, the articles and essays come together as a theoretical and empirical exploration of the role of social movements in a set of transforming spaces of political communication, spaces also known as public spheres. Following Habermas's seminal conception of the public sphere outlined in *The Structural Transformation of the Public Sphere* (1989) and later work (1996, 2004, 2006), the public sphere is conceived, ideally, as a space or arena in which individuals and groups, on the basis of equality, discover and deliberate in a rational and non-coercive manner, public issues of common concern. The exercise of public reason through interaction in the public sphere is a basis for democratic governance insofar as it contributes to the formation of public opinion and the legitimization of political institutions within democratic systems. The public sphere may also have integrative properties, where individuals constitute themselves collectively as democratic communities.

This ideal conception of the public sphere has been rightly criticized for implausible assumptions about the extent of rational deliberation among citizens, who, despite varying social, political and economic circumstances, are to be considered equal interlocutors; for a failure to recognize the coexistence of plural, overlapping and competing publics within the same communicative spaces; and for anchoring of the notion of public sphere within a 'Westphalian political imaginary' assuming a bounded political community with its own territorial state (e.g., Alexander, 2006; Fraser, 1992, 2007 and for a summary of other critiques see Calhoun, 1992, pp. 33–36; de Vrees, 2007, p. 5).

Building on such criticisms, recent scholarship embraces more complex conceptualizations of the public sphere and explicitly problematizes the consequences of European integration and globalization. This literature addresses both the normative implications of political communication among citizens in Europe or beyond for the democratic legitimacy of supranational political authorities, as well as the conceptual underpinnings of transnational public spheres and implications for understanding the nature and development of EU and global governance (e.g., Della Porta & Caiani, 2009; Fossum & Schlesinger, 2007; Fraser, 2007, 2013; Gerhards, 2001; Koopmans & Statham, 2010; Risse, 2010, 2014; Salvatore, Schmidtke, & Trenz, 2013; Statham & Trenz, 2013, 2015; Trenz & Eder, 2004; Wessler, Peters, Brüggemann, Kleinen von Könignslöw, & Stifft, 2008). In this literature, an empirical and theoretical focus on the mass media as a forum for public debate dominates. However, many authors acknowledge that political communication also takes place elsewhere, including online, in public meetings, through public protest and within political movements and organizations themselves. Of these alternative fora, social movements constitute a particularly interesting case because they simultaneously serve both as spheres of political communication in their own right and as actors – indeed, sometimes highly influential – within broader public spheres. Moreover, as 'arenas', social movements may perform different functions in democratic governance than the functions they perform when they engage as 'actors' within broader spheres of communication.

Social movements conceived as arenas, or as Fraser put it, 'subaltern counterpublics', provide 'parallel discursive arenas where members of subordinate social groups invent and circulate counter discourses to formulate oppositional interpretations of their identities, interests and needs' (1992, p. 123). As such, social movements may be seen as venues of empowerment permitting those excluded from official public spheres to 'find the right voice or words to express their thoughts' (Fraser, 1992, p. 123). They may become laboratories for testing alternative means of socialization, intercultural communication, reflexive identity formation and collective learning (Salvatore et al., 2013, p. 7). Social movements have also contributed to the transformation of public spheres by serving as fora for reimagining the very conceptual underpinnings of democratic practices defining the public sphere both within the state and transnationally (Della Porta, 2013; Della Porta & Caiani, 2009).

On the other hand, social movements aim to disseminate their discourses to wider arenas and, as such, are simultaneously actors within civil society. They, among others, take part in what Fraser terms weak publics 'whose deliberative practices consist exclusively in will formation' (1992, p. 134). However, modern public spheres also include an institutionalized component or strong publics, such as sovereign parliaments (or supranational authorities), 'whose discourse encompasses both opinion formation and decision-making' (Fraser, 1992, p. 134). As actors, social movements may thus provide an important 'discursive check' on the state by seeking to influence such strong publics. Social movements may also be conduits for activist citizenship, where subjects transform themselves into 'citizens' through claims to justice and political struggle (Balibar, 2004; Isin, 2009). The dissemination and advocacy of social movement identities and new conceptions underpinning democratic practices may also give social movements a role in the transformation of public spheres (Della Porta, 2013; Della Porta & Caiani, 2009).

Conceptions of social movements as civil society actors predominate in much public sphere scholarship, including recent work reflecting on contentious politics, politicization and the public sphere in the context of economic crisis (e.g., de Wilde & Zürn, 2012; Koopmans & Statham, 2010; Statham & Trenz, 2015). And yet, as many social movement scholars have observed, one of the distinctive features of the current wave of mobilization – and the practice which gave its name to the Occupy movement – is the physical occupation of public space in order to establish alternative political arenas to debate causes, consequences and appropriate responses to political and economic crises (e.g., Castells, 2012; Flesher Fominaya, 2014). In different, but complementary ways, the articles and invited essays in this special issue substantiate the point that social movements perform a dual role as both arenas and actors in evolving and transnationalizing public spheres.

My own article, 'Social movements and the transnational transformation of public spheres', draws on the existing literature focusing on the mass media as carriers of the public sphere to develop a series of indicators for observing and measuring the role of social movements in the transnational transformation of public spheres. I argue that as 'arenas', or counterpublics, social movements may contribute to transnational public sphere transformation when, among other things, activists evaluate political developments in other countries; frame claims in a comparative manner; participate in the meetings of other movements abroad; seek to learn from or copy movements abroad (diffusion); frame issues as common problems of transnational scope; and consider themselves members of transnational communities of identity. As 'actors' in broader public spheres, social movements may contribute to transnational public sphere transformation when they, among other things, direct claims to political authorities beyond, and claim to represent interests broader than, the state and when they focus on similar issues as, and use similar frames of reference and meaning structures to, movements abroad. A key argument is that it is not necessary for social movements to be transnational in scope in order for them to contribute to the transnational transformation of public spheres.

Baumgarten and Díez's article, 'More than a copy paste: The spread of Spanish frames and events to Portugal', analyses diffusion from the Spanish 15M (or indignados) movement to the Portuguese anti-austerity movements between 2011 and 2014, of action forms (e.g., occupation of public space) movement labels (Indignados/the indignant; or the Mareas/Marés/Waves; or PAH housing movements) and ideational frames (e.g., themes of democracy, deliberation and political participation). The authors show how both 15M and the Portuguese movements that emerged beginning in 2011, consciously sought to set themselves up as subaltern publics or arenas to debate pressing public matters in their countries (particularly political and economic crises), but nevertheless sought to collaborate with, share ideas with and learn from like-minded movements abroad. Factors such as esteem for existing parties of the left and perceptions of differences between activists abroad were cited as factors limiting the wholesale importation of movement models to Portugal from Spain. In all, the interest of the article follows from the evidence of diffusion between the Spanish and Portuguese movements, whether carried by activists' communication with each other online, personal contacts, meetings and collaboration in international platforms, or indirectly through knowledge acquired secondhand. Diffusion processes are necessarily an outcome of, and thus an important indicator for, the salience of transnationalized public spheres.

Dunphy's article, 'Beyond nationalism? The anti-austerity social movements in Ireland: Between domestic constraints and lessons from abroad', examines the Irish Right2Water and Right2Change campaigns, which built on protest against austerity conditionality required by the EU and IMF and accepted by the government in exchange for a financial bailout in 2010. The article focuses on the political moment when movements contemplate entering political institutions by forming new parties and, more specifically, when the Irish movements contemplated the creation of an Irish equivalent of the Spanish party *Podemos*. Dunphy argues that the strategy employed to achieve these goals contributed to the transnationalization of the public sphere in Ireland, as activists sought to learn lessons from *Podemos*' successes, incorporated key *Podemos* positions into their manifesto, invited speakers from Spain, Greece and Germany to their rallies, sent representatives to conferences and rallies abroad, and established links with similar movements in North America. Addressing the failure of the initiative hitherto, however, the article identifies the constraints of political culture (conservativism, localism and personalism) and the electoral system, traditional weakness of the left, as well as divisions within the Right2Water and Right2Change movements regarding the appropriateness of the *Podemos* paradigm for Ireland. Nevertheless, looking beyond the 'blocked' Irish party system and addressing common European problems in a common European language with activists from other countries is, according to Dunphy, a new mode of activism for Irish social movements.

The article by Roose, Kanellopoulos and Sommer, 'National anti-austerity protests in a European crisis: comparing the Europeanizing impact of protest in Greece and Germany during the Eurozone crisis', examines whether protests against austerity in the context of the Eurozone crisis became a driver of public sphere Europeanization. The authors focus on public attributions of responsibility for the crisis as an indicator of public sphere Europeanisation. Such attribution is considered analogous to horizontal communication involving the reporting or evaluation of policy developments abroad if blame attribution centres on actors and institutions beyond the state; territorial decision-making targeting such actors and institutions beyond the state; as well as simultaneous claim-making and discourse convergence if similar attributions are made across countries at the same time. The authors argue that there was some evidence that protests (and thus social movements and civil society organizations) were drivers of discourse convergence focusing on the role of EU institutions, austerity policy and socio-economic consequences of the crisis, although evidence that protest events were drivers for other kinds of Europeanisation were weak in both the Greek and German cases. More generally, they argue that while there is strong evidence, such as that in this special issue and elsewhere in the literature, that social movements have increased their transnational links in recent years, the authors argued that they have found it difficult to make their voices heard in broader mass media-dominated public spheres.

David and Côrte-Real Pinto's article, 'The Gezi protests and the Europeanization of the Turkish public sphere', analyses the modalities and degree of Europeanization of civil society organizations present at the 2013 Gezi park mobilizations. It is a case of particular interest given the EU's direct intervention, through the EU accession process, in Turkish civil society with funding for organizations, transnational network creation, norm diffusion and pressure to liberalize regulation of associational life. The authors argue that although the territorial scope of claim-making during the Gezi protests was predominantly local and national, there was some evidence of public sphere Europeanization among pro-Gezi supporters, including a framing of claims in a wider European or global context; lifestyles and pluralistic values and norms shared with EU counterparts; and, despite low levels of activist linkage, a high degree of international media support, providing an international frame of solidarity sparking reciprocity from Turkish pro-Gezi activists. Nevertheless, David and Côrte-Real Pinto also highlight the heterogeneity of Turkish civil society organizations' degree of Europeanization, depending on their history, ideology and the nature of their relations with the EU and Turkish state.

García's article, 'European counterpublics? DiEM25, Plan B and the agonistic European public sphere', examines the nature and goals of the transnational networks and movements A Plan B for Europe (Plan B) and the Democracy in Europe Movement 2025 (DiEM25). García argues that despite their differences, these separate political initiatives seek to create a European counterpublic in which an alternative to the contemporary EU is discussed and elaborated. Although Plan B is principally conceived as an alternative deliberative 'arena' to the European Parliament open to other actors supporting a different kind of Europe, DiEM25 was born as an actor disseminating its preference for political change at the transnational level as well as promoting new public arenas for deliberation. These initiatives illustrate the point that transnational social movements and networks may explicitly set out to reimagine and transform the very underpinnings and democratic practices defining public spheres; in these cases, focusing on the transformation of an exclusive, elite-directed European public sphere dominated by a hegemonic neo-liberal discourse into one approximating a more pluralist, inclusive, demos of 'European peoples' in which neo-liberal discourses are subject to more substantial public contestation.

Feenstra's essay, 'Rethinking global civil society and the public sphere in the age of pro-democracy movements', argues that the concept global civil society ought to be conceived as analogous to transnational public spheres. In the article, global civil society is defined as constituting a transnational arena of politics, interaction and debate, albeit with a specific form resembling Fraser's conception of a 'weak public' (1992, p. 134), or a domain distinct from governmental authority typically encompassing activists from social movements and non-governmental organisations. Feenstra argues that the utility of this mode of 'rethinking global civil society' is illustrated by a consideration of the claim-making, political practices and strategies employed by a range of pro-democracy movements emerging in the 'global wave' of protest since 2011, including some of those addressed elsewhere in this special issue. Feenstra argues that this reconceptualization of global civil society helps address critiques that the concept is more theoretical than real without a coherent global political state against which it can mobilize. It does so by drawing attention to the broader contribution of civil society actors to influencing and incorporating new themes in public discussion and to monitoring and scrutinizing a range of actors, not just governmental authorities. It also permits a theorization of the impact of transnational dimensions of a revitalization of domestic civil society.

Boje's concluding essay, 'Social activism against austerity – the conditions for participatory and deliberative forms of democracy', wraps up the special issue. It identifies four core themes raised in the articles relating to democratic participation and emancipation, themselves core themes in normative debates about the public sphere. The four themes include the strong demand for a participatory and deliberative culture with more inclusive forms of democracy at multiple territorial levels; declining confidence in traditional channels for public decision-making and calls for 'real democracy'; an emphasis on protest formats favouring direct participation of citizens, openness, publicity and equality rather than mobilization predominantly through networks of associations; and a cosmopolitan vision with a recognition of the need for global solutions to global problems. He then turns to contextualize these developments as part of a transition in the institution of citizenship, adapting to changing conditions for governance and democratic representation in societies dominated by global economic transactions and transnational communication. Here contemporary social movements may become channels for activist citizenship, disrupting already defined orders, practices and statuses, and thereby intervening not only in favour of groups excluded from the established norms of citizenship, but also calling into question the immutability or givenness of a particular body politic. Boje further reflects on the public sphere of civil society – now, he argues, the core institution for deliberative and emancipatory actions among the citizens at local, national and transnational levels – and the conditions affecting active participation of citizens therein. In this regard he points to the key role of civil society organizations, among other things, in the achievements of the normative principle of 'parity of participation' (Fraser 2005) and inclusion and empowerment of all groups of citizens regardless of their formal citizenship. Nevertheless, he cautions that this remains an important challenge for many civil society organizations, which internally tend to replicate prevailing social and economic inequalities.

Disclosure statement

No potential conflict of interest was reported by the author.

References

Alexander, J. C. (2006). *The civil sphere*. New York, NY: Oxford University Press.
Balibar, E. (2004). *We, the people of Europe? Reflections on transnational citizenship*. Princeton, NJ: Princeton University Press.
Bourne, A., & Chatzopoulou, S. (2015). Europeanization and social movement mobilization during the sovereign debt crisis: The cases of Spain and Greece. *Recerca*, 17, 33–60.
Calhoun, C. (1992). Introduction: Habermas and the public sphere. In C. Calhoun (Ed.), *Habermas and the public sphere*, 1–49. Cambridge: MIT Press.

Castells, M. (2012). *Networks of outrage and hope: Social movements in the internet Age*. Cambridge: Polity.
de Vrees, C. H. (2007). The EU as a public sphere. *Living Reviews in European Governance, 2*, 3. Retrieved from http://www.livingreviews.org/lreg.html
de Wilde, P., & Zürn, M. (2012). Can politicization of European integration be reversed? *Journal of Common Market Studies, 50*(1), 137–153.
Della Porta, D. (2013). Social movements and the public sphere. In A. Salvatore, O. Schmidtke, & H. J. Trenz (Eds.), *Rethinking the public sphere through transnationalizing processes: Europe and beyond* (pp. 107–136). Houndsmills: Palgrave Macmillan.
Della Porta, D. (2015). *Social movements in times of austerity*. Cambridge: Polity Press.
Della Porta, D., & Caiani, M. (2009). *Social movements and Europeanization*. Oxford: Oxford University Press.
Della Porta, D., & Mattoni, A. (Eds.). (2014). *Spreading protest*. Essex: ECPR Press.
Della Porta, D., & Tarrow, S. (2005). *Transnational protest and global activism*. Lanham: Rowman and Littlefield.
Flesher Fominaya, C. (2014). *Social movements and globalisation*. Houndsmills: Palgrave Macmillan.
Flesher Fominaya, C., & Cox, L. (2013). *Understanding European movements*. London: Routledge.
Fossum, J. E., & Schlesinger, P. (2007). *The European Union and the public sphere: A communicative space in the making?* London: Routledge.
Fraser, N. (2005). Re-framing justice in a globalizing world. *New Left Review, 36*, 69–88.
Fraser, N. (1992). Rethinking the public sphere: A contribution to the critique of actually existing democracy. In C. Calhoun (Ed.), *Habermas and the public sphere* (pp. 109–142). Cambridge: MIT Press.
Fraser, N. (2007). *Scales of justice: Reimagining political space in a globalising world*. New York, NY: Columbia University Press.
Fraser, N. (2013). A triple movement? *New Left Review, 81*, 119–132.
Gerhards, J. (2001). Missing a European public sphere. In M. Kohli, & M. Novak (Eds.), *Will Europe work? Integration, employment and social order* (pp. 145–158). London: Routledge.
Habermas, J. (1989). *The structural transformation of the public sphere*. Cambridge: MIT Press.
Habermas, J. (1996). *Between facts and norms*. Cambridge: MIT Press.
Habermas, J. (2004). Why Europe needs a constitution. In E. O. Eriksen, J. E. Fossum, & A. J. Menéndez (Eds.), *Developing a constitution for Europe* (pp. 17–33). London: Routledge.
Habermas, J. (2006). *Time of transitions*. Cambridge: Polity Press.
Imig, D., & Tarrow Sidney, S. (2000). Political contention in a Europeanizing polity. *West European Politics, 23*(4), 73–93.
Isin, E. (2009). Citizenship in flux: The figure of the activist citizen. *Subjectivity, 29*, 367–388.
Kaldor, M., Selchow, S., Deel, S., & Murray-Leach, T. (2013). *The 'bubbling up' of subterranean politics in Europe*. London: Civil Society and Human Security Research Unit London School of Economics and Political Science June.
Koopmans, R., & Statham, P., (Eds.). (2010). *The making of a European public sphere: Media discourse and political contention*. Cambridge: Cambridge University Press.
Risse, T. (2010). *A community of Europeans? Transnational identities and public spheres*. Ithaca: Cornell University Press.
Risse, T. (2014). No demos? Identities and public spheres in the euro crisis. *Journal of Common Market Studies, 52*(6), 1207–1215.
Salvatore, A., Schmidtke, O., & Trenz, H. J. (2013). Introduction: Rethinking the public sphere through transnationalizing processes; Europe and beyond. In A. Salvatore, O. Schmidtke, & H. J. Trenz (Eds.), *Rethinking the public sphere through transnationalizing processes: Europe and beyond* (pp. 1–25). Houndsmills: Palgrave Macmillan.
Statham, P., & Trenz, H. J. (2013). *The politicization of Europe: Contesting the constitution in the mass media*. London: Routledge.
Statham, P., & Trenz, H. J. (2015). Understanding the mechanisms of EU politicization: Lessons from the Eurozone crisis. *Comparative European Politics, 13*(3), 287–306.

The Guardian. (2015). ThisIsACoup: Germany faces backlash over tough Greek bailout demand, 13 July 2015.

Trenz, H. J., & Eder, K. (2004). The democratizing dynamics of a European public sphere. *European Journal of Social Theory, 7*(1), 5–25.

Wessler, H., Peters, B., Brüggemann, M., Kleinen von Königslöw, K., & Stifft, S. (2008). *Transnationalization of public spheres*. Houndsmills: Palgrave Macmillan.

Social Movements and the Transnational Transformation of Public Spheres

Angela Bourne

ABSTRACT
This article presents a theoretical framework for the empirical study of social movements as agents in the transnational transformation of public spheres. It draws on the existing literature on transnationalization of public spheres, which predominantly focuses on the broadcast media as carriers of the public sphere, to conceptualize transnational public spheres and mechanisms of public sphere transformation and to identify indicators for measuring the degree of that transformation. It then turns to argue that conceptualization of transnational public spaces as complex, multilayered, and overlapping permits analysis of social movements as agents of public sphere transformation in the form of actors or arenas, either within transnational spaces or through more routine forms of contestation within the nation state. I then adapt indicators developed to measure the degree of transnationalization of public spheres and illustrate their applicability for the study of social movements using contemporary examples of movement practices and discourses.

Introduction

As many commentators have observed, one of the distinctive characteristics of the wave of social movement mobilizations in the wake of the financial crisis of the late 2000s were efforts to construct new spaces for public debate (Castells, 2012; della Porta & Mattoni, 2014; Flesher Forminaya, 2014; Flesher Forminaya & Cox, 2013). The occupation of public squares—and indeed the emergence of the global Occupy movement—provides a potent contemporary illustration of efforts by social movements to create alternative agora for discussion of public issues, although they are by no means isolated examples. Social media platforms and transnational networks like ATTAC, Blockupy, or the Alter Summit provided additional civil society fora for discussion of public issues of common concern to transnational communities (Castells, 2012; Chatzopoulou & Bourne, 2017). These practices illustrate the point that social movements may serve, on the one hand, as public spheres in themselves, or what Nancy Fraser called 'subaltern counter publics' (1992, p. 134), and on the other, as actors within broader national and transnational public spheres coalescing around institutionalized arenas of governance. They also provide a pertinent setting in which to examine the role of social movements in the transformation of public spheres, and more specifically the transnationalization of public spheres, given the interrelation of local, state, European, and global contexts of crisis contestation. This is the topic I address in this article, which aims to present the theoretical foundations of an approach for studying social movements as agents in the transnational transformation of public spheres.

I begin with a discussion of foundational insights drawn from the existing theoretical and empirical literature regarding conceptualization of transnational public spheres, mechanisms of public sphere transformation, and indicators for measuring the degree of that transformation. In the next part, I argue that conceptualization of transnational public spaces as complex, multilayered, and overlapping permits analysis of social movements as agents of public sphere transformation as either actors or arenas within transnational spaces or more routine forms of contestation within the nation state. I then adapt indicators developed to measure the degree of transnationalization of public spheres and illustrate their applicability for the study of social movements using examples of practices and discourses of social movements discussed elsewhere and in this special issue—namely the transnational anti-austerity movement, Blockupy (Chatzopoulou & Bourne, 2017), the Spanish housing movement, Platform for Mortgage Affected People and 15 M (or indignados movement) (Feenstra, 2017, see also Bourne & Chatzopoulou, in press), and the Irish Right2Water and Right2Change campaigns (Dunphy, 2017)—as well as substate nationalist movements that mobilized during Catalan and Scottish independence campaigns (Bourne, 2014) and a prisoner amnesty group of the radical Basque nationalist movement.

Social movements, public spheres, and the transnational transformation of public spheres

Following Habermas' (1989) seminal contribution in the *Structural Transformation of the Public Sphere*, a public sphere can be conceived in ideal terms as a space or arena in which people, on the basis of equality, discover and deliberate in a rational and non-coercive manner public issues of common concern. The possibilities for exercising 'public reason' are intimately linked to possibilities for democratic governance insofar as they provide a site for formation of public opinion and the legitimization of political institutions in democratic systems. A public sphere may also have integrative properties, where individuals constitute themselves as a democratic political community.

Building on critiques that Habermas' early conception of the public sphere failed to recognize the coexistence of plural, overlapping, and competing publics within the same communicative spaces, and its anchoring within a 'Westphalian political imaginary' assuming a political community bounded by its own territorial state, recent scholarship has embraced more complex conceptualizations of the public sphere (for such critiques, see Calhoun, 1992, pp. 33–36; de Vrees, 2007, p. 5; Fraser, 1992, 2007). This has included an effort to understand the implications for political communication and democratic practices of new political arenas emerging in Europe and beyond, with particular attention directed to the impact of the European Union (della Porta & Caiani, 2009; Fossum & Schlesinger, 2007a; Fraser, 2007, 2013; Gerhards, 2001; Koopmans & Statham, 2010; Risse, 2010, 2014; Salvatore & Trenz, 2013; Statham & Trenz, 2013, 2015; Trenz & Eder, 2004; Wessler, Peters, Brüggemann, Kleinen von Königslöw, & Stifft, 2008). In this literature, a key underlying normative concern has been the quality of democratic politics in the EU and more specifically the validity of the common assumption that democratic quality is constrained by the absence of an EU 'demos' due, at least in part, to the absence of a sufficiently developed transnational space for political communication. This literature provides a number of foundational insights for understanding the role social movements play in the transnational transformation of public spheres, namely a complex, multilayered conception of public spheres, theoretical proposals identifying mechanisms of public sphere transformation, and the development of indicators for observing transnational transformation of public spheres.

Conceptualizing transnational public spheres: 'Top-down' versus 'bottom-up' approaches

One of the major contributions of the more recent literature has been theoretical work conceptualizing public spheres as complex, multilayered, overlapping spheres of communication. Eriksen's (2007) work on the EU as a sphere of public debate, for instance, identified three different kinds of European public spheres, each of which cross cuts national and transnational governance arenas. Eriksen distinguished between 'strong publics', 'a general European public sphere' and 'segmented publics' (2007, pp. 32–37). A 'strong public' entailed 'legally institutionalised and regulated discourses specialized in collective will formation at the policy centre' (Eriksen, 2007, p. 32). In the EU, these take the form of institutionalized deliberative spaces such as the European Parliament or the 2002–2003 Convention on the Future of Europe (Eriksen, 2007, p. 36). A second type was a 'general European public', or 'communicative spaces of civil society in which all may participate on a free and equal basis and, due to proper rights entrenchment, can deliberate subject only to the constraints of reason' (Eriksen, 2007, p. 32). These two kinds of public are effectively modelled on the EU conceived as 'a rights-based federal union, based on core tenets of the democratic constitutional state' (Fossum & Schlesinger, 2007b, pp. 12, 14–16). 'Segmented publics', in contrast, 'evolve around policy networks constituted by a selection of actors with a common interest in certain issues, problems and solutions' (Eriksen, 2007, p. 33). Here no 'unifying form of discourse develops but rather discourses that vary according to the issue fields that reflect the institutional structure of the EU' (Eriksen, 2007, p. 33). This is effectively founded on the conception of the EU as a regulatory system based on transnational networks or issue-oriented and relatively self-contained epistemic communities and in which 'a European public space ... is nationally segmented' (Fossum & Schlesinger, 2007b, pp. 13–14).

While Eriksen's conception of 'segmented publics' explicitly models a transnational public sphere (the EU) as an overlapping and multilayered arena, this and his other models might nevertheless be considered top-down models, insofar as they superimpose transnational onto national public spheres. An alternative approach, which might be called 'bottom up', starts from national public spheres and considers how they may develop new or more significant transnational dimensions. It follows the observation on the part of many scholars that the absence of a common transnational language, a transnational media system, or shared identities limited prospects for the development of 'national public sphere writ large' as conceived in Habermas' (1996a) early work (for further discussion, see de Vrees, 2007; Zimmermann & Favell, 2011). Transnationalization of national public spheres involved an extension of the scale of political communication through, among other things, an increasing awareness of publics in other states, a synchronization of political debates across national spheres, a convergence in meaning structures, the circulation of ideas between speakers in different countries, and for some, multilayered identities encompassing national and transnational communities (Koopmans & Statham, 2010; Risse, 2010; Statham & Trenz, 2013; Wessler et al., 2008).

Transformation of public spheres

Another major contribution of the existing literature has been theoretical work on the processes through which public spheres may be transformed to encompass transnational communities of political communication. Theoretical accounts of the processes by which public spheres may acquire transnational dimensions emphasize both the impact of broader changes in the structure of governance as well as social processes whereby individuals engaged in critical public debate redefine and reconstitute existing public spheres. The former argument is essentially founded on the expectation that emergence of authoritative supranational institutions, with the EU as the primary example, creates conditions in which new patterns of contestation and communication emerge (Gerhards, 2001; Statham & Trenz, 2013, p. 9, 2015, p. 288; Wessler et al., 2008, p. 1).

This line of argument has been developed in greatest depth in recent research on the 'politicization' of the EU, which focuses on a shift from elite-dominated contestation over EU politics to one involving wider publics in contestation and debate over EU policy, processes of decision-making as such, and the purposes of the EU itself (de Wilde & Zürn, 2012, p. 139; Statham & Trenz, 2013, p. 7, 2015). Statham and Trenz argue, for instance, that in addition to the role of the media as carriers of an expanding public debate about Europe (2015, pp. 292, 294), the consolidation of the EU as an advanced governance system alters political opportunity structures (Statham & Trenz, 2013, p. 9): It gives some collective actors access to new supranational decision fora, while constraining mobilization opportunities in the domestic arena for other actors (Statham & Trenz, 2013, p. 9). Furthermore, insofar as European integration may create 'winners' and 'losers'—in material terms, political authority, and identities—it provides incentives for broader public contestation about Europe (Fligstein, 2008; Hooghe & Marks, 2008; Statham & Trenz, 2013, p. 9, 2015, p. 299). These may come to 'structure political conflict along pro-and anti-European lines' (Statham & Trenz, 2015, p. 294). Member state elites have often sought to dampen public engagement in EU politics, but mass publics may come to engage in contestation in response to EU-level processes like new treaties (notably referenda on the Constitutional Treaty), and 'external shocks' like the financial crisis (de Wilde & Zürn, 2012; Statham & Trenz, 2013, 2015). Features of national political systems may also be important for understanding these processes, such as the degree of media receptiveness to EU affairs, dynamics of party competition, and the nature of national narratives, myths, and stories about the EU (de Wilde & Zürn, 2012; Hooghe & Marks, 2008; Statham & Trenz, 2013, 2015).

A second approach focuses on intersubjectivity of social actors, who may disseminate new or adapted practices and discourses that redefine identities, social bonds, and practices of political communication (Calhoun, 2002; Eder, 2007; Risse, 2010). As Risse put it, public spheres emerge in the process during which people debate controversial issues ... The more we debate issues, the more we leave the position of neutral observers [of others beyond the national spheres]—thereby creating and/or reifying political communities in the process. (2010, p. 120)

Such processes are likely to be conflictual: Political contestation over matters of public concern open possibilities for critical self-reflection, reflexivity, and social learning. Social learning may take place when people argue together in public as equals, which may create reciprocal obligations and bind them together into a process of 'collective will formation' (Eder, 2007, p. 49). Reflexivity is important insofar as 'members of the public are speakers who debate and deliberate not only by reflecting on their own interests and values but also on their own identity as autonomous agents' (Salvatore & Trenz, 2013, p. 2). Moreover, 'affirmation of the normative legitimacy of the public sphere itself has a structuring effect on the emergence of "world society"' insofar as the 'public sphere is evoked as a normative horizon of a cosmopolitan community of citizens' (Salvatore & Trenz, 2013, p. 4; see also Eder, 2007, p. 46).

Measuring transnationalization of public spheres

A further major theoretical contribution of this literature is the wealth of insights it provides into observing and measuring the transnationalization of public spheres. Here I briefly review three of the most sophisticated approaches, namely those by Koopmans and Statham (2010), Risse (2010) and Wessler et al. (2008). Koopmans and Statham's approach (2010), which draws on Koopmans and Erbe's (2004) work on vertical and horizontal Europeanization, identifies progressively wider territorially based spheres of communication arranged in concentric circles around individual national public spheres. The spatial reach and boundaries of political communication are investigated in relation to the patterning of 'communicative flows' and 'the relative density of public communication within and between different political spaces' (Koopmans & Statham, 2010, p. 38). In the model, a centrally located national space is surrounded by the national spaces of separate European countries, which is in turn surrounded by a supranational European political space where the institutions and polices of organizations like the EU, the Council of Europe, or the European Free Trade Association (EFTA) are the focus of communication. Beyond this, a broader sphere includes the national political spaces of countries outside Europe, while an outer sphere contains global institutions such as the International Monetary Fund (IMF), G8, or United Nations (UN) (Koopmans & Statham, 2010, pp. 39–40). The communicative flows of interest in Koopman and Statham's approach are 'political claims', defined as 'public speech acts (including protest events) that articulate political demands, calls to action, proposals, or criticisms, which, actually or potentially, affect the interests or integrity of the claimants or other collective actors' (Koopmans & Statham, 2010, p. 55). The presence or relative importance of arenas of political communication are determined empirically in different ways depending on whether these theoretically defined public spheres are arenas of governance—invested with authoritative political institutions—or of horizontal communication across national public spheres.

In a (theoretical) public sphere entirely bounded by the territory of a nation state all claims make demands on national addressees (e.g. national or local governments) on behalf of nationally defined interests (e.g. the poor in Britain, gay and lesbian communities in Spain, ethnic minorities in Germany). In contrast, in a supranational public sphere, European claimants make demands on European addressees in the name of European interests (Koopmans & Statham, 2010, p. 49)—as for example, when pan-European movements like Blockupy make anti-austerity demands on EU institutions (Chatzopoulou & Bourne, 2017). However, rather than serving as a hermetically sealed political arena, communication patterns indicating the presence of supranational public spheres also include instances where a national actor directly addresses European institutions, for instance, through the local interest group lobbying of the European Commission or European Parliament; where national actors indirectly lobby supranational institutions via their national representatives; or when European actors address national actors, such as, when EU Commissioner Barosso supported the Spanish and British governments' view that an independent Catalonia or Scotland would have to reapply for EU membership (Bourne, 2014). Similarly, the emergence of transnational public spheres could be observed from claim-making addressing international bodies, like North Atlantic Treaty Organization (NATO) or the UN, in the name of international groups and interests, but could also include media coverage of communication between international institutions or media coverage of actors from non-European countries and their demands on international institutions.

Consequential horizontal communication *across* nationally constituted public spheres—i.e. when it occurs across public spheres in either Europe or beyond—can take a weak or a strong form. Weak forms of horizontal communication 'occurs when the media report on what happens within the national political spaces of other European countries' which does not take the form of a direct communicative link, but nevertheless, 'bring foreign claims to the attention' of a national public (Koopmans & Statham, 2010, 41). A stronger variant of horizontal communication involves direct linkages between national actors in two or more European countries, or between national actors in two or more countries outside Europe (Koopmans & Statham, 2010, 41). Examples of direct linkages could include support by other European states for the Spanish government's positions on Catalan independence and EU membership (Bourne, 2014). It may also include claims framed in a comparative way, such as when national groups point to European and extra-European examples as benchmarks for criticizing their own government.

Risse's approach, in contrast, focuses on the spatial, temporal, and semantic simultaneity of political debates, with indicators of public sphere transnationalization resting on Habermas' (1996b, p. 306; cited in Risse, 2010, p. 116) contention that a public sphere enables citizens to take positions at the same time on the same topics of the same relevance. Risse identifies five criteria for identifying what he calls a 'transnational' European sphere. Firstly, there is a visibility criterion, under which 'the same (European) themes are controversially debated at the same time at similar levels of attention across national public spheres and media' (Risse, 2010, p. 125). It can be observed by examining whether the valleys and troughs in issue cycles of media attention in different European countries follow similar patterns (Risse, 2010, p. 116). A second indicator concerns whether speakers in different states employ the same 'criteria of relevance', that is, whether similar frames of reference, meaning structures, or patterns of interpretation are used across national public spheres and the media. It does not necessarily involve a shared European perspective, but an awareness of the different frames under which it is possible to discuss a political issue, or common interpretations of a problem that include controversial opinions on a particular question (Risse, 2010, p. 119). For example, despite profound disagreements over the 2003 Iraq war, debaters in different countries nevertheless employed the same 'criteria of relevance', by which 'compliance with international law, on the one hand, and respect for basic human rights, on the other, are significant in debating questions of war and peace' (Risse, 2010, p. 119; see also Habermas & Derida, 2005). Three further indicators concern the extent to which a community of communication emerges in which:

> ... (a) European or other national speakers regularly participate in cross-border debates, (b) speakers and listeners recognize each other as legitimate participants in transnational discourses that (c) frame the particular issues as common European problems. (Risse, 2010, p. 126)

A third approach is Wessler et al.'s (2008). It identifies four dimensions on which a possible transnationalization of public spheres can be observed. The first, monitoring governance, occurs when 'European or other international governance processes become visible on a national level and can thus be monitored by citizens' (Wessler et al., 2008, p. 10). It occurs when European or international political institutions, decision processes, or policies become an object or reference point for public debate, usually when they are covered or discussed in the national news media (Wessler et al., 2008, pp. 10–11). A second indicator of the transnational dimensions of public spheres concerns discourse convergence, or whether national discourses become more similar over time. This convergence can be observed if 'speakers in different national public spheres identify the same issues as important, accord them similar relevance and employ similar problem definitions' (Wessler et al., 2008, p. 11). It may also be observed in a convergence of 'discourse constellations', that is 'particular sets of actors who use specific justifications to bolster their positions' (Wessler et al., 2008, p. 11). Convergence of discourse constellations may be observed in similarities of justification employed across national boundaries or similarities in the membership of such constellations—such as whether all anti-austerity constellations include trade unionists, social democratic parties, or anti-poverty groups. A third dimension, discursive integration, concerns more direct communication across national borders, that is a combination of 'attention to political developments in other countries (mutual observation ...)' and 'the circulation of ideas between speakers in various countries (discursive exchange)' (Wessler et al., 2008, p. 12). It involves the diffusion of opinions and justifications across national spheres. A final indication of transnationalization is collective identification, which can occur if speakers simply acknowledge a transnational collectivity, expressing a sense of belonging to that collectivity by 'including themselves in a collective "we"' or by 'pointing to (or inventing) historical or cultural commonalities or by setting it apart from other communities which are often devalued in the process' (Wessler et al., 2008, p. 12).

This literature is largely focused on the transformation of national public spheres, which despite acknowledgements that internal differentiation exists within them, nevertheless tends to conceptualize territorial units of governance and typically the state as the unit of analysis. As I turn to argue in the next section, however, the insights of this literature can be employed to examine the role of social movements as both 'actors' in the transformation of public spheres and as transnationalizing public spheres in themselves.

Social movements as 'agents' and 'arenas' in the transnational transformation of public spheres

As I have just proposed, existing scholarship provides important insights for examining the role of social movements as agents in the transnational transformation of public spheres. In the first place, work on the conceptualization of transnational public spheres points to the possibility that social movements, as actors within what Eriksen (2007) calls a 'general European public' or 'segmented publics', may contribute to a shift in the scale of political communication. Social movements, whether national in scope or as part of transnational networks, may contest the actions and legitimacy of transnational authorities. However, as research on the transnationalization of national public spheres suggests, social movements may also be agents of scale shift when engaging in more routine forms of contestation within the nation state. In short, it is not necessary for social movements to be transnational in scope to contribute to transnational transformation of public spheres.

Secondly, the existing literature suggests that the modalities by which social movements may contribute to public sphere transformation may take two forms. The first modality concerns their role as civil society actors participating in political contestation as a response to changing political opportunity structures and an awareness that transnational governance may have consequences in material or identitarian terms, or for their political influence. Here, as actors within 'weak publics', they contribute to deliberative practices principally consisting in 'will formation' (Fraser, 1992, p. 134) centred on issues which include topics with transnational dimensions. In so doing, social movements may contribute to the dissemination of new practices, discourses, and identities redefining the contours of existing public spheres (della Porta, 2013; della Porta & Caiani, 2009). This is the role envisaged for social movements in the literature on politicization of the EU with a public sphere perspective: As Statham and Trenz argue, for instance, social movements, among others, may mobilize claims in public with transnational dimensions and 'the more public claims are mobilized by collective actors, the more this leads to a public debate characterized by an intensified communication over the EU and an increase in the reflexive public evaluation and monitoring of the EU polity' (2015, p. 293).

Furthermore, if the critique that existing empirical studies tend to reify the national public sphere at the expense of more complex, multilayered conceptions is taken seriously, it also becomes appropriate to examine whether social movements themselves may be arenas in which individuals and groups undertake the work of redefining the scale of spheres of political communication. This is the second modality by which social movements may contribute to public sphere transformation. In this regard, social movements can be conceived as 'subaltern counterpublics', which according to Fraser may provide sites for 'social groups to invent and circulate counter discourses to formulate oppositional interpretations of their identities, interests and needs' (1992, p. 123). As such they may become 'laboratories for testing alternative means of socialization, intercultural communication, reflexive identity formation and collective learning' (Salvatore & Trenz, 2013, p. 7). In other words, social movements may be one of the sites in which social actors disseminate new or adapted practices and discourse that redefine identities, social bonds, and practices of political communication.

And finally, conceptual work identifying appropriate indicators of public sphere transnationalization may be adapted for empirical analysis with social movements as an object of analysis. Indicators can be grouped depending on whether they provide evidence of social movements engaging in transnational public debates as actors, or whether they provide sites for transnationalized public deliberation themselves. These are summarized in Table 1.

Territorial scope of claim-making

Perhaps the most straightforward indicator that social movements play a role as actors engaged in political communication beyond the state can be drawn from Koopmans and Statham's (2010) focus on the strategies of political actors, including whether they target national, EU or transnational authorities, and the territorial scope of interest represented. It is relatively easy to find instances of protests targeting transnational authorities, such as EU institutions, or the IMF; targeting other member states; or involving collaboration among movements in other countries. Blockupy emerged in 2012 when it began the first of a series of actions targeting the European Central Bank's financial base and the financial district in Frankfurt, Germany. These actions aim to block operations of banks and make anger over Troika policy apparent (Facebook, Blockupy, 16 May 2012). Substate nationalist movements, including pro-independence campaigners from Scotland and Catalonia (unsuccessfully), initiated a European Citizens' Initiative to enshrine the Universal Right of Self-determination within the EU's legal framework (Bourne, 2014). The Spanish housing movement, *Plataforma de Afectados por la Hipoteca* (PAH), has an international committee seeking to engage with pro-housing affinity

Table 1. Indicators for empirical analysis of the role of social movements as agents in the transnational transformation of public spheres.

	Focus of analysis	Research questions
Social movements as actors	Territorial scope of claim-making	At what territorial levels are a social movement's claim-making directed?
		What is the territorial scope of the interest they claim to represent?
	Simultaneous claim-making	To what extent do social movements of similar types in different countries focus attention on similar issues at the same time?
	Criteria of relevance/discourse convergence	To what extent do social movements in different countries use similar frames of reference and meaning structure?
		To what extent do discourse coalitions in different countries contain similar types of political actors?
Social movements as arenas	Weak horizontal communication/ monitoring governance	To what extent do social movements report on what happens within the national spaces of other European countries?
	Strong horizontal communication	To what extent do social movements evaluate political developments in other countries?
		To what extent do social movements frame claims in a comparative manner?
	Community of communication/ collective identities	To what extent do European or other national speakers regularly participate in cross-border debates?
		To what extent do speakers and listeners recognize each other as legitimate participants in transnational discourses?
		To what extent are ideas diffused across national spheres?
		To what extent are issues framed as common European problems?
		To what extent do social movements include themselves in transnational communities?

groups, collectives, and organizations across Europe and beyond and regularly participates in workshops and contentious actions with such groups (PAH, 2016). The 'Free Otegi, Free Them All' campaign, which principally targets Spanish and French governments and pursues the release of imprisoned members of the radical Basque nationalist movement, launched an initiative involving artists from the Basque Country and abroad to record a song and video for an international campaign, sung in various languages (Free Otegi, Free Them All, 2017a). This kind of mobilization has been the subject of various studies already (see for example, Bourne & Chatzopoulou, 2015; della Porta & Caiani, 2009; Imig & Tarrow, 2000; see also Roose, Kanellopoulous, & Sommer, 2017), most of which nevertheless conclude that contentious politics predominantly focuses on the domestic arena (della Porta & Caiani, 2009, p. 79; Imig & Tarrow, 2000, p. 84; Koopmans, Erbe, & Meyer, 2010). Nevertheless it is only one of a number of possible indicators of public sphere transnationalization.

Simultaneous claim-making

Other indications that social movements play a role as actors in the transnationalization of public spheres can be drawn from indicators focusing on convergence in the content of claims made by social actors in different member states. These include Risse's 'simultaneous claim-making' indicator (2010), focusing on the extent to which media issue cycles are aligned in different countries. This indicator can be adapted to examine whether social movements of similar types focus attention on similar issues at similar times. An example of such 'simultaneous claims-making' includes mobilization against the Transatlantic Trade and Investment Partnership not just by pan-European movements like Blockupy (Chatzopoulou & Bourne, 2017), but also national movements such as the Irish Right2Water campaign (Right2Water, 2016) and the Spanish platform *Democracia Real Ya* (DRY) (DRY, 2014), among others. Another example is mobilization, referred to in the opening of this special issue, by movements around the world in support of Greek 'Oxi' (No) voters in the July 2015 referendum on the conditions for a third EU-IMF bailout (e.g. Blockupy, in Chatzopoulou & Bourne, 2017; in the UK, 'Oxi to Osbourne,' 2015; in Ireland, 'Thousands Turn Out,' 2015; and in Germany, 'Angela Merkel,' 2015).

Criteria of relevance/discourse convergence

Similarly, Risse's 'criteria of relevance' and Wessler et al.'s 'discourse convergence' indicators, where similar frames of reference and meaning structures are employed across national public spheres, can be applied to the social movement discourses as easily as they can to broader discourses reported in the media. A comparative study of discourses of Euroscepticism among three Spanish and three Greek movements mobilizing for 'real democracy' or against 'austerity' since 2011 observed similar discourses of 'critical Euroscepticism' (Bourne & Chatzopoulou, in press). Although there were differences in conceptions of the nature of crisis, cultural and historical references, and practices of protest, similarities could nevertheless be observed in a position of soft Euroscepticism, framing the EU as a neo-liberal enterprise lacking 'real democracy' but nevertheless capable of transformation into 'another', better Europe (Bourne & Chatzopoulou, in press).

Weak horizontal communication/monitoring governance

Indicators that social movements play a role as arenas reimagining the territorial scale of political communication include Koopmans and Statham's horizontal communication indicators, also reflected in both Risse's first two and Wessler et al.'s first indicators of transnational public sphere transformation. Koopmans and Statham's 'weak horizontal communication' indicator, essentially the same as Wessler et al.'s 'monitoring governance' indicator, focuses on reporting of what happens in the national political spaces of other countries. It can be adapted, however, to provide an indicator of the visibility of foreign claims within social movement spheres of communication. There are many examples of news stories posted on websites, Facebook, or other social media about events in other countries, including activities of like-minded movements. Indeed, movements including Blockupy, Free Otegi, Free Them All, PAH, and Right2Water, included 'International' pages on their websites, advertising events or movements in other countries, and all but the latter opened themselves to monitoring by international audiences by publishing in multiple languages.

Strong horizontal communication

Similarly, the existence of what Koopmans and Statham define as strong forms of horizontal communication, such as commentary or evaluations on policy developments abroad and comparisons across countries, could be employed in empirical analysis of social movements' political communication. In a study of Scottish and Catalan independence movements' pro-independence campaigns, for instance, there were frequent references to actors or policies of other European countries, to portray opponents in a negative light by comparing them with an exemplary other; portray the speaker's movement in a positive light by comparing themselves with an exemplary other; mobilize participants in the speaker's movement by relating successes of similar movements to their own experiences; warn opponents of undesirable but possible future scenarios; underline the viability of Catalonia and Scotland as viable independent states; or undermine the validity of opponent's arguments (Bourne, 2014).

Community of communication/discursive integration

Risse's two indicators regarding a 'community of communication', that is, the extent to which European or other national speakers regularly participate in cross border debates and the extent to which speakers and listeners recognize each other as legitimate participants in transnational discourses, could likewise be adapted. An example of such a transnational 'community of communication' includes European Parliamentarians, willing to endorse the prisoners' campaign, Free Otegi, Free Them All, and accept a conflict-resolution frame which saw Arnaldo Otegi and other leaders of the banned party, *Batasuna*, as central figures of a Basque 'peace process' imprisoned for 'political' reasons (Free Otegi, Free Them All, 2017b). The campaign's website also included a long list of people from other countries endorsing their campaign, including senior politicians from Northern Ireland, Uruguay, Paraguay, Honduras, Mexico, and Turkey, Nobel Peace Prize winners (e.g. Desmond Tutu and Mairead Maguire), and Members of the European Parliament (Free Otegi, Free Them All, 2017c).

Wessler et al.'s 'discursive integration' indicator, similar to those in Risse's work, but which additionally involves the diffusion of opinions and justifications across national spheres, could also be employed in analysis of social movements' political communication. Such processes are, of course, already well documented in the literature on social movements (della Porta & Diani, 2006; McAdam & Rucht, 1993; Snow, 2004; Tarrow, 2005). An important theme in much existing work on protests following the Arab Spring focuses on transnational diffusion, addressing for instance the spread of mobilization frames (e.g. calls for 'real democracy'), tactical repertoires (e.g. occupation of public spaces, assemblies), and movement labelling (e.g. Indignados and Occupy) (della Porta & Mattoni, 2014; Flesher Forminaya, 2014; Kousis, 2014; Tejerina, Perugorria, Benski, & Langman, 2013).

And finally, Risse's and Wessler et al.'s 'transnational identity' indicators could be usefully adapted in analysis of the role of social movements in re-imagining the boundaries of public spheres. These indicators focus on the extent to which issues are defined as a common European problem, or as Wessler et al. (2008) put it, the extent to which speakers acknowledge a transnational community by pointing to (or inventing) historical and cultural commonalities or by setting such a transnational community apart from other communities. For instance, calls for 'real democracy' in Spain were extended to Europe and beyond (Bourne & Chatzopoulou, in press). DRY (Real Democracy Now), one of the platforms involved in the 2011 15 M mobilization in Spain (Romanos, 2013), issued a Citizen Declaration on the Fraud of Public Debt, signed by 8632 people, which argued: 'Europe can't constitute itself or have a future if it is not on the basis of real democracy' (DRY, 2011a). Similarly, its website showed many appeals for transnational solidarity, mostly encompassing groups beyond Europe. A list of slogans submitted by the public included various references to universal ethical standards and rights, such as 'people first, markets afterwards', 'fundamental rights for everyone', 'global attacks, global response', or 'for a world that is free and social for all' (DRY, 2011b).

Conclusion

In the foregoing I have sought to outline theoretical foundations for empirical research on the role of social movements as agents in the transnational transformation of public spheres. An advantage of this approach is that it permits analysis of a wide range of transnational dimensions in social movement activism, including that of local movements which may rarely look beyond the state in their claim-making or alliance strategies. As a consequence, it permits researchers to both acknowledge and move beyond Tarrow's (2012) contention that transnational activists are at best 'rooted cosmopolitans', a claim which tends to be supported by most empirical studies of transnational mobilization. In other words, accepting that instances of transnational collaboration and mobilization targeting transnational governance authorities may be relatively rare does not necessarily exclude the possibility that over the longer term, social movements, along with others, of course, may plant the seeds of subtle, but consequential, transformations in discourses, practices, and repertoires of political communication, as well as conceptions of citizenship and the boundaries of communities of communication. As della Porta and Caiani observe, social movements may, at least theoretically, play a role in the construction of transnational public spheres in a similar manner to which they did so in the realm of the nation state (2009, pp. 12–13).

As indicated above, the existing literature acknowledges that processes of transnationalization are complex and likely to be mediated by existing social and political practices, including media receptiveness to transnational affairs, dynamics of party competition, and the nature of national narratives, myths, and stories about transnational governance structures (like the EU or the Troika) (de Wilde & Zürn, 2012; Hooghe & Marks, 2008; Statham & Trenz, 2013, 2015). To this we might also add that the role of social movements as agents in transnationalization of public spheres is likely to be mediated by factors facilitating or limiting transnational activism, such as the availability of material and cultural resources and communication technologies, shared histories, culture and world views, or pre-existing social networks, relationships of trust and reciprocity (della Porta & Diani, 2006; Imig & Tarrow, 2000, p. 80).

Furthermore, a focus on social movements as agents in the transformation of public spheres helps to address criticisms levelled at the predominant interest of existing studies of public claim-making in broadsheet newspapers, hitherto the principal source of data on public debate employed in empirical analysis of public sphere transformation. This strategy is rightly defended on the grounds that the media serves as the most important source of political information for most people and that it reflects the dominance of the mass media as a sphere of political communication in modern societies (Statham & Trenz, 2013, p. 10; Wessler et al., 2008, p. 4). Nevertheless, as Zimmermann and Favell put it in a point about the EU that is nevertheless relevant for broader processes of transnationalization, this research strategy 'only grasps a very small part of the EU as a novel political environment, because so much of what is interesting in the EU takes place well beyond the eye of the national media' (2011, p. 505). While such critiques do not foreclose the utility of the traditional media as a source of data on public sphere transformation in general or social movements in particular (see for example Roose et al., 2017), a focus on social movements as an object of inquiry favours the use of other sources of data, including interviews with activists (see, for example, David and Côrte-Real Pinto, 2017) as well as social media, online publications, and debate fora of social movements themselves. Indeed, as the articles in this special issue further illustrate, the indicators presented in Table 1 may be analysed empirically using a wide range of methods including diachronic studies of single or small numbers of movements from a single country examining change over the longer term; synchronic studies of movements in paired or multiple case studies; or studies examining single or multiple indicators.

Disclosure statement

No potential conflict of interest was reported by the authors.

References

Angela Merkel shuts down group of Greek anti-austerity protesters. (2015, July 4). *The Telegraph*.
Bourne, A. (2014). Europeanization and secession: The cases of Catalonia and Scotland. *Journal on Ethnopolitics and Minority Issues in Europe, 13*(3), 94–120.
Bourne, A., & Chatzopoulou, S. (2015). Europeanization and social movement mobilization during the European sovereign debt crisis: The cases of Spain and Greece. *Revista de pensament i Anàlisi, 17*, 33–60.

Bourne, A., & Chatzopoulou, S. (in press). *Euroscepticism and the crisis: 'Critical Europeanism' and anti-austerity social movements, Routledge handbook of Euroscepticism*. London: Routledge.

Calhoun, C. (1992). Introduction: Habermas and the public sphere in Calhoun. In C. Calhoun (Ed.), *Habermas and the public sphere* (pp. 1–50). Cambridge, MA: MIT Press.

Calhoun, C. (2002). Imagining solidarity: Cosmopolitanism, constitutional patriotism and the public sphere. *Political Culture, 14*(1), 147–171.

Castells, M. (2012). *Networks of outrage and hope: Social movements in the internet age*. Cambridge, MA: Polity.

Chatzopoulou, S., & Bourne, A. (2017). Transnational mobilization and critical Europeanisation: The cases of ETUC, ALTER SUMMIT, and BLOCKUPY: The cases of ETUC, ALTER SUMMIT and BLOCKUPY. In J. FitzGibbon, B. Leruth, & N. Startin (Eds.), *Euroscepticism as a transnational and Pan-European phenomenon: The emergence of a new sphere of opposition* (pp. 80–96). Abingdon, OX: Routledge/Taylor & Francis Group.

David, I., & Côrte-Real Pinto, G. A. (2017). The Gezi protests and the Europeanization of the Turkish public sphere. *Journal of Civil Society, 13*(3), 307–322. doi:10.1080/17448689.2017.1359887

de Vrees, C. H. (2007). The EU as a public sphere. *Living Reviews in European Governance, 2*, 3. Retrieved from http://www.livingreviews.org/lreg.html

de Wilde, P., & Zürn, M. (2012). Can politicization of European integration be reversed'? *Journal of Common Market Studies, 50*(1), 137–153.

della Porta, D. (2013). Social movements and the public sphere. In A. O. S. Salvatore & H. J. Trenz (Eds.), *Rethinking the public sphere through transnationalizing processes: Europe and beyond* (pp. 107–136). Houndsmills: Palgrave Macmillan.

della Porta, D., & Caiani, M. (2009). *Social movements and Europeanization*. Oxford: Oxford University Press.

della Porta, D., & Diani, M. (2006). *Social movements: An introduction*. Malden, MA: Blackwell.

della Porta, D., & Mattoni, A. (Eds). (2014). *Spreading protest*. Colchester: ECPR Press.

Democracia Real Ya. (2011a). *Declaración ciudadana ante la Estafa de la Deuda Publica*. Retrieved November 10, 2014, from http://declaraciondeuda.democraciarealya.es/

DRY. (2011b). *Lemas*. Retrieved November 10, 2014, from http://www.democraciarealya.es/promocion/lemas/

DRY. (2014). *#NoAlTTIP*. Retrieved November 10, 2014, from http://international.democraciarealya.es/2014/09/15/noalttip-on-the-11th-of-october-2014-join-the-decentralised-european-day-of-action-to-stop-ttip-ceta-tisa

Dunphy, R. (2017). Beyond nationalism? The anti-austerity social movements in Ireland: Between domestic constraints and lessons from abroad. *Journal of Civil Society, 13*(3), 267–283. doi:10.1080/17448689.2017.1355031

Eder, K. (2007). The public sphere and European democracy: Mechanisms of democratization in the transnational situation. In J. E. Fossum & P. Schlesinger (Eds.), *The European Union and the public sphere* (pp. 44–65). London: Routledge.

Eriksen, E. O. (2007). Conceptualising European public spheres: General, segmented and strong publics. In J. E. Fossum & P. Schlesinger (Eds.), *The European Union and the public sphere* (pp. 23–43). London: Routledge.

Feenstra, R. (2017). Rethinking global civil society and the public sphere in the age of prodemocracy movements. *Journal of Civil Society, 13*(3), 337–348. doi:10.1080/17448689.2017.1359886

Flesher Forminaya, C. (2014). *Social movements and globalisation*. Houndsmills: Palgrave Macmillan.

Flesher Forminaya, C., & Cox, L. (2013). *Understanding European movements*. London: Routledge.

Fligstein, N. (2008). *Euroclash – the EU, European identity and the future of Europe*. Oxford: Oxford University Press.

Fossum, J. E., & Schlesinger, P. (2007a). *The European Union and the public sphere: A communicative space in the making?* London: Routledge.

Fossum, J. E., & Schlesinger, P. (2007b). The European Union and the public sphere: A communicative space in the making? In J. E. Fossum & P. Schlesinger (Eds.), *The European Union and the public sphere* (pp. 1–20). London: Routledge.

Fraser, N. (1992). Rethinking the public sphere: A contribution to the critique of actually existing democracy. In C. Calhoun (Ed.), *Habermas and the public sphere* (pp. 109–142). Cambridge, MA: MIT Press.

Fraser, N. (2007). *Scales of justice: Reimagining political space in a globalising world*. New York, NY: Columbia University Press.

Fraser, N. (2013). A triple movement? *New Left Review, 81*, 119–132.

Free Otegi, Free Them All. (2017a). *Free Otegi, free them all*. Retrieved January 20, 2017, from https://www.youtube.com/watch?v=xNxVQsa-Fws

Free Otegi, Free Them All. (2017b). *26 MEPs endorse the declaration*. Retrieved January 20, 2017, from http://freeotegi.com/24-meps-endorse-the-declaration

Free Otegi, Free Them All. (2017c). *Endorsements*. Retrieved January 20, 2017, from http://freeotegi.com/endorsements/

Gerhards, J. (2001). Missing a European public sphere. In M. Kohli & M. Novak (Eds.), *Will Europe work? Integration, employment and social order* (pp. 145–158). London: Routledge.

Habermas, J. (1989). *The structural transformation of the public sphere*. Cambridge, MA: MIT Press.

Habermas, J. (1996a). *Between facts and norms*. Cambridge, MA: MIT Press.

Habermas, J. (1996b). *Die Einbeziehung des Anderen*. Frankfurt am Main: Suhrkamp.

Habermas, J., & Derida, J. (2005). February 15 or what binds Europeans together: A plea for a common foreign policy, beginning in the core of Europe. *Constellations, 10*(3), 291–297.

Hooghe, L., & Marks, G. (2008). A postfunctional theory of European integration from permissive consensus to constraining Dissensus'. *British Journal of Political Science, 39*(1), 1–23.

Imig, D., & Tarrow, S. (2000). Political contention in a Europeanising polity. *West European Politics, 23*(4), 73–93.

Koopmans, R., & Erbe, J. (2004). Towards a European public sphere? Vertical and Horizontal Dimensions of Europeanized Political Communication, Innovation. *The European Journal of Social Science Research, 17*(2), 97–118.

Koopmans, R., Erbe, J., & Meyer, M. (2010). The Europeanization of public spheres: Comparison across issues, time and countries. In R. Koopmans & P. Statham (Eds.), *The making of a European public sphere: Media discourse and political contention* (pp. 63–96). Cambridge, MA: Cambridge University Press.

Koopmans, R., & Statham, P., eds. (2010). *The making of a European public sphere: Media discourse and political contention*. Cambridge, MA: Cambridge University Press.

Kousis, M. (2014). The transnational dimension of the Greek protest campaign against troika memoranda and austerity policies, 2010–12. In D. Della Porta & A. Mattoni (Eds.), *Spreading protest* (pp. 137–170). Essex: ECPR press.

McAdam, D., & Rucht, D. (1993). The cross-national diffusion of movement ideas. *The Annals of the American Academy of Political and Social Science, 528*, 56–74.

Oxi to Osbourne. (2015, July 7). *The Guardian*.

Plataforma de Afectados por la Hipoteca. (2016). *PAH international committee*. Retrieved January 20, 2017, from http://afectadosporlahipoteca.com/2016/11/03/pah-international-committee/

Right2Water. (2016). *TTIP and CETA*. Retrieved January 20, 2017, from http://www.right2water.ie/events

Risse, T. (2010). *A community of Europeans? Transnational identities and public spheres*. Ithaca, NY: Cornell University Press.

Risse, T. (2014). No demos? Identities and public spheres in the euro crisis. *Journal of Common Market Studies, 52*(6), 1207–1215.

Romanos, E. (2013). Collective learning processes within social movements. In C. Flesher Fominaya & L. Cox (Eds.), *Understanding European movements: New social movements, global justice struggles, anti-austerity protest* (pp. 203–219). London: Routledge.

Roose, J., Kanellopoulous, K., & Sommer, M. (2017). National anti-austerity protests in a European crisis: Comparing the Europeanizing impact of protest in Greece and Germany during the Eurozone zrisis. *Journal of Civil Society, 13*(3), 284–306. doi:10.1080/17448689.2017.1362137

Salvatore, A. O. S., & Trenz, H. J. (2013). Introduction: Rethinking the public sphere through transnationalizing processes; Europe and beyond. In A. O. S. Salvatore & H. J. Trenz (Eds.), *Rethinking the public sphere through transnationalizing processes: Europe and beyond* (pp. 1–25). Houndsmills: Palgrave Macmillan.

Snow, D. (2004). Framing processes, ideology and discursive fields. In D. A. Snow, S. A. Soule, & H. Kriesi (Eds.), *The Blackwell companion to social movements* (pp. 380–412). Malden, MA: Blackwell.

Statham, P., & Trenz, H. J. (2013). *The politicization of Europe: Contesting the constitution in the mass media*. London: Routledge.

Statham, P., & Trenz, H. J. (2015). Understanding the mechanisms of EU politicization: Lessons from the Eurozone crisis. *Comparative European Politics, 13*(3), 287–306.

Tarrow, S. (2005). *The new transnational activism*. Cambridge, MA: Cambridge University Press.

Tarrow, S. (2012). *Strangers at the gate*. Cambridge, MA: Cambridge University Press.

Tejerina, B., Perugorria, I., Benski, T., & Langman, L. (2013). From indignation to occupation: A new wave of global mobilization. *Current Sociology, 61*(4), 377–392.

Thousands turn out for Greek protests in Dublin. (2015, July 4). *Irish Times*.

Trenz, H. J., & Eder, K. (2004). The democratizing dynamics of a European public sphere. *European Journal of Social Theory, 7*(1), 5–25.

Wessler, H., Peters, B., Brüggemann, M., Kleinen von Königslöw, K., & Stifft, S. (2008). *Transnationalization of public spheres*. Houndsmills: Palgrave Macmillan.

Zimmermann, A., & Favell, A. (2011). Governmentality, political field or public sphere? Theoretical alternatives in the political sociology of the EU. *European Journal of Social Theory, 14*(4), 489–515.

More than a Copy Paste: The Spread of Spanish Frames and Events to Portugal

Britta Baumgarten and Rubén Díez García

ABSTRACT
The article contributes to the literature on diffusion by focusing on two recent cases of social movements in Spain and in Portugal, identifying different stages of cooperation and diffusion. Our specific contribution to the diffusion literature is the temporal perspective: Processes were observed over several years. This allows for an in-depth analysis of factors of success and failures of diffusion and how activists deal with such processes over time. We further ask how activists deal with a lack of success in some processes of diffusion and why this was no obstacle of further diffusion processes.

Occupation of public spaces, public assemblies, and the frames 'Democracy Now!', 'Podemos', and the 'Platform against Evictions (PAH)' – these are some of the many examples of ideas and models imported from Spanish to Portuguese anti-austerity movements. In our article, we analyse this spread of ideas, events, and action frames from Spain to Portugal.

We compare the framing of the Spanish Indignados movement to the Portuguese anti-austerity movements at different times of the development of each movement and show possible diffusion of framing. Both cases are part of a worldwide protest wave starting from the Arab Spring (Dufour, Nez, & Ancelovici, 2016; Flesher Fominaya & Cox, 2013; Tejerina, Perugorria, Benski, & Langman, 2013). Based on a comparison of events and frames of the Spanish 15M and Portuguese anti-austerity protests and movements between 2011 and 2014, we, firstly, identify similarities and differences between the cases. Then, based on interviews with Portuguese activists, we analyse the importing of frames and action forms from Spain to Portugal and the mechanisms that supported and hindered such diffusion processes.

Portugal and Spain are both third-wave democracies that are characterized by a low degree of political participation, but their civil societies differ.[1] In terms of historical events, there are many references of the Portuguese activists to the Carnation Revolution in 1974 (Baumgarten, 2017), while the Spanish 15M/Indignados, as well as other large mobilizations since the mid-1990s, have been reflecting the unintended consequences and 'black holes' of political transition to democracy in Spain (Laraña, 2009; Laraña & Díez, 2009, 2012).

Since May 2011, the Spanish Indignados became an important actor inspiring activists in other countries (Castañeda, 2012; Díez García, 2017; Romanos, 2016). While the large protests of the Geração à Rasca ('Desperate Generation') in several Portuguese cities in March 2011 had some impact on activism in other countries, the Portuguese activists imported action forms from Spain rather than exported them.[2] The international resonance of the Spanish movement's frames and values is linked with the existence of common problems and demands across different countries, as well as a common lack of confidence in political leaders' ability to solve and handle them (Díez García, 2017; Laraña & Díez, 2012). The rapid and large-scale expansion of the movement, which became very visible worldwide following the protests in May 2011, also inspired social movement activism in many other countries. In this process, two aspects have played a central role: (i) 15M's resonance through the media and digital social networks – sometimes with activists with digital technology skills pursuing stimulus communication strategies[3] and (ii) the emergence of transnational networks of indignados activists and organizations – some of them already active since the alter-globalization movement of the 1990s (Díez García, 2017).

This article contributes to the literature on diffusion by focusing on two recent cases of social movements and identifying different stages of cooperation and diffusion, starting from contacts at the individual level and diffusion mainly via the web 2.0, and developing into closer cooperation including meetings and the creation of international platforms. Our specific contribution to the diffusion literature is the temporal perspective of diffusion. Observation of these processes over several years allows for an in-depth analysis of factors leading to the success or failure of diffusion and how activists deal with such processes over time. In addition, we not only analyse factors of success and failure of diffusion, but further ask how activists deal with a lack of success in some processes of diffusion and why this lack of success (in our case) was no obstacle to continue diffusion processes.

The diffusion of ideas, action forms, and framing: A transnational view on anti-austerity movements

Social movements are deeply embedded in their national contexts even in the case of global protest waves like the one observed starting with the Arab Spring in 2011. National borders are important, for example, because of different political contexts and different histories of social movement organization. Transnational differences are an important source of inspiration for social movements, especially in times when information on events and practices travels fast via the Internet (Baumgarten, 2014; Castells, 2012; Romanos, 2016). Such inspiration is necessary to fulfil the task of constantly innovating action forms in order to stay attractive for the mass media (Cottle, 2008) and potential new supporters, but also to find new forms of organizing protest in times when 'the old recipes' do not work out well (Baumgarten, 2016). In this article, we employ the distinction between 'international resonance' and 'transnational diffusion'. A frame or idea can have a resonance or an echo in the international sphere, but the diffusion of such a frame or idea is transnational. International resonance is a first step that does not guarantee diffusion.

Diffusion is a more complex process, which does not embrace the entire globe, but only some countries in which certain frames, ideas or forms of action are adapted through different channels.

The spread of particular practical knowledge, ideas, strategies, or frames among social movements, as well as cultural and discursive continuities over time and in different contexts, is not new (Díez García, 2017; McAdam & Rucht, 1993; Snow & Benford, 1988). However, the diffusion of ideas, forms of action, and frames is an issue that acquired importance particularly since the 1990s, following the emergence of the alter-globalization social movement and the expansion of digital technologies (Castells, 2012; Della Porta, Kriesi, & Rucht, 1999; Earl, 2010; Givan, Roberts, & Soule, 2010; Soule, 2004; Tarrow, 2005).

There are two forms of diffusion: Direct and indirect. While direct diffusion depends on the strength of the connections between actors, indirect diffusion can take place when the adapter identifies with the submitter or when the mass media act as transmitters (Soule, 2004, pp. 295–296). Along these lines, Tarrow (2005) distinguishes between non-relational channels (e.g., mass media and digital social networks) and interpersonal contacts. Mass media has enabled and encouraged such diffusion in the past, as well as today, playing an important role as non-relational channels of diffusion (McAdam & Rucht, 1993; Romanos, 2016; Tarrow, 1994).

In the Information Age, digital communication technologies have become powerful tools for diffusion of knowledge and information (Castells, 2012). Earl (2010) describes the dynamics of diffusion processes of protest via the Internet. She distinguishes between diffusion of information, protest-related innovations, and protest itself. According to Earl, 'Innovations cannot be broadcast like information, but rather must be learned about and then adopted' (2010, p. 214).

In our country comparison (McAdam, McCarthy, & Zald, 1996), we build upon social movement approaches that take a closer look at movement practices and organizational structures, namely the framing approach (Benford & Snow, 2000; Snow & Benford, 1988; Snow, Rochford, Worden, & Benford, 1986), and that focus on repertoires of action (Tilly, 2008). Frames were analysed in both cases based on manifestos and calls for protest.[4] Both cases are further developed on the basis of ethnographic fieldwork: 47 activist meetings and 13 demonstrations and other protest events (between September 2011 and March 2013) in Portugal and more than 50 actions and events, among them meetings, demonstrations, teach-ins, marches and assemblies (between May 2011 and 2014) in Spain. In both cases, events were followed by periods of intensive fieldwork.

Our analysis also included in-depth interviews with activists. In Portugal, 17 interviews with activists were carried out mainly in 2012. The Spanish database includes (i) the analysis of 10 in-depth interviews with activists, supporters, and sympathizers, and 8 focus groups from a study carried out by the Centre of Sociological Research (CIS) during the second half of 2011 (ES2921) and (ii) quantitative data analysis of a survey carried out by the CIS (ES2920).[5]

This material allows us to analyse frames and forms of action over time, and in different contexts, starting with the emergence of the 15M in Spain and the 2011 Portuguese anti-austerity movement. The data collection and fieldwork took place mainly between the first half of 2011 and 2014, although it has continued through 2016.

The Spanish case: The Indignados movement or how frames may change

The search for new participatory forms of representation is central to the Indignados project of political change and regeneration. Indeed, this central demand gave the name to one of the movement's major organizations Democracia Real Ya! (DRY) (Real Democracy Now!), which played a key role in the 15M movement with its call to mass demonstrations on 15 May 2011. A rejection of the power structure – which activists called 'partitocracy' – and their search for alternatives became the main motivation for action against what they viewed as a closed system of participation, burdened by inefficiency.

Political themes had a greater presence and influence in the Spanish movement's framing activities than did economic ones. For example, the movement demanded suppression of the privileges of the 'political class' and changes to the electoral law by, for instance, introducing open lists and a distribution of seats more in proportion to the number of votes received. Likewise, in the Puerta del Sol Square, activists collected signatures supporting central proposals in their prognostic frame explaining the cause of people's current problems as political corruption, the party system and elections in Spain (Laraña & Díez, 2012).

A large number of spontaneous proposals were collected in Puerta del Sol in 2011. A year later they were compiled and released by the Sol's Proposal Commission. Of a total of 14,679 proposals, political matters prevailed (33%) over economic (22%), environmental (15%), and educational issues (13%). Among the 20 most frequent proposals, the first 3 made reference to political issues: (i) 'suppression of politicians' privileges', (ii) 'reform of the electoral law', and (iii) 'measures against corruption'; the fourth and the fifth referred to 'public education' and 'improvement in labour conditions', while the 'regulation of banks and financial institutions' appeared in the sixth place.[6]

A key feature in the emergence of the 15M lied in its prognostic frames, in its order of priorities to solve economic problems, and the way these frames focused on political regeneration as a precondition for such solutions, which linked critique of current politics with pressing economic problems (Laraña & Díez, 2012). These prognostic frames are significant for understanding this phenomenon in a broad sense, and its resonance among audiences in Spain and other countries (Díez García, 2017).

This order of priorities is supported by statistical analyses of aggregate data from the above-mentioned CIS survey: Dissatisfaction with the political situation and the way in which formal democracy is running became a distinguishing element among those survey respondents who had decided to channel their disaffection and outrage through the 15M movement. These political claims contributed more significantly to their participation in the movement, than did their negative perceptions of the economic situation (Díez, 2015). In summary, data show that the political elements of the 15M mobilization frame played a key role in its emergence, in its continuity and in the social support it received; and they fulfilled a fundamental role in this movement because they were the basis of its collective identity (Díez, 2014, 2015; Laraña & Díez, 2012).

15M's mobilization frames were strongly influenced by DRY claims, which included not only political aspects but also economic ones that were expanded during the camps and beyond. Among the economic problems that activists included in their diagnostic frames in particular were issues which affected many citizens' life chances, especially those of young people, which contributed to the resonance of DRY's claims. For example, the issues of precariousness and unemployment affected an important part of the movement's supporters and sympathizers, as did controversy over the payment of mortgages and evictions. This controversy, in addition to cuts in public services such as education and health, had high resonance among citizens. Subsequently, the *Plataforma de Afectados por la Hipoteca* (PAH) (Platform of People Affected by Mortgages) and the *Mareas Ciudadanas* (Citizens' Tides or Waves) – or protests – in defense of public services became important actors mobilizing citizens following the emergence of the 15M in 2011. Therefore, the 15M not only confronted the political power structure but also the main economic organizations of the country (Díez, 2015; Laraña & Díez, 2012).

In mid-June 2011, after the camps were dismantled, a large number of neighbourhood and local assemblies emerged.[7] These assemblies participated in the Euro-Pact protests (on 19 June 2011) and in the Marcha Popular Indignada (Indignant People's March) and the 15M Social Forum of July 2011, as well as in the international events of October 2011 and May 2012. In 2012, PAH began to gain visibility and other new initiatives also emerged, such as the 'Coordinadora 25-S',[8] those that led to the 'Mareas' in defense of public services, or the Platform that called in 2014 for the Marchas de la Dignidad (Marches of Dignity). Among the groups, networks, and organizations that shaped these platforms and attended their calls, we can find great diversity. People joining these groups came from the new networks that emerged with the 15M and the assemblies, but there were also many others already active before the 15M, who had participated in that movement – some from the beginning, others joining later – (at least not in a leading role, e.g., people from minor political parties, unions, and activists with previous experience).

Changes in demands and frames that came along with the emergence of new actors and subsequent events provide evidence of open and dynamic processes of mobilization, in which labels and categories can quickly lose their utility as a way to understand reality, including the category 15M itself. These are processes in which we can expect the existence of alliances, confluences, controversies, conflicts, and fragmentations,[9] if we take into account that the impulse to articulate citizens' indignation was supported in a movement whose origins showed an inclusive and plural character.

Consequently, mobilization frames changed over time – in particular, producing an amplification and extension of frames (Benford & Snow, 2000; Díez, 2015; Snow, 2004).[10] Some aspects of the original frames have been constant over time or implicitly informed subsequent episodes of protest in a context of mobilization shaped by 15M since its emergence in May 2011. Some, however, changed considerably, with new claims, manifestos, and proposals no longer emphasizing explicitly and clearly the key aspects with the greatest potential for collective persuasion; namely, its order of priorities for solving everyday problems of the citizens, focused on political changes and democratic regeneration as a precondition for such solutions. In this process, the increasing prominence of experienced pre-15M activists and groups from Spanish social movements' scene of the 2000s as well as 15M's transnationalization has played an important role.

Regarding its international resonance, two main events were milestones: The 15O (15 October 2011) and the 12M (12 May 2012). In October 2011, under the slogans 'United for Global Change', 'United for Global Democracy', and 'Global Revolution', DRY and the 15M international group launched a first call for mobilization. People from all over the world demonstrated 'to claim their rights and demand a true democracy'.[11] The call emphasized the gap between the ruling classes and the people, and denounced the connivance between 'politicians, and the financial elites they serve', using the DRY slogan: 'We are not goods in the hands of politicians and bankers who do not represent us'. Some months later in May 2012, another call also denounced the aforementioned connivance between economic and political elites, emphasizing that 'democratic political systems have been emptied of meaning, put to the service of those few interested in increasing the power of corporations and financial institutions'.[12] In the Spanish case, this second call was supported through demonstrations and other public actions by several thousand people of many different age and social positions. Nevertheless, in contrast with October 2011 call, it showed an amplified prognostic and mobilization frame. Under the broad slogan: 'For global democracy and social justice! Take to the streets in May 2012!', proposals were made to democratize the economy and to put it to the service of the people, to democratize the political system and international institutions, and to renew the Universal Declaration of Human Rights, to make it fit for the twenty-first century, written in a participatory, direct, and democratic way.

Building on the minimum consensus[13] regarding the values, claims, and goals from which 15M found its social bases – its high capacity of resonance and the collective expression of citizens' indignation – , the original or initial frames subsequently experienced a process of extension and amplification. This was due to the movement's inclusive, open, and plural character. Thus, in the interplay of differing definitions of the situation coming from different networks, the emphasis on its original, initial, and more powerful resonant frames have gradually led to a diversification of frames. Some of them are classic issues and themes of the activist setting of the 1990s and 2000s in Spain and the autonomous and alter-globalization movement that became important at that time (Flesher Fominaya, 2015). In this context, different actors spread new collective definitions, demands, and frames, while the political and economic context also changed (e.g., further austerity measures and cuts in public services, rising unemployment and evictions, an increasing European debt crisis and difficulties in accessing credit, new corruption cases, and bank frauds, among other issues).

To what extent has this diversification of frames affected the movement's capacity to maintain the alignment of its values and goals with its initial audiences and contributed to the movement's gradual loss of visibility? A plausible answer to this question is that this wide range of different claims and proposals might have had some impact on the 15M's gradual loss of visibility. However, it might also have contributed to reinforcing 15M's transformation and fragmentation into different, heterogeneous, and yet recurrent episodes of more atomized and less visible demonstrations, protests, and public actions, in addition to other latent initiatives such as those managed by housing activists, Mareas, Centros Sociales Ocupados (Squatter Social Centres), pensioners affected by bank frauds, workers, republicans, LGTB groups, or feminists, among many other collectives (Díez, 2015).

These atomized mobilizations, however, seemed to gain more visibility in the less frequent but large demonstrations and marches that brought them together (Flesher Fominaya, 2014). This is the case of the Marches of Dignity that took place on 22 March 2014 in Madrid. In particular, the actors joining these marches developed a new framing that proposes a new constituent process, since the Spanish democracy is a corrupted and illegitimate one inherited from Franco's dictatorship, which was kidnapped by the Troika, thanks to the collaboration of the two main large parties in Spain.[14]

During these years therefore, the lack of policies to resolve the everyday problems of the citizens has led different activists, branches, and supporters to pursue a complementary strategy which goes beyond social mobilization: To go into politics. The most relevant initiatives that have emerged are Podemos and those parties grounded in municipalism. In fact, many of the members and sympathizers of these initiatives share this new framing. However, the new framing includes several very controversial issues in Spanish politics and among citizens, and do not seem a call to inclusiveness and pluralism, two essential characteristics of the 15M movement.

The Portuguese case (2011–2014) and its relation to the Spanish 'Indignados' movement

In Portugal, a large protest event, the so-called Geração à Rasca (Desperate generation) protest, took place on 12 March 2011, some nine weeks before the occupation of Puerta del Sol in Madrid. It put an end to a period of about 35 years in which the trade unions were the only actors capable of organizing mass demonstrations (Accornero & Ramos Pinto, 2015; Baumgarten, 2013a, 2013b, 2016; Estanque, Costa, & Soeiro, 2013). In May 2011, inspired by the Spanish 15M, protestors occupied Rossio, a central square in Lisbon. During the Rossio occupation 15O – a platform of more than 30 activist groups and associations against the Portuguese government's austerity program – was created in order to organize the international day of protest on 15 October 2011 in Portugal – an international day of protest initiated by 15M. 15O continued to meet regularly after the October protest to organize further protest events. The events in May in particular contributed to the creation of new citizen groups, assemblies, and activist groups, among them Democracia Verdadeira Já, which organized a first international meeting in July 2011.[15]

In May 2012, protesters occupied a large park in Lisbon for three days to commemorate the first anniversary of the founding of the 15M movement in Spain. This event was part of the international event 'Global Spring'. Greater sacrifices and loss of fundamental rights were diagnosed by the Portuguese organizers as key problems facing ordinary citizens and the solution proposed was that all have to be part of the solution; reflected in the slogan 'people over profit'. Global action and the strength of protest activities in other countries were used to motivate people in Portugal to be part of a strong movement, as expressed in the event's slogan 'Global Spring is arriving'.

'Que se lixe a troika (QSLT)' (Screw the Troika), a small group of activists, called for a protest on 15 September 2012 that was followed by further protests that were often very successful in bringing large numbers of people to the streets in Portugal up until 26 October 2013. The most prominent series of activities of that time was 'grandolar' (a word coined during the protests): After a group of activists interrupted the Prime Minister's speech in the Parliament by singing the famous revolutionary song 'Grândola', various groups all over the country began to practise this creative form of protest against their local and national politicians from the conservative party in government, who were often accused not only to foster austerity but also to be involved in cases of corruption.[16]

The years 2013 and 2014 are dominated by protests and strikes of branches of the trade unions, for example, on behalf of teachers, the public transport workers, or health professionals. The social movement sector organized a few demonstrations – mainly on international issues like solidarity with Palestine or against the Spanish king – that all remained small compared those demonstrations in 2011–2013. In 2014, a protest in commemoration of the 40th anniversary of the Revolution of the Craves that started in the night of 24 April 1974 was organized in the form of a demonstration march from different starting points. The commemoration was regarded as an opportunity to claim that the goals of the Revolution and the revolutionary process had not been fully accomplished in Portugal and that they were endangered by austerity. The image used was that of different rivers flowing towards the symbolic place 'Largo do Carmo' in Lisbon, where the dictator finally gave up and left the country.[17]

We argue that the Spanish protests have influenced the Portuguese protests since May 2011, but the impact varied over time. The events most influenced by the Spanish case were the occupation of Rossio in May 2011 and the international demonstrations. In the following, we shed light on the different kinds of impact that became visible between 2011 and 2014 (see Table 1 for an overview).

Action forms and activist groups

Choosing the action form 'occupation of a public space' and the organizational form of public assemblies, the Portuguese activists in May 2011 followed the Spanish Indignados with the help of information from the Internet, personal contacts, and Spanish persons living in Portugal. Moreover, 'first, when it started there were more Spaniards than Portuguese' (Luis, Lisbon). But some action forms that became internationally prominent following the emergence of the Spanish 15M could be found in Portugal even before 15 May 2011 and have developed independently from the Spanish 15M. Public assemblies, for example, had been employed already in 2010 and squatting as such has a longer history in Portugal, going back to the Revolution in 1974. In Oporto, an empty school building had already been occupied in April 2011 and was used as a cultural centre in 2011 until its occupants were evicted in 2012.

The Spanish example, however, promoted these action forms in prefigurative terms as pointers of success. Especially the public assemblies and the occupation of public space were now practised with the aim of building up a large movement for democracy and against austerity. Occupations, however, were rare cases in Portugal, which is explained by the fear of police repression. Here, activists rather rented spaces for projects and often organized benefits to be able to pay the rent, or owners let them use their empty buildings for free. Furthermore, associations have the possibility of getting access to spaces from the municipality for free.

Many Portuguese political groups were founded inspired by Spanish examples. In the months after May 2011, a lot of new activist groups were created, most of them in Lisbon. Most prominently, we find the emergence of Indignados in Portugal from May 2011 and local assemblies from the same year. But not all of the groups followed the model of the Spanish Indignados. Indeed, we find the coalescence of varying old and new forms of organization, internal practices and issues, and new and experienced activists (unlike in Spain, in Portugal the term activist was not challenged by many people). The platform 15O was created with the aim of copying the Spanish assemblies, but in practice it was

Table 1. Overview of the Spanish and Portuguese cases and diffusion.

Temporal progress	Ideal (type) character and (noticeable) repertoire		Leading networks, groups and organizations		Predominant frame and themes		Factors explaining diffusion
	Spain	Portugal	Spain	Portugal	Spain	Portugal	
2011 Spring	Youth Without Future Demonstration (April 2011) & Indignados 15M movement (May 2011)	Geração à Rasca (12 March 2011), public assemblies in Oporto	A Facebook Platform & preliminary meetings since the beginning of 2011, Real Democracy Now (DRY), Youth Without Future (JSF), Acampada Sol & Acampada Barcelona (among other camps), & Indignados sympathizers and supporters among citizens	Facebook call followed by organization of existent groups (Lisbon) and assemblies (Oporto)	National focus on Spanish democracy & citizens' life chances in DRY & JSF Manifestos and during the assemblies in the camps. But also an international scope that gained progressive importance with other manifestos, commissions & very active, globally oriented groups	Right to employment, improvement of working conditions end of precarious life situations, right to education	No diffusion
	Occupation of public squares, assemblies, sit-ins, & demonstrations	May 2011 occupation of public squares, occupation of public building Oporto		Spontaneous decision after demonstration in front of Spanish consulate		Portuguese adaptation of the Spanish manifesto: introduction of democracy frame, against the global phenomenon of the actual loss of rights and opportunities	Success of 15M and resonance of at least its broad mobilization frames, personal contacts with Spanish activists, travelling Portuguese activists, Web2.0, few Spaniards invited to events in Portugal
2011 Fall	Spreading out of the camps & internationalization Neighbourhood and local assemblies, marches & international protest events	Demonstrations, international protest day, assemblies, some smaller attempts of local assemblies	DRY, JSF, Take the Square & International Commissions, as well as local and neighbourhood assemblies	15O, public assemblies, few neighbourhood assemblies	Continuity of the original frame & progressive emergence of global and European concerns and more social and economic issues than political ones	Continuation of participative democracy, transparency in political decisions, end to precarious existences	International protest events, more personal contacts, visits of Spanish activists

(Continued)

Table 1. Continued.

Temporal progress	Ideal (type) character and (noticeable) repertoire		Leading networks, groups and organizations		Predominant frame and themes		Factors explaining diffusion
	Spain	Portugal	Spain	Portugal	Spain	Portugal	
2012–2013	Housing, defense of public services, symbolic, & public pressure on politicians and political institutions. Neighbourhood & local assemblies, actions against evictions, demonstrations, 'escraches', international events & marches	Occupation of a public park, occupation of a building. Large demonstrations, institucionalization of former activist groups (associations, cultural centres), new political parties, alternatives to occupation (rent or use space for free), European general strike	Neighbourhood & local assemblies, Platform against Evictions (PAH), Citizens' Tides or Waves (Mareas Ciudadanas), Coordinadora 25-S Platform, 'Social Centres', JSF and its collectives in other countries, & Partido X (X Party)	Until May 2012 event 'Global Spring' planned by open assemblies. Since August 2012 QSLT (including Mareas)	Anti-austerity frame in the context of the European Debt crisis and Europeanization/ transnationalization of social movements; as well as a wide range of themes from the 1990s and 2000s Spanish social movements' scene, alter-globalization & autonomous movements	Shift to international frames, reinvent democracy: participation, sharing, transparency, social justice and environmental protection	International protest events and meetings, international group of 15M, more direct contacts than before, strength of protest in Spain, smaller scale of the Portuguese mobilization
2014–2015	Marches of Dignity & emergence of new political organizations. Marches & demonstrations	Few demonstrations, mainly organized by different branches of the trade unions and little groups instead of platforms; event linked to the ideas of Podemos	Marches of Dignity Platform, new political organizations: Podemos and those grounded on municipalism, Coordinadora 25-S & 'Social Centres'	No dominant group	Anti-austerity frame & national focus on Spanish economy and politics, and controversial issues among parties and citizens: Type of Government/State, constituent processes, territorial organization	National focus against cuts in salaries, privatization, housing	Success of Podemos, existing contacts, smaller scale of the Portuguese mobilization

dominated by activist groups rather than individuals, as was the case in Spain (Baumgarten, 2013b, 2016).

The idea of the Marés – the Spanish Mareas that mainly emerged in Spain in 2012[18] – came up in Portugal in the QSLT movement. Especially in the protest on 2 March 2013, many different Marés became visible in Lisbon and Oporto in the areas of health, education, pension, culture, human rights, precariat, and unemployment. In the beginning of 2015, the Portuguese PAH started activities in Lisbon, following the Spanish PAH model, but it never became a large actor. Also in the case of Podemos, the diffusion did not result in the foundation of a political party like that in Spain. There was a citizen assembly for the project Juntos Podemos, 12–13 December 2014, which borrowed its name from the very successful Spanish Podemos, but the organizational principle differed from the Spanish case. Attempts to create a party like that in Spain failed because of the existing structures of party affiliation of many Portuguese activists.[19]

Framing

Some of the most important protest events in Portugal (2011–2014) were inspired by Spanish events or related to international events. In all of these events, the framing is similar regarding the broad mobilization frames, but there are differences in the more specific diagnostic, prognostic, and motivational framing as well as in blame attribution. We observed parallel developments of new action forms and organizational strategies often with a time lag that indicates to us the direction of the travel of ideas from Spain to Portugal. In some cases, the Portuguese mobilizations profited from the popularity and size of the Spanish movements and their protests.

Similarities in framing between movements in Spain and Portugal could be observed mainly in the international events where they both participated. In the other events in Portugal, frames depended on the structure of the groups engaged in organizing the protest (Baumgarten, 2013b). In the first large Portuguese demonstration on 12 March 2011, which took place before the momentous protest events in Spain, we find diagnostic frames closely related to the socio-economic problems of the country: The precarious situation, especially of young people, and the connected problem of not having the opportunity to realize their potential. For example, the manifesto of the protest claims:

> We are the highest-qualified generation in the history of our country. For this reason, we won't let down to tiredness, frustration or lack of future perspectives. We do believe we have all the resources and tools to provide a bright future to our country and ourselves.[20]

We find a discourse emphasizing a waste of resources and the blocking of aspirations of young people, similar to the claims of the Spanish key organization behind the 15M, 'Youth without Future',[21] which held a demonstration on 7 April 2011 under the slogan: 'No house, No Job, No Pension, No fear'. These discourses were highly compatible with the dominant discourse of the European Union aiming at young people finding jobs suited to their education and experience.[22] For the events that followed, we observe various kinds of relationships between the Spanish and the Portuguese protests, which point towards different phenomena of diffusion.

The most obvious import from Spain was the democracy frame from the time of the 15 October 2011 international protests. This frame had not been present in Portugal before.

In fact, the democracy frame is rarely connected in Portugal to the idea of rejecting political parties as such. An activist from Lisbon explained this in an interview in 2012 as follows:

> in the social movements there are more people that [...], more or less directly participate or are members of a political party. I think here in Portugal the political parties of the Left, like the Left Bloc or the Communist Party are respected and thus the idea of non-partisanship resonates better in Spain than in Portugal. (Antonio, Lisbon)

Various other issues gained importance in 2012 because of the Spanish model, for example, housing, deliberation, and inclusive political participation. Already in 2012, the activist group 'Habita' that defends the right to housing became active and turned into an association in 2014. The new frames, however, did not result in the decreasing importance of older ones: Frames related to the socio-economic situation of the country remained important and became more concrete. For example, posters for the demonstration and the general strike on 22 March 2012 included the following issues: Debt, austerity, precariousness, unemployment, poverty (a photo of the poster is available at https://ephemerajpp.files.wordpress.com/2012/03/dsc09763.jpg?resize=500%2C375).

The continuing importance of older frames is explained by their continuing relevance for the countries' situation, but also because they were the result of a longer preparation process that involved many different activist groups and individuals that to a great extent belonged to the classical field of social movement activism (Baumgarten, 2013b). Calling for protest on 2 March 2013 the organizers (QSLT) published the statements of activists, artists, and others about why they participate in the protests. So a central call was avoided and a plurality of voices – most of them including frames related to the socio-economic situation of the country – was presented instead.

Furthermore, beginning in May 2011, there have been similarities with the Spanish case in the attribution of blame: Politicians were blamed for not listening to the people and the issue of collusion between politicians, employers, and bankers was raised in Portugal for the first time. While in March 2011 direct blame was absent, from October 2011 it became more detailed and more international: Attributed not only to the actual governments and the economic system, but also to markets, financial speculation, and (in the QSLT protests) a lack of social and environmental consciousness on the part of the government and businesses. The solutions proposed in May and October 2011 are concrete, many of them resembling the Spanish ones.[23] Later such detailed frames are not apparent. The QSLT protests in particular remain vague, which reflects the difficulty of the Portuguese activists to agree on common solutions, and 'importing' ideas from Spain was not the solution to this problem.

The Portuguese framing was often independent from Spanish frames and referred to national peculiarities, such as references to the Carnation Revolution (Baumgarten, 2017). The import of frames was stronger at the 'international demonstrations', such as 15 October 2011, the Global Spring (May 2012), and the Global Noise (October 2012) which were themselves often mainly initiated by Spanish activists, with the help of activists and groups from transnational networks (Díez García, 2017). Portuguese frames here are to a great extent similar to the Spanish frames, and some calls were simply translated into Portuguese from the international calls. Coordination of international protests at that time did not include international planning meetings, like those we find in some of the later protests, but there was an exchange of ideas via the Internet. QSLT was maybe the group that put most effort in attempts to internationalize protests. Many protests were explicitly named 'international', and a first 'European' general strike took place on 14 November 2012. We also find parallel developments in Portugal and in Spain that were fostered by these international events. At the Global Spring, for example, there was a shift towards more international frames, but also a loss of detail in prognostic frames, reduced to 'all have to be part of the solution' and 'people over profit'.

Large protests in Spain inspired Portuguese activists to organize protests in Portugal on the same day, but these events often remained small in the end. Different external as well as organizational factors help to explain why large Spanish protests could not be copied successfully. For example, protests on 19 June 2011 against the so-called Euro Pact were very large in Spain but remained small in Portugal. As the protests were mainly directed towards the government, and were held only two days before the Portuguese parliamentary elections, not much resonance with movement frames from Spain could be expected in Portugal. In addition, the activists had just started to organize themselves. The occupation of Rossio had ended only two weeks earlier, and the planning of events as well as the development of internal organization structures of some very young activist groups was focused on the international protest coming up on 15 October.

Channels of exchange of ideas

All of the Portuguese activists we interviewed in 2012 mentioned that they did not have any formal, institutionalized contact with Spanish groups. At that time action forms and frames were diffused mainly via the Internet, personal contacts, visits to Spain, and visits from Spanish activists in Portugal. While the Internet remained the main channel for exchange of information, cooperation was organized via face-to-face meetings and phone calls. Spaniards were invited as speakers at Portuguese events, as, for example, in the case of a representative of Acampada Salamanca who spoke at the international meeting 'Real democracy and Austerity Plans' in Lisbon in June 2011. Those invitations became more frequent with the availability of funding and the institutionalization of contacts after 2012.

By 2013, there were some international meetings with financial support, e.g., a meeting in Amsterdam in October 2013 with funding from the Transnational Institute that allowed activists from Portugal to travel. Members of the group on internationalization of the Spanish 15M took part in the national meeting of the public assemblies in Coimbra in February 2013, talked about their work in Spain and gave advice on organizational issues. Portuguese and Spanish activists met at loosely coordinated events, like the European Strike Meeting in September 2014,[24] the Blockupy meeting in Brussels in October 2014, and the Blockupy Protests in Frankfurt in Spring 2015.[25]

Construction of otherness

The construction of otherness is an important factor in processes of diffusion: Such constructions help activists to explain why certain forms of action work or do not work in their case and why other movements are more or less successful (Baumgarten, 2014). Starting from May 2011, frequently drawn comparisons between activism in Portugal and Spain led to frustration because the Portuguese events were smaller and fewer people participated in public assemblies, the (Portuguese) Indignados and newly created political groups, such as the unemployed movement (Movimento Sem Emprego) or the movement of generations (Movimento Gerações). Interviews conducted in 2012 showed that many Portuguese activists regarded the Spanish people as more active and explained the lack of participation in protest events in Portugal in relation to cultural differences. Also the Spanish movement was regarded as more open to differing political views and new participants. Regarding the degree of radicalism, many Portuguese activists described the Spanish as more radical and the Portuguese as looking for compromises even with the police: 'Here you do a demonstration, then comes the time, that time agreed upon with the police was from three to six, at six o'clock you tidy up your banners and we go home. That was what we did' (Rui, Oporto).

These constructions helped to overcome frustration when an action form imported from Spain did not work out. They were, however, only used as an explanation after a failed diffusion and not as an argument against trying out action forms from Spain.

Conclusions

In this article, we have emphasized the importance of national contexts, cultural aspects, and a longitudinal perspective in the spread of frames and events between Spain and Portugal. Literature on diffusion of social movements' ideas sometimes underestimates such differences, since it focuses analyses on media and digital technologies that are attributed the main role in the diffusion of frames and ideas across borders. Also, that literature tends to categorize complex and changing frames as one static 'anti-austerity' frame.

Over the whole time period examined, we find a mixture of direct and indirect diffusion, but the mechanisms of direct diffusion changed. In 2011, the Portuguese activists depended on Spaniards living in Portugal and on personal contacts rather than institutionalized contacts. Institutionalized contacts and the number of international meetings and visits grew especially throughout 2012. Thus, in addition to the existing, almost accidental direct contacts, we now observe contacts between experienced people that in some cases even specialized in diffusion of the 15M practices.

Based on our data, we have singled out factors that enabled diffusion and factors that were obstacles to it. Going beyond explaining success and failure, we have analysed why in the Portuguese case failures in some cases of diffusion were no obstacle for diffusion of other ideas.

Among the enabling factors for diffusion we have found:

(1) The success of the Spanish case, its strategies, and frames:[26] Success works as a motivational factor that in Portugal, for example, led to the promotion of action forms such as public assemblies that formerly were only practised on a small scale.
(2) As noted above, we find a mixture of direct and indirect diffusion over time but change in the mechanisms of direct diffusion. In 2011, when there were almost no international meetings or institutionalized contacts between activist groups or assemblies, the Portuguese activists turned to Spaniards that lived in Portugal and relied primarily on personal, almost accidental contacts. With the increase of institutionalized contacts, international meetings, and visits throughout 2012, contacts between

experienced people also increased. A specific enabling factor was the international group of the 15M that was present at the Portuguese Indignados meeting and explained as well as demonstrated in detail practices from the Spanish 15M. This was probably the most intensive form of diffusion. The indirect diffusion via the Internet was the main channel since it was an inexpensive way to stay informed about what was happening in Spain.[27]

(3) There is a trend towards more international frames in the international protests in both countries: Joint events favour similar framing. This mechanism works mainly for the international events, but does affect protest events following the respective international protest. There is, however, a slight trend towards more international frames as a result not only of a more international process of organizing, but also of a growing realization regarding the insight about the interconnectedness of the world and the need to adapt framing to this interconnectedness. This insight about interconnectedness might result from observations of the experiences of leftist governments, especially the Greek Syriza and their difficult struggle with the international institutions.

Among the obstacles to diffusion are:

(1) National context: The different national contexts pose an obstacle to successful diffusion. This can be a context that is less favourable for the idea to be diffused, but it can also be a context that favours alternatives: In the Portuguese case, for example, since it is much easier to rent a space or to convince the owner to let a group use a space for free, occupation is a risk that is often not necessary to take. Another example, since a large portion of Portuguese activists accepted political parties, the democracy frame there was different from the Spanish frame: It was rather directed against the government than against all political parties.
(2) Existing organizational structures and practices: These can have a great impact on the success of diffusion. In Lisbon, for example, the public assemblies soon lost their character as spaces of individual participation due to the dominance of existing groups.
(3) Lack of success: The Portuguese activists faced difficulties with the imported action forms: The existing contexts of activism in Lisbon and new people's limited interest in joining action forms other than the large protests are the main factors that hampered the successful import of Spanish models. The lack of success of certain imports caused frustration but only in some cases did it have direct consequences for diffusion. In this case, activists mainly tried out small changes, instead of abandoning the idea entirely.

With our long-term perspective, we have described in greater detail how diffusion works after the first step of import until the point a diffused frame or action form becomes established (or not) in the new context. We have also been in a better position to evaluate whether developments in action forms or frames are caused by diffusion, or – like we have shown for the introduction of more socio-economic frames in the Spanish case – whether they are explained by internal developments, e.g., changes in the national framework or in the organizational structure of the protests. Furthermore, we have shown mechanisms by which activists deal with failure of diffusion and why this does not necessarily mean that diffusion cannot happen in the future. The construction of the Spaniards as a different kind of people helped to overcome frustration. Construction of otherness was only used in this sense as a specific, functional explanation after a failed diffusion and not as an argument against trying out action forms from Spain. So, 'construction of otherness' is not regarded as an obstacle to diffusion but rather as a mechanism of shifting blame away from the Portuguese activists.

Notes

1. In our country comparison, we leave aside the historical aspect of having two countries with different paths of democratization, which has been described elsewhere (Fernandes, 2014; Fishman, 2011).
2. The most repeated sources of inspiration among the Spanish Indignados were the Arab Spring and the 'Iceland Revolution' (Study ES2921; Toret, 2012; Díez García, 2017), even though several demands focused on life chances were framed by networks of activists and organizations in different European countries in their collective definitions regarding the economic crisis since the late 2000s. In those countries, as well as in Spain, protests and mobilizations emerged before May 2011, e.g., Iceland, UK, Greece, or Portugal (Geração à Rasca in March 2011); however, the frame that emerged in the spring of 2011 by way of the Spanish Indignados went beyond such issues and claims as we show in this text. This fact does not mean that mutual inspiration among them did not exist, but temporal precedence and mutual inspiration do not guarantee a mechanic and causal transmission or diffusion of frames and forms of action.
3. Such as online meetings on Mumble or mainstream and alternative digital social networks, streaming of protests and other public actions, or online connections with other public actions in other countries during the occupation of public spaces in Spain.
4. Especially between mid-2011 and mid-2012 those calls result from long debates among activists about how to frame the calls for protest and manifestos. Thus, except the framing from smaller outsider groups that did not join the platforms and events, the frames reflect all those frames important at the respective moments in time.
5. This survey is based on a national representative sample of more than 6000 individuals, of which 592 participated in the actions organized by the movement from May 2011 to January 2012.
6. Madrid15M, jun.12, n° 4: 13, http://madrid15M.org/%20publicaciones/madrid15M_n_4.pdf
7. Puerta del Sol camp was dismantled on 12 June after a lengthy assembly at which the decision was made.
8. And its call to *Rodear* (to enclose) and *Ocupar* (to occupy) the Parliament in September 2012.
9. For instance, the conflict and the breakup of Real Democracy Now! in 2012, the conflicts inside 'Marea Ciudadana', or the rejection of some organizations and groups of the 15M to join the siege of the Parliament organized by the 'Coordinadora 25-S' in 2013.
10. Frame amplification refers to the idealization, embellishment, clarification, or invigoration of existing values, beliefs, and frames. Frame extension involves extending the boundaries of primary frames to include issues and concerns that are presumed to be of importance to potential adherents. Although these processes aim to promote and strengthen social movements, they are also subject to risks and constraints, and do not always yield the desired results (Snow et al., 1986; Benford & Snow, 2000).
11. Call to action: united for global change on October 15! available at: https://web.archive.org/web/20120302131333/ http://roarmag.org/2011/09/call-to-action-united-for-global-change-on-october-15 (accessed: 30 November 2016).
12. The 'GlobalMay manifesto' of the International Occupy assembly, available at: http://www.theguardian.com/commentisfree/2012/may/11/occupy-globalmay-manifesto (accessed: 30 November 2016).

13. This notion was used by activists in the camps and has similarities to the concepts of 'working consensus' from Goffman and 'consensus mobilization' from Klandermans (1984).
14. March of Dignity Manifesto, available at: https://marchasdeladignidadmadrid.wordpress.com/2014/03/08/manifiesto-marchas-de-la-dignidad/ (accessed: 30 November 2016).
15. Reunião internacional 'Democracia Verdadeira e Planos de Austeridade', available at: https://acampadalisboa.wordpress.com/2011/07/17/reuniao-internacional-%E2%80%9Cdemocracia-verdadeira-e-planos-de-austeridade%E2%80%9D/ (accessed: 7 July 2016).
16. We also find this sort of form of action in Spain, known as 'escraches' and inspired by the Argentinian form of action of the same name. There were some significant 'escraches' in Madrid, for instance in June 2011 and July 2012, but this form of action gained visibility once the PAH included it among its repertoire in 2013. This shows how in both cases activists share similar forms of action that are adapted to the political culture of each country. In the Portuguese case, this form of action is inspired by the song Grândola Vila Morena. This song was played, among many other songs, by the '15M Orchestra', the Spanish 'La Solfónica' (Díez, 2013), in what seems a recognition or tribute to the Revolution of the Craves and the neighbor country. The *set list* is available at: https://solfonica.wordpress.com/nuestras-letras.
17. The framing of the calls for the event 'Rios to Carmo' on 24 April 2014 to celebrate the 40th anniversary of the Revolution of the Craves is very much related to the event of the Carnation Revolution. For a detailed analysis of this event, see Baumgarten (2017).
18. Although the 'Marea' on Public Education already emerged in autumn 2011.
19. Many activists are active in the Left Bloc (BE) and smaller political parties like the Movement for a Socialist Alternative (MAS), while there is a great proximity between the Communist Party (PCP) and the trade union confederation CGTP. In 2013, the left-libertarian, pro-European, green political party FREE – Time to move on (LIVRE) was created and participated for the first time in the elections in 2014.
20. English translation of the manifesto of Geração à Ràsca, available at: https://geracaoenrascada.wordpress.com/manifesto/english/ (accessed: 9 January 2017).
21. Juventud Sin Futuro (JSF).
22. See, for example: European Commission: Addressing youth unemployment in the EU, available at file:///C:/Users/Britta/Downloads/YG%20leaflet%2001%202015.pdf (accessed: 9 January 2017).
23. In detail, we find in May 2011: equality, progress, solidarity, cultural liberty, sustainable development, good living, happiness; right to housing, employment, culture, health, education, political participation, consumers rights; direct political participation with the aim of broad participation; for an ethical revolution; people over profit. They are different from the prognostic frames of the Geração à Rasca that more vaguely called for dignity and a future with stability and security in all areas of people's lives.
24. Call from the Strike Meeting to the European Movements and Networks, available at: http://www.connessioniprecarie.org/2014/11/08/call-from-the-strike-meeting-to-the-european-movements-and-networks/ (accessed: 30 November 2016).
25. Blockupy, available at https://blockupy.org/en/ (accessed: 30 November 2016).
26. Success refers in this case to the high number of participants in the mobilization, the spread and growth of the movement all over the country, its high resonance in the mass media and impact on the political and cultural agendas, and the wide range of groups and organizations that have emerged and acted in the public sphere since May 2011 (see Table 1).
27. Much has been written about diffusion via web 2.0, so we will not add new things here.

Acknowledgement

The authors would like to thank the participants of the two workshops 'Studying Social Movements against EU Austerity' organized by the Global Dynamics research cluster on 'Structural Adjustment comes to Europe' in Roskilde 2015 and 2016 for their comments on previous versions of this article.

We are also very grateful for comments by Tiago Carvalho and Robert Fishman and by the two anonymous reviewers of this article. Both authors, moreover, wish to thank their research subjects for accepting us as participant observers and taking the time for interviews with us.

Disclosure statement

No potential conflict of interest was reported by the authors.

Funding

The work of Britta Baumgarten was supported by the FCT [grant number IF/01311/2014/CP1250/CT0001].

ORCID

Britta Baumgarten http://orcid.org/0000-0002-7323-1833
Rubén Díez García http://orcid.org/0000-0002-8022-5343

References

Accornero, G., & Ramos Pinto, P. (2014). 'Mild mannered'? Protest and mobilisation in Portugal under austerity, 2010–2013. *West European Politics, 38*(3), 491–515.
Baumgarten, B. (2013a). Anti-austerity protests in Portugal. *CritCom*. Retrieved October 3, 2013, from http://councilforeuropeanstudies.org/critcom/anti-austerity-protests-in-portugal/
Baumgarten, B. (2013b). Geração à Rasca and beyond: Mobilizations in Portugal after 12 March 2011. *Current Sociology, 61*(4), 457–473.
Baumgarten, B. (2014). Culture and activism across borders. In B. Baumgarten, P. Daphi, & P. Ullrich (Eds.), *Conceptualizing culture in social movement research* (pp. 91–112). Basingstoke: Palgrave Macmillan.
Baumgarten, B. (2016). Time to get re-organized! The structure of the Portuguese anti-austerity protests. *Research in Social Movements, Conflicts and Change, 40*, 155–187.
Baumgarten, B. (2017). The children of the carnation revolution? Connections between Portugal's anti-austerity movement and the revolutionary period 1974/1975. *Social Movement Studies, 16*(1), 51–63.
Benford, R., & Snow, D. (2000). Framing processes and social movements: An overview and assessment. *Annual Review of Sociology, 26*, 611–639.
Castañeda, E. (2012). The indignados of Spain: A precedent to occupy wallstreet. *Social Movement Studies, 11*, 309–319.
Castells, M. (2012). *Networks of outrage and hope: Social movements in the Internet Age*. Cambridge: Polity Press.
Cottle, S. (2008). Reporting demonstrations: The changing media politics of dissent. *Media Culture and Society, 30*(6), 853–872.
Della Porta, D., Kriesi, H., & Rucht, D. (Eds.) (1999). *Social movements in a globalizing world*. Basingstoke: Palgrave Macmillan.
Díez, R. (2013). Music and social movement activism in urban space, *BlogURBS, estudios urbanos y ciencias sociales*. Retrieved from http://www2.ual.es/RedURBS/BlogURBS/music-and-social-movement-activism-in-urban-spaces
Díez, R. (2014). Does the Spanish 15M have an ideology? Issues of method and measurement". *Athenea Digital: Revista de Pensamiento e Investigación Social, 14*(3), 197–215.
Díez, R. (2015). Las bases sociales de la indignación: una perspectiva agregada sobre los factores asociados a la participación ciudadana en el movimiento 15M. *Sistema: Revista de ciencias sociales, 238*, 41–84.

Díez García, R. (2017). The 'indignados' in space & time: Transnational networks & historical roots. *Global Society, 31*(1), 43–64.

Dufour, P., Nez, H., & Ancelovici, M. (2016). From the indignados to occupy: Prospects for comparison. In M. Ancelovici, P. Dufour, & H. Nez (Eds.), *Street politics in the age of austerity: From indignados to occupy* (pp. 11–40). Amsterdam: Amsterdam University Press.

Earl, J. (2010). The dynamics of protest-related diffusion on the web. *Information, Communication & Society, 13*, 209–225.

Estanque, E., Costa, H., & Soeiro, J. (2013). The new global cycle of protest and the Portuguese case. *Journal of Social Science Education, 12*, 31–40.

Fernandes, T. (2014). Rethinking pathways to democracy: Civil society in Portugal and Spain, 1960s–2000s. *Democratization, 22*(6), 1–31.

Fishman, R. (2011). Democratic practice after the revolution: The case of Portugal and beyond. *Politics & Society, 39*(2), 233–267.

Flesher Fominaya, C. (2014, March 25). *Spain's marches of dignity, 22M, 2014: Not anti-politics*, www.openDemocracy.net. Retrieved November 30, 2016, from https://www.opendemocracy.net/can-europe-make-it/cristina-flesher-fominaya/spain%E2%80%99s-marches-of-dignity-22m-2014-not-antipolitics

Flesher Fominaya, C. (2015). Debunking Spontaneity: Spain's 15M/Indignados as autonomous movement. *Social Movement Studies, 14*(2), 142–163.

Flesher Fominaya, C., & Cox, L. (Eds.) (2013). *Understanding European movements: New social movements, global justice struggles*. London: Routledge.

Givan, R., Roberts, K., & Soule, S. (Eds.) (2010). *The diffusion of social movements: Actors, mechanisms, and political effects*. Cambridge: Cambridge.

Klandermans, B. (1984). Mobilization and participation: Social-psychological expansisons of resource mobilization theory. *American Sociological Review, 49*(5), 583–600.

Laraña, E. (2009). *Is Spain a statist society? A research perspective on organizations, reflexivity and collective action* (Institute for the Study of Social Change, ISSC Project Reports and Working Papers). Berkeley: University of California. Retrieved from http://repositories.cdlib.org/issc/reports/ISSC_VS_WP_01

Laraña, E., & Díez, R. (2009). *The social construction of citizenship: Voluntary organizations and social movements in the Spanish transition to democracy*. Center for Iberian and Latin American Studies, University of California, San Diego.

Laraña, E., & Díez, R. (2012). Las raíces del movimiento 15M: Orden social e indignación moral. *Revista Española del Tercer Sector, 20*, 105–144.

McAdam, D., McCarthy, J. & Zald, M. (Eds.) (1996). *Comparative perspectives on social movements: Political opportunities, mobilizing structures, and cultural framings*. Cambridge: Cambridge University Press.

McAdam, D., & Rucht, D. (1993). The cross-national diffusion of movement ideas. *The Annals of the American Academy of Political and Social Science, 528*, 56–74.

Romanos, E. (2016). From Tahrir to Puerta del Sol to wall street: The transnational diffusion of social movements in comparative perspective. *Revista Española de Investigaciones Sociológicas, 154*, 103–118.

Snow, D. (2004). Framing processes, ideology and discursive fields. In D. A. Snow, S. A. Soule, & H. Kriesi (Eds.), *The Blackwell companion to social movements* (pp. 380–412). Malden: Blackwell.

Snow, D., & Benford, R. (1988). Ideology, frame resonance and participant mobilization. In B. Klandermans, H. Kriesi, & S. Tarrow (Eds.), *From structure to action: Comparing social movement research across cultures. International Social Movement Research* (1, pp. 197–217). Greenwich: JAI Press.

Snow, D., Rochford, E., Worden, S., & Benford, R. (1986). Frame alignment processes, micromobilization, and movement participation. *American Sociological Review, 51*(4), 464–81.

Soule, S. (2004). Diffusion processes within and across movements. In D. A. Snow, S. A. Soule, & H. Kriesi (Eds.), *The Blackwell companion to social movements* (pp. 294–310). Malden: Blackwell.

Tarrow, S. (1994). *Power in movement: Collective action, social movements and politics*. Cambridge: Cambridge University Press.

Tarrow, S. (2005). *The new transnational activism*. Cambridge: Cambridge University Press.

Tejerina, B., Perugorria, I., Benski, T., & Langman, L. (2013). From indignation to occupation: A new wave of global mobilization. *Current Sociology, 61*(4), 377–392.

Tilly, C. (2008). *Contentious performances*. Cambridge: Cambridge University Press.

Toret, J. (2012). Una mirada tecnopolítica sobre los primeros días del #15M. In Alcazan, ArnauMonty, Axebra, Quodlibetat, Simona Levi, SuNotissima, & TakeTheSquare y, Toret (Eds.), *Tecnopolítica, internet y r-evoluciones. Sobre la centralidad de redes digitales en el #15M*. Barcelona: Icaria.

Beyond Nationalism? The Anti-Austerity Social Movement in Ireland: Between Domestic Constraints and Lessons from Abroad

Richard Dunphy

ABSTRACT
The European financial crisis has inspired a wave of social activism, challenging established party politics. In Ireland, a large social protest movement produced a Right2Change political campaign in 2015 that confronted the right-wing consensus in Irish politics. Some activists sought to emulate and learn from the example of new parties like Spain's *Podemos*. Yet, to date, the traditional party structure remains intact, and hopes of emulating the success of activists elsewhere remain muted. At the same time, anti-austerity activism in Ireland has seen a conscious attempt to engage in intense dialogue with the pan-European experience. Irish activists have looked to Europe before for inspiration and a sharing of experiences; but the most recent attempt to create a Europeanised public space in response to the perceived 'blockage' in the Irish party system is something fairly innovative. This article, based in part on ten semi-structured interviews with politicians and social movement activists, considers the achievements and failings of the Irish anti-austerity movement to date.

Introduction

For much of the twentieth century, since gaining independence from Britain in 1920 until the 1990s, the state now known as the Republic of Ireland was regarded as amongst the most conservative in Europe. From the consolidation of the party system in the late 1920s and early 1930s until the general election of 2011, between 80% and 90% of the electorate regularly voted for two big centre-right Catholic nationalist parties—*Fianna Fáil* (FF) and *Fine Gael* (FG)—with the Irish Labour Party, one of the most centrist social democratic parties in western Europe, polling an average of around 10% of the national vote. Ireland was inhospitable territory for progressive, radical, left, liberal or secular politics of any variety. Political stagnation was matched by economic stagnation. Until the so-called Celtic Tiger economic lift-off of the late 1990s and early 2000s, Ireland was one of the most economically backward and underdeveloped countries in Western Europe. The absence of an industrial revolution meant that persistently high unemployment was matched by large-scale emigration which became an accepted facet of Irish life. From the 1920s to the 1990s, large numbers of Irish citizens emigrated to North America and the UK in search of a better life. Emigration had the effect of further reducing any pressure for political change at home, by removing the youngest and most dynamic groups in Irish society.

Several other aspects of Irish political culture tended to defuse pressure for change—and render Ireland less given to the politics of social protest found in many other European countries. As has often been noted (see, e.g. Kirby & Murphy, 2011), Irish political culture displays a strong tendency towards both localism and personalism. The former refers to a tendency to 'think locally' when voting nationally. It tends to favour the election of well-known or colourful local personalities who are seen as defending local interests. Often it encourages maverick politicians, elected on a party list, to defy the party whip in defence of local interests, knowing that, their reputation as a local hero thus secured, even if deselected by their party they will be re-elected at the next election as an 'independent' and can negotiate the terms of their re-entry to their party of origin—or continue with a successful political career as an Independent. As Weeks (2009) points out, the number of Independents returned to the Irish parliament often is greater than the combined total returned to all other West European parliaments taken together; their importance in Irish political life, therefore, should not be underestimated. Personalism refers to the tendency to favour the politics of personality over that of ideology (or sometimes even party). An unknown candidate, perhaps with weak local roots, has very little chance of success against a candidate with a strong personal following, regardless of the appeal of ideology or political message.

Both these tendencies are encouraged by the Irish electoral system. The Single Transferable Vote (STV) system of proportional representation forces candidates from the same political party to compete against one another in multi-member constituencies and thus to build up personal machines. A major way in which Irish politicians do this is by emphasizing their brokerage role—their willingness to act as intermediaries between constituents and the bureaucracy, helping to obtain for constituents their legal entitlements (Komito, 1984, 1992). Such a role, deemed by politicians to be essential to their (re-)election, can be enormously time-consuming and leave little time or energy for initiating or supervising legislation or, in the case of politicians, attempting to create new, radical parties, the business of party-building.

The ways in which STV combines with aspects of Irish political culture also makes it difficult for new, radical or anti-system parties to emerge and transform the politics of street protest into a challenge to the existing party system. At first sight, STV is fairer than, for example, a first-past-the-post electoral system; and might be deemed to facilitate minority party representation (for a discussion of the STV electoral system see Farrell, 2011). However, there is another side to this. First, in order to make an initial electoral breakthrough, new (and almost, by definition, small) anti-system parties must rely upon building up the profiles of popular local activists—and a small new party dominated by a handful of well-known personalities can be prone to fissile tendencies. Second, STV allows voters, even in times of mass alienation and disillusionment with traditional politics, to cast a first preference (protest) vote for an Independent or new party candidate whilst reverting with their second, third, fourth, etc., preferences to the party of their traditional allegiance. Thus, attempts to subvert traditional party identifications are made more difficult. These issues are crucial in understanding why the anti-austerity social movement in Ireland has not yet produced a successful challenge to the party system. But they are not the only reasons, as we will see.

Social movements in Ireland

According to Connolly and Hourigan (2006, pp. 2–3)

> it is often inaccurately assumed that N[ew] S[ocial] M[ovement]s could not and did not flourish in societies 'like Ireland' (a country with a small, predominantly rural, population on the periphery of Western Europe), either before or after the 1960s, because of the social and political dominance of the Catholic Church and its close relationship with the State.

However, as many of the contributors to their edited volume make clear, this is far from the truth. The power of the Catholic Church over Irish society and politics has been 'a catalyst as well as a constraint' for the emergence of social movements. Ireland has seen a large number of new social movements (NSMs) emerge and make their impact on Irish societies since the 1960s. Examples have included: the Irish Women's Liberation Movement, launched in its modern form in 1970, which has campaigned for gender equality in general but for the legalization of contraception, divorce and abortion in particular (for a full account of its emergence and campaigning activities see Stopper, 2006); the Irish gay and lesbian liberation movement, which campaigned for several decades for the decriminalization of homosexuality and the enactment of full legal equality for all sexualities; groups protesting against the marginalization of the Irish language; environmental action and anti-nuclear groups; anti-racism and anti-war groups; housing action and unemployment action groups; and, of course, the civil rights movement in Northern Ireland. Indeed, the very variety of NSMs that has been part of the political landscape in Ireland since the 1960s points to the problem of arriving at an agreed definition of NSM that can cover most, if not all, of them.

A 'health check' of Irish civic activism carried out by the think-tank, TASC, in 2007 paints a picture of a vibrant civil society with high levels of community activism, above all in the voluntary sector. The report argues that 'Ireland shows higher levels of engagement in informal social networks and community activism than the UK, higher levels of involvement in membership organisations, and greater confidence that ordinary people can make a difference to public decision making.' Moreover, it found that 'women were more likely than men to be "community activists"' even though they were greatly under-represented in public office (Hughes, Clancy, Harris, & Beetham, 2007, p. 440). The Irish citizenry, then, displays considerable social capital accumulation and is far from being passive. However, until recently very few social movements have directly challenged the neo-liberal consensus that has underpinned Irish economic policy in recent decades—a consensus that has been shared by all three of the Republic of Ireland's largest political parties.

All of this was to change with what Laurence Cox refers to as 'the movement of movements', a term he adopts to signify the 'coming together of different groups, campaigns and individuals which have realised that their different areas of concern—racism and war, economic exploitation and environmental destruction, patriarchy and state power—are interlinked' (Cox, 2006, p. 212). The movement of movements, or movement against capitalist globalization, exploded upon the Irish political scene in the early years of the twenty-first century, even when the so-called Celtic Tiger economy was still in the ascendant. The catalyst may well have been the Iraq war, which drew 100,000 on the streets of Dublin in 2003 in the largest demonstration seen for two decades, and the visit of President George W. Bush to Ireland a year later, which again drew tens of thousands on the streets in protest. But, quickly, the movement spread to encapsulate protest against economic inequality and what were perceived as the unfair nature of the neo-liberal policies that underpinned the Celtic Tiger phenomenon. A genuinely popular movement that challenged the neo-liberal consensus head-on was emerging, which would later (after 2008) help give birth to a mass movement of anti-austerity activism.

The first manifestation of this new wave of activism came with the anti-bin changes movement in 2003, which followed the decision of local authorities in Ireland to introduce additional charges for domestic refuse collection, which activists deemed to fall heaviest on working class communities. A large number of local protest groups were formed, especially in Dublin, and a campaign of non-payment, backed up by disruption of refuse collections and blockades of bin lorries, was launched. The campaign saw the imprisonment by the Irish courts of 22 activists, including Joe Higgins, a parliamentary deputy (*Teachta Dála*—TD) for the small Trotskyist Socialist Party (SP), Clare Daly (later also to be elected a SP TD—and later still an Independent left TD) and several activists of the Irish Socialist Network, a democratic socialist splinter from the orthodox communist Workers' Party. Although ultimately a failure, the anti-bin charges movement made household names in Dublin of several of those imprisoned and can be seen as both paving the way for the modest electoral success that the 'hard left' would enjoy in the decade ahead as well as for the larger anti-austerity movement that would emerge after 2008.

The anti-austerity movement in Ireland, 2008–2011

The Republic of Ireland officially entered recession in September 2008. Unemployment soared, reaching 15.1% by 2012. Large-scale emigration resumed. Tens of thousands of families were left with crippling negative equity as house prices slumped. The country was scarred by unfinished large suburban housing estates, and by huge cuts to public spending (see Dunphy, 2016, for a more detailed discussion of these points). When the economic collapse occurred, Ireland was governed by the FF party, a centre-right populist, nationalist and Catholic party with strong clientelist ties to the construction and banking sectors, in coalition with a small Green Party. These parties established a National Asset Management Agency (NAMA) in 2009, which effectively took over the debts of the banking sector, sending the national debt spiralling upwards and condemning future generations to pay off the private banking sector's debts. In December 2010, the Irish *Taoiseach* (prime minister), Brian Cowen, signed an Economic Adjustment Programme with the Troika (European Commission, European Central Bank and International Monetary Fund). A Memorandum of Understanding, signed by the Irish government, committed the country to adhere to 'tight supervision of expenditure commitments' (IMF, 2011, p. 62). In practice, this involved agreement to impose an austerity programme of public sector cuts, chiefly to health, education, pensions and social welfare, in addition to introducing a household tax on every family who owned their own home, and domestic water charges—all in return for a Troika loan of 85 billion Euros.

In response to these developments, a truly mass anti-austerity protest movement emerged, with small radical left parties, trade unions (or, at least, those which had broken their traditional ties to the pro-austerity Labour Party), and numerous community and activist groups participating. In 2010, 100,000 participated in one of the biggest demonstrations ever organized by Ireland's trade unions. Forty thousand took part in student protests. An estimated 30,000 farmers took to the streets in protest. They were followed by teachers, civil servants, police officers, taxi drivers and many groups that had not previously been drawn into political protest. In 2011, Occupy camps were established in Dublin, Cork, Galway and Waterford, emulating protest movements in other countries (Dunphy, 2016, p. 192).

Yet, in the period 2008–2011, none of this activism or popular protest really impacted on the party political system. At the level of party politics, the neo-liberal consensus seemed to hold. The three big parties (and the Greens), which all backed austerity, continued to dominate political life. Indeed, during the period 2008–2013, Ireland 'was widely seen as a so-called poster child for austerity', delivering swingeing cuts while minimizing political protest and maintaining political consensus (Dellepiane-Avellaneda & Hardiman, 2015, p. 209). Indeed, the insensitivity of the Irish political elite to mass anti-austerity demands from below increased the feeling of many activists that Ireland suffered from a dysfunctional political system; and that the politicization of public spaces, such as the streets and town squares, through mass demonstrations and protest camps offered the only way of bringing the anti-austerity message to ever greater numbers of people.

The failure to translate mass anti-austerity activism into radical political change during the period 2008–2011 was deeply disappointing to many activists. There are a number of reasons why this happened. The FF party, which had dominated the political life of Ireland for much of the period since the early 1930s, bore the brunt of voters' anger at the 2011 general election, falling to 17% (from around 40%). But disillusioned Irish voters turned not so much to the radical left or even the nationalist-populist *Sinn Féin* (SF), which sought to deploy anti-austerity rhetoric to harness support for its traditional project of a united Ireland,[1] as to the other big centre-right party FG and the centrist Labour Party, both of which, after the election, committed to the same austerity programme as FF. In part, this reflects the conservative nature of Irish political culture and the weakness of any radical left in Ireland. In part, it is because the two small radical left parties that played such a prominent role in the anti-austerity movement—the SP, which began fighting elections under the banner of the Anti-Austerity Alliance (AAA), and the Socialist Workers' Party, which did the same under the banner of the People Before Profit Alliance (PBPA)—were riven by internecine sectarian rivalries. Furthermore, according to some activists and trade union leaders outside the ranks of these parties, both gained a reputation within the wider anti-austerity movement for extreme political dogmatism and sectarian posturing. In particular, according to activists interviewed for this research, the SP/AAA was suspected of trying to destroy any movement that it could not control. Brendan Ogle, a Unite union leader who played a prominent role in the movement, said, 'I often got the impression that [the SP/AAA] saw in any mass movement that they could not control the spectre of reformism'. Further, interviewee Ruth Coppinger, an SP/AAA TD, indicated that the SP/AAA resented the presence within the movement of SF, which it suspected of trying to subordinate anti-austerity activism to bourgeois nationalism and of trying to capture the leadership of the movement. These divisions, mutual suspicions and rival leadership aspirations considerably weakened the chances of a new political phenomenon emerging from the ranks of the anti-austerity movement in the run-up to the 2011 general election.

Table 1 demonstrates the extent to which mass agitation had failed to unsettle traditional Irish voters' behaviour after three years of austerity. The important point to note here is that at the general election of 2009, the four parties that explicitly implemented and defended austerity policies—FF, FG, Labour and Greens—had polled 83.7% and won 154 seats out of 166. In 2011, these same parties polled 74.7% and won 133 seats out of 166. In fact, these figures underestimate the neo-liberal consensus as between one-third and one-half of the Independents elected on both occasions also shared in it. Despite the collapse of FF, the election represented, in the words of Shaun McDaid, 'a redistribution of the existing party system, rather than its "destruction"' (McDaid, 2016, p. 190). The decision by the Labour Party to form a coalition with FG further blocked any left-versus-right realignment in Irish politics and guaranteed 'business as usual' since non-FF coalitions have always revolved around FG and Labour (McDaid, 2016, p. 191). These points are important because, as Massey has argued,

> An economic crisis is not enough. You also need a fracturing of the ideological and the political … because one of the main bases of the ideological hegemony of neoliberalism is the way in which it removes the economic from political and ideological contest, the way in turns the economic into a matter of technocratic expertise. (Massey, 2015, pp. 13–14)

The anti-austerity movement in Ireland after 2011

In the aftermath of the 2011 general election in Ireland, anti-austerity social protests were stepped up, drawing yet greater numbers of previously unpoliticized people into politics, and the movement, at the same time, began to take on new directions, partly influenced by activism elsewhere. On 22 December 2011, the Campaign Against Home and Water Taxes (CAHWT) was launched, supported by the small radical left parties, independent left parliamentary deputies and some members of SF. Above all, it would be the issue of water charges that would galvanize the movement and rally mass public support. Mass grassroots community activism included resisting meter installation and boycotting registration. The CAHWT called for a boycott of household and water taxes, established a national anti-household tax helpline and organized protests in every major town and

Table 1. Summary of 2011 Irish general election results (with 2009 results for comparison).

Party	% of votes	Seats in Dáil	2009 election %	2009 seats
Fine Gael	36.1	76	27.3	51
Labour	19.4	37	10.1	20
Fianna Fáil	17.4	20	41.6	77
Sinn Féin	9.9	14	6.9	4
Marxist parties[a]	2.7	5	1.3	0
Greens	1.8	0	4.7	6
Independents	12.7	14	8.1	8
Total	100	166	100	166

[a]Socialist party (1.2%—2 seats), People Before Profit Alliance (1%—2 seats), Unemployed workers' Action Group (0.4%—1 seat), Workers' party (0.1%—0 seats).

city in Ireland. However, the CAHWT found itself badly divided by the SP/AAA's insistence on non-payment of household charges even though the government had enabled legislation allowing payment to be deducted from wages or welfare payments. As Brendan Ogle noted in our interview, critics of the SP/AAA argued that this tactic risked plunging many people into debt and hardship. The internal difficulties faced by the CAHWT risked leaving large numbers of activists feeling disillusioned—and, arguably, paved the way for the emergence of the separate and distinctive Right2Water campaign (see below).

Finn (2015, p. 49) claims that Irish political elites and Troika officials who favourably compared the 'solid, dependable Irish, who would do as they were told and ask for nothing in return', with the troublesome Greeks were taken 'entirely by surprise' by the new and more forceful wave of anti-austerity activism. Acts of civil disobedience and grass roots activism followed in many Irish towns that had never seen protests against neoliberalism before, with over 100,000 marching against the bank debts in February 2013, and the launch of the Right2Water campaign in late 2014 leading to further mass protests throughout 2014–2016. Indeed, the period since 2014 has seen the biggest protests, and water charges has proven to be the issue that has acted as a focal point for the entire anti-austerity movement in Ireland.

Ireland formally exited the Economic Adjustment Programme in late 2013 and exited the recession in 2014 when it returned to modest economic growth. The ruling coalition of FG and Labour proudly boasted that its pursuit of austerity had been a success, and Labour privately hoped that the exit from recession might be in time to save it from political meltdown at the next election (which was held in 2016). On the contrary, anti-austerity protests underwent an 'eruption' in late 2014 (Finn, 2015, p. 49). Although unemployment fell from nearly 15% in 2012 to 10% in summer 2015, mass emigration was behind this fall. According to Finn (2015, pp. 50–51), nearly 475,000 workers left the country between 2008 and 2014, a higher rate of emigration than the Baltic states, and without which unemployment in Ireland would have reached Spanish and Greek levels. The recovery, then, was 'partial and tentative' and left much of the population unaffected.

The government established Irish Water in 2013 with plans to introduce charges for domestic consumption of water in 2014. By taking responsibility for such charges out of the hands of local authorities and placing them in the hands of a company, the government was clearly, in many people's eyes, preparing for the privatization of water, thus removing Irish Water's borrowings from the state's books. Finn argues that the government's handling of this issue contributed to the anti-water charges campaign becoming the focal point of the entire movement. First, the introduction of water charges had the effect of targeting a wide range of different social groups simultaneously and thus forcing them to coalesce. Second, the decision to award a contract to install water meters to a company owned by one of the country's wealthiest and most controversial businessmen, Denis O'Brien, provoked widespread anger. Third, Irish Water's decision to spend 85 million Euros on consultant fees generated public anger over perceived corporate greed (Finn, 2015, pp. 54–55).

Right2Water was launched in September 2014, with two of the big trade unions most autonomous from the Labour Party, Mandate and Unite, playing a large role. A march in Dublin in October brought 100,000 to the streets with 200,000 taking part in national marches in November. A parliamentary by-election in Dublin South West in October was fought almost entirely on the issue: the SP won the seat, defeating SF, which had been expected to take the seat. Although both parties had declared support for Right2Water, the SP called uncompromisingly for a boycott of water charge payments which SF did not—only reversing its position in the wake of by-election defeat. The message was clear: in working class constituencies in particular, the water charges movement had unleashed fierce anti-austerity anger.

In his detailed study of the Irish anti-war charges movement,[2] Hearne (2015) reports that the mass nature of the protests was fuelled by a sense of anger, desperation, real life suffering and a sense that austerity had 'gone too far'. Moreover, he claims that austerity 'had reached a tipping point in 2013 and 2014 … and … had extended out to impact a broad section of the population by the end of the troika bailout' (Hearne, 2015, p. 9).

In early 2015, some of those involved in the campaign, inspired by the renewed and seemingly redoubled energy of social activism, felt that the time was ripe to enter the electoral arena. Hearne's study of those involved in the anti-water charges movement lends support to their view, in that he found that 79.5% of activists taking part in his survey felt that there was a need for a new political party in Ireland (Hearne, 2015, p. 25). He argues that this is consistent with polls showing high levels of disillusionment with existing parties, even amongst those who continue to vote for them, and the fact that many people who had begun voting for SF or the Trotskyist parties were still looking for a new alternative that might better represent their views. Hearne concluded that

> it is clear that the respondents want a new party that stands on a platform of anti-austerity; is for radical political reform involving a 'clearing out' of the 'establishment' political parties from power; that is anti-corruption, anti-cronyism and for democracy where government acts for the people and not the elite or 'golden circle' … . (Hearne, 2015, pp. 26–27)

With a general election due in early 2016, some activists felt that this time, perhaps, it would be possible to challenge the political and electoral consensus around neoliberalism and give Ireland what it had never had in its history—a left-of-centre government that would reject austerity and stand up to the demands of the Troika. Under trade union leadership, a conference was held to transform Right2Water into Right2Change—a broader-based political movement that published a list of principles that should underpin a progressive Irish government (see next section, for a detailed discussion of this). Boosted by Irish Water's admission in July 2015 that less than 50% of Irish households had paid the water charges, and by further mass rallies and demonstrations at the end of the summer, they focussed on the forthcoming election. The electoral strategy was nebulous, however, with no clear agreement on whether a new political formation, along the lines of either Syriza or Podemos, was needed; moreover, divisions between supporters of the Trotskyist parties and others, and between SF supporters and others, and disagreement over how to interpret the lessons to be learned from other countries' experience, all hampered the initiative. In the event, all that could be managed was agreement to invite existing parties and Independents to sign up to supporting the principles behind Right2Change. SF, the PBPA and many left Independents did so; the SP/AAA declined. Candidates and parties who agreed to sign up were further divided over whether they featured the common principles prominently (or at all) in their electoral campaign. For example, as Brendan Ogle explained in our interview, neither the PBPA manifesto

(PBPA, 2016) nor the joint declaration of common principles by the AAA and PBPA (2016) made any reference to the Right2Change principles. Nor did SF electoral propaganda make any reference to the campaign.

As Table 2 demonstrates, the 2016 general election saw a modest advance by the Trotskyist parties, a significant advance by SF on the basis of that party's espousal of anti-austerity rhetoric (which was nonetheless less than SF had hoped for) and a big advance by the Independents grouping which now included a recently formed radical left, Independents4Change group of parliamentary deputies, most of whom had been prominent in the anti-austerity social movements. And yet, no convincing, united or coherent new force has burst on to the party political scene. The parties favouring austerity—FF, FG, Labour, Greens and *Renua*—polled 61.4% and won 103 seats out of 158. These figures are again boosted by the fact that many Independents are centre-right or centrist and favour austerity also. The consensus around neoliberalism was badly dented by the 2016 election—but still not fractured.

Nevertheless, Murphy (2016) has argued that voting figures disguise the fact that levels of trust in politics, traditional parties and the institutions of government are low; and that, with a values-led discourse that challenges neoliberalism, a mass movement for change that emphasizes gender and social reproduction issues, environmental concerns and concerns over social justice and income inequality might yet mobilize a wide range of actors, create new alliances and change the political system. In other words, the outcome of the 2016 general election by no means marks the exhaustion of the movement for change in Ireland.

In the next section, we will explore the extent to which the Irish anti-austerity movement has been able to incorporate lessons from abroad—and the reasons why an Irish Podemos has, so far at least, failed to emerge.

From a new way of doing politics to a new political formation?

As we have seen, the period since 2014 saw an up-turn in anti-austerity protests in Ireland with the Right2Water campaign giving birth to a broader Right2Change movement in 2015. Many of those involved in Right2Change have explicitly acknowledged the

Table 2. Summary of the 2016 Irish general election results.

Party	% of votes	Seats in Dáil
FG	25.5	50
Labour	6.6	7
FF	24.4	44
SF	13.9	23
Marxist parties[a]	3.9	6
Greens	2.7	2
Independents[b]	17.8	23
Renua[c]	2.2	0
Social Democrats[c]	3.0	3
Total	100	158[d]

[a]The AAA and the PBPA presented a joint list at the 2016 elections, despite publishing separate election manifestos.
[b]Independents includes the left-wing, anti-austerity Independents4Change group.
[c]Renua and the Social Democrats are two new parties, of the centre-right and centre-left, respectively.
[d]Total number of parliamentary seats reduced from 166 to 158 in 2016.

importance of the Spanish and Greek examples and have tried to draw political lessons from the experiences of other countries. In Spain, *Podemos* grew out of a broad-based citizens and democracy movement and registered as a political party in March 2014. As Heilig (2016, p. 22) argues, *Podemos* had its origins in a manifesto signed by around 30 intellectuals and social activists, calling for candidates to be fielded in European Parliament elections scheduled for June and arguing for

> the redistribution of wealth in Spain from top to bottom, the maintenance of the public character of education and healthcare, the raising of salaries, the creation of a stock of public housing, as well as resistance to the tightening of Spain's abortion legislation. The movement also demanded Spain's exit from NATO.

The influence of this manifesto on the Right2Change movement, launched in early 2015, can be readily seen in its founding document, *Policy Principles for a Progressive Irish Government* (see Right2Change, 2015). This, too, was a manifesto in embryonic form that echoed many of the founding demands of *Podemos*. It went beyond the water charges issue to call for:

- *A Right2Jobs and Decent Work* including the introduction of a Decent Work Act that tackled low pay and precarity, introduced a Living Wage, enshrined the right to collective bargaining in law, and strengthened the social protection system by bringing in pay-related benefits and childcare payments;
- *A Right2Housing* that called for new legislation that waged war on homelessness and provided for the construction of new social housing, regulated rents and non-speculative house building;
- *A Right2Health* involving the creation of 'a universal health care system free at the point of entry';
- *A Right2Debt Justice* that would see the convening of a European Debt Conference to restructure sovereign debt throughout the Eurozone, the introduction of a Financial Transaction Tax to repay states that had written off private banks' debts and a restructuring of mortgage debt;
- *A Right2Education* that would see massive investment in education and the reduction of class sizes from among the highest to the lowest levels in the EU;
- *A Right2Democratic Reform* that would seek to reform and reinvigorate political decision-making process, local and national, by giving citizens the right of recall of their elected representatives, allowing citizens to propose constitutional changes and referenda on legislation, measures to relax the party Whip system and to strengthen parliamentary committees from party patronage, and—a measure that chimes well with *Podemos's* populist attacks on existing political elites which it branded *The Caste*—the introduction of breathalysers ahead of votes in parliament.

In the case of the Irish manifesto, the initiative had been taken largely by the trade unions, Mandate and Unite. Perhaps for this reason, and in support of their call for maximum participation in both the political system and the process of formulating a full programme for a new type of politics, the document was declared to be an attempt to inaugurate a discussion about what type of society Ireland should be. Contributions to the discussion were invited from all interested individuals and groups, and a further conference was called by the Unions for 13 June 2015.

As we will see, one of the groups within the movement most open to studying the lessons of Spain and Greece was the group of Independent left parliamentary deputies, chief amongst them Clare Daly and Joan Collins. Both these deputies had risen to prominence, long before their election to the Irish parliament, as leading activists in the anti-austerity protest movement; and both had resigned or been expelled from the two small Trotskyist parties—Daly from the SP/AAA and Collins from first the SP and then the PBPA—which they came to see as sectarian, dogmatic and obstacles to further progress by the anti-austerity movement. In a contribution to the Right2Change debate (issued as United Left, a name they briefly used) these activists and parliamentary deputies echoed that 'a radical mass movement in Ireland has to link up with similar movements in Europe, such as Syriza in Greece and Podemos in Spain'. They called for a new vision for the European Union—as opposed to the Trotskyist parties' uncompromising call for Ireland to leave the EU. Acknowledging that 'one of the more significant movements against austerity in Europe since the onset of the economic crisis … has the potential to be the key factor in the development of a new and mass radical left movement', they emphasized that such a development would take time, would not emerge in time for the 2016 elections and would need to learn from experiences elsewhere in Europe. A new formation would have to repudiate any coalition with FF, FG or Labour and act autonomously. Echoing *Podemos*'s manifesto, the activists called for strong opposition to NATO, repeal of Ireland's constitutional ban on abortion, separation of Church and State, and public ownership of some of the leading banks (United Left, 2015).

From the outset, the organizers of Right2Water invited representatives from the social movements in, for example, Greece, Spain and Germany to address rallies in Ireland. According to Brendan Ogle, Irish activists had engaged in new tactics and methods of challenging the political establishment, but lacked any clear structure. Above all, they struggled to find mechanisms of democratic input. Irish trade unions had traditionally abstained from any involvement with social activism; indeed, their involvement in social partnership programmes with successive Irish governments had led, in the eyes of left-wing critics, to their virtual cooption as part of the state apparatus (see Allen (2000) for an espousal of this view). Social Partnership Agreements have operated in Ireland since 1987, and have involved leading trade unions, farmers' and employers' organizations and the government meeting regularly under the auspices of the National Economic and Social Council (NESC) to discuss, for example, targets for wages, prices and fiscal stability (Coakley & Gallagher, 2010, pp. 336–340). Ogle argued in our interview that the social partnership agreements, especially recently, have contributed to a progressive deradicalization of trade unions and an abandonment of any real oppositional stance. Those unions most critical of such 'institutionalization'—Mandate and Unite—now found themselves thrust into a leadership role almost by accident. In the aftermath of the local and European elections in June 2014, a conference was held, attended by the unions, community activists' groups and the political parties—SF, SP, PBPA and Left independents. Ogle described the atmosphere amongst the politicians as 'poisonous', with the two Trotskyist parties allegedly blaming each other for lack of success in the European elections, and both highly suspicious of SF. The unions, he claims, stepped forward at this juncture and offered to design the subsequent Right2Change campaign. For trade unions, this was a new departure. The relationship between unions and the NSMs has not always been an easy one. Unite (UK) spokesperson, Simon Dubbins, in conversation with Doreen Massey, admits that unions have been slow to engage with the Occupy movement and are accustomed to dealing with formal structures and leadership elites—and so are sometimes uneasy with informal, grass roots-led movements. Learning different methods and different ways of 'doing' democracy is often a steep learning curve for those who come from this tradition (Massey, 2015, p. 26). It might be argued that in Ireland, union leadership of the Right2Water and Right2Change campaigns carried risks of stultifying grass roots energy as well as new challenges.

Ogle argued in our interview that the unions looked outside Ireland for inspiration, sending representatives to attend conferences in Marseilles, Thessaloniki, Berlin and Brussels. They sought to establish links with North American campaigns, seeking to learn from the Detroit Water brigade that campaigned against water shut-offs, and linking up with Canadian activists such as Maude Barlow's Blue Planet Project. Right2Change then, as we have seen, was launched with a statement of common principles for a progressive government. All of this, together with the invitations to representatives from the European movements to address rallies and demonstrations in Ireland, can be seen as a conscious effort to create the sort of transnational European sphere that Risse (2010) talks of. Risse mentions five criteria for the existence of such a sphere: visibility of common themes, common criteria of relevance, speakers engaging in cross-border debates, speakers from different countries recognizing each other as legitimate interlocutors and speakers framing the issues at stake as common European problems (Risse, 2010, p. 126). There can be no doubt that all of these criteria were present in Ireland, certainly during the second main wave of anti-austerity activism since 2014.

What Ogle described as the 'dysfunctional' nature of the Irish left parties—their alleged dogmatism and tendency towards in-fighting—helps explain why many activists were attracted, not only by new ways of intervening in politics but by the idea of a new political formation. Right2Change's first major conference was attended by representatives from Podemos, Syriza and the Berlin water charges protest movement. The Podemos representative defended his movement's presentation of itself as 'neither left nor right' and urged Irish activists to look beyond old ways of thinking and to develop new mechanisms of ensuring mass, democratic participation in politics. While such messages were welcomed by some activists, they were anathema to others.

The two Trotskyist parties in Ireland have drawn rather different lessons from Europe. In their view, the anti-austerity movement can only advance and succeed if it is under the leadership of a Marxist-Leninist vanguard party. Otherwise, it runs the risk of two forms of 'betrayal'. First, it risks falling into a form of populism—defined as 'lacking a clear political programme as your backbone' and lacking a class perspective (Fitzgerald, 2015). The charge of populism is one that the SP explicitly levels against those left independents most favourably disposed to Podemos—and, by implication, at Podemos itself. Second, it runs the risk of working within the capitalist system and thus leading the working class to defeat, as, they argue, has happened with *Syriza* (Murphy, 2015). According to the PBPA's Kieran Allen, 'Syriza embraces a reformist strategy ... it operates within the framework of capitalism ... at the core of its strategy was a belief that the machinery of the state could be used to ameliorate the lives of workers' (Allen, 2015). *Syriza* and *Podemos* were therefore examples of what not to do.

Moreover, the rules of both parties prevent them from participation in any government that includes 'pro-capitalist' or reformist parties (which include Labour and the Greens and possibly SF, depending on how SF evolves in the years ahead). Thus, after months of wrangling, the SP/AAA withdrew from the Right2Change discussions altogether. The PBPA signed up to the principles but remains hostile to any new political formation which it cannot control and determined to remain aloof from any coalition, as recounted in my interview with one of its recently elected TDs, Gino Kelly, who adds that 'any new formation arising from that [Right2Change] is likely to be reformist, not revolutionary, and we don't believe that Ireland needs another reformist party'.

SF is also hostile to the emergence of any new political formation and seeks to draw upon the energy of the anti-austerity movement to increase its own electoral fortunes. Indeed, SF sees itself as the Irish equivalent of Podemos, already formed. This claim is made explicitly in SF campaign leaflets in 2015: 'In Spain, it is called Podemos, in Greece, Syriza, and in Ireland, Sinn Féin' (cited in Dunphy, 2016, pp. 204–205). However, many anti-austerity and left activists outside of SF's ranks have three problems with this claim. First, they see SF as a nationalist party, much more than a left party. Second, its ministers in coalition government in Northern Ireland have actually implemented austerity politics and, in the Republic, it has positioned itself in recent years for possible participation in coalition government with FF, as indicated in my interviews with Daly and McCann. Third, they see its future political direction—leftwards or rightwards—as being as yet undecided. Anti-austerity activist and Independent left TD (and ex-SF member), Thomas Pringle, declared in our interview that SF 'has no internal democracy at all and is completely focussed on getting into power'.

Some Left independent deputies tend to be amongst those most open to a new political formation. In our interview Clare Daly said that

> the Syriza model, with political elites from a number of different parties building a new formation from the top down, would never work in Ireland. It will have to be the Podemos model—building from the grass roots up. A huge number want something different. A vanguard party is completely out of date and can only dissipate the energies of the movement.

Daly is clearly referring here to the fact that Syriza, unlike Podemos, 'did not come out of the [social] movements' but pre-dated them and was formed by existing political parties and elites (Massey, 2015, p. 17). By contrast, Podemos was formed by people who had 'come from social movements, and the demands and lessons from the squares have been incorporated into Podemos's ideas, structures, and mechanism.' As Podemos member Sirio Canos Donnay explains, in conversation with Doreen Massey, 'anybody, even if they belong to another party, can join one of its locally-held, horizontally-organised meetings, and vote in its internal processes.' Moreover, it is a loose-knit organization, without formal membership or fees, which tries to stay close to its grass roots origins, with maximum discussion of policies, programmes and principles and open votes on strategies and coalitions (Massey, 2015, pp. 21–22). Online registration allows permanent participation with a personal voting code, and the tactic of 'drawing nebulous borders between the inside and the outside of the party' helped increase membership to nearly 400,000 within a year, facilitating a truly mass mobilization of energies (Della Porta, Fernández, Kouki, & Mosca, 2017, pp. 78–79). Clearly, it is this loose-knit, bottom-up approach to building a new political organization that some activists felt most appropriate to the Irish context—as opposed to either the 'democratic centralist' model of the Leninists (and, arguably, SF) or the idea of creating another top-down party like the others (as arguably happened when three Independent TDs created the Social Democrats in July 2015).

For Thomas Pringle TD, increasing democratic participation and control is the key. As he said in our interview, 'We have to learn from *Podemos* and do something similar. The mobilisation against austerity has made people more open to alternatives.' These views were echoed by Deputy Joan Collins in our interview: 'We need a new political movement, linked to the unions and the social movements, and built from the grass roots up.'[3]

In the aftermath of the disappointing 2016 general election in Ireland, activists were adamant that the conditions for a new politics were still ripening. Three pillars of the anti-austerity movement were identified: the trade unions, the politicians (very divided, as we have seen, over the extent to which a new formation was desirable or possible), and the community activists and grass roots groups. According to two activists interviewed for this research, the community activists who form the third pillar of the movement in this analysis constitute, in some ways, both its greatest potential strength and its potential weakness, in that they often lack the necessary skills and experiences in dealing with professional politicians and bureaucrats and may be open to manipulation or disillusionment. In 2015 and 2016, both the Unite union and the Left independents sought to strength the third pillar, fearing that its relative weakness might imperil the project of encouraging new forms of democratic participation and control. Unite has organized two- and three-day-long education workshops on political economy for non-party community and anti-austerity activists, not wanting them to be at a disadvantage. By the summer of 2016, Ogle claimed in our interview, a democratic structure in the community pillar was beginning to emerge, although it remains unclear as to how this claim may be verified. All future scenarios remained under review, including the possibility of a new party, in which some members of the Independents4Change group that had emerged in parliament might play a role.

The Independents4Change group remains fairly heterogeneous, however. Not all of its members believe that a new party can succeed. One of those who is most favourably disposed to the idea—Deputy Joan Collins—decided to use part of her salary as a parliamentary deputy to pay for a young Unite activist to work for the community pillar of the anti-austerity movement, touring the country to organize grass roots groups. The goal is to sustain and expand community activism and democratic participation in generating new ideas about politics by focussing on specific actions—such as the national rallies on 17 September 2016, the most recent (at time of writing) mass demonstrations by the Right2Water campaign. As Collins argued in our interview, 'the aim now is to set up a movement for social change—not a party yet. That has to emerge organically'.

Clearly, the relationship between social movements and political parties is, as Della Porta et al. (2017) make clear, a complex and multi-faceted one. Citing McAdam and Tarrow (2010), they mention six forms that this relationship can take:

> Movements introduce new forms of collective action that influence election campaigns. Movements join electoral coalitions or, in extreme cases, turn into parties themselves. Movements engage in proactive electoral mobilization. Movements engage in reactive electoral mobilization. Movements polarize political parties internally. (Della Porta et al., 2017, pp. 3–4)

The Right2Change movement has attempted the first of these but with limited success. Some activists continue to hope that conditions may yet facilitate the birth of a new party that can express the hopes and aspirations of part of the social movement, at least.

Conclusion

This article has sought to understand why the anti-austerity movement in Ireland has not yet succeeded in effecting more far-reaching and wide-ranging change to the party system, and how some activists within the movement have sought to learn lessons from activists in other countries, above all Spain and Greece. The relative failure to date by what is arguably the biggest, most sustained and most vibrant mass social movement that Ireland has yet seen to really shake the political system is due to numerous factors. The conservative nature of Irish political culture, the operations of the STV electoral system in a country dominated by traditions of personalism and localism, the weakness of the Irish left, the self-interest of existing parties involved in anti-austerity activism and political divisions amongst activists have all contributed to this relative failure. Nevertheless many activists in all three pillars of the Irish anti-austerity movement—trade union, politicians and communist grass roots activists—have looked abroad, to Europe and to North America, for lessons to be learned.

While it is difficult to assess just how direct the influence of groups like *Podemos* has been, it is clear that many activists have absorbed some central lessons from aboard. These include the necessity to sustain and increase mass democratic participation in politics and the desirability of creating new mechanisms of democratic control and accountability. In addition, the anti-austerity protest movement in Ireland has seen Ireland consciously join in the creation of a transnational European space, with activists and leading speakers from other countries invited to Ireland to address mass rallies of activists, and Irish representatives attending conferences and rallies elsewhere in Europe. This awakening of a political awareness that activists need to look beyond a 'blocked' Irish party system and address common European problems in a common language with activists from other countries is something relatively new in Ireland and its full ramifications have yet to be realized. Whether or not a new political party emerges organically from the anti-austerity movement and what the prospects might be for such a new party if it did emerge are open questions. But the Irish anti-austerity movement, now well into its second decade, has not yet exhausted its potential to surprise and innovate and has already injected new thinking about politics into Irish society.

Notes

1. Albeit in a somewhat inconsistent and vacillating way (see below for SF's contradictions on the water charges issue).
2. Hearne's online survey gathered the responses of 2556 people involved in the movement, making it perhaps the biggest and most representative survey of participants in the anti-water charges movement.
3. Of course, it could be argued that Syriza's radicalism has been tempered if not indeed broken in Greece, and that Podemos has reached a ceiling in Spain without being capable of delivering its promise to unseat the ruling 'caste' and fundamentally upset the Spanish party system. But the formidable obstacles in the way of new political forces turning anti-austerity activism into successful challenges to the political system is another story.

Acknowledgements

The author would like to acknowledge the cooperation of the following who agreed to be interviewed: Joan Collins TD (ex-SP, ex-PBPA, now Left independent—Independents4Change), Ruth Coppinger TD (SP/AAA), Clare Daly TD (ex-SP/AAA, now Left independent—Independents4Change), Gino Kelly TD (PBPA), Eamon McCann MLA (Member of the Legislative Assembly of Northern Ireland—PBPA), Thomas Pringle TD (ex-SF, now Left independent—Independents4Change), and Brendan Ogle, full-time official with Unite—the Union and key figure behind the Right2Change campaign, and three other anti-austerity movement activists who requested anonymity. All interviews were conducted, face to face, in Dublin in June and July 2015 and July 2016, apart from that with McCann which was conducted in Derry in July 2016.

Disclosure statement

No potential conflict of interest was reported by the author.

References

Allen, K. (2000). *The Celtic tiger: The myth of social partnership in Ireland*. Manchester: Manchester University Press.

Allen, K. (2015). *The defeat of Syriza and its implications for the Irish left*. Retrieved August 23, 2015, from www.peoplebeforeprofit.ie/2015/07/the-defeat-of-syriza-and-its-implications-for-the-irish-left

Anti-Austerity Alliance, & People Before Profit Alliance. (2016). *Common principles: Radical alternatives and real equality*. Dublin: Author.

Coakley, J., & Gallagher, M. (Eds.). (2010). *Politics in the republic of Ireland* (5th ed.). Oxon: Routledge.

Connolly, L., & Hourigan, N. (Eds.). (2006). *Social movements and Ireland*. Manchester: Manchester University Press.

Cox, L. (2006). News from nowhere: The movement of movements in Ireland. In L. Connolly, & N. Hourigan (Eds.), *Social movements and Ireland* (pp. 210–229). Manchester: Manchester University Press.

Della Porta, D., Fernández, J., Kouki, H., & Mosca, L. (2017). *Movement parties against austerity*. Cambridge: Polity.

Dellepiane-Avellaneda, S., & Hardiman, N. (2015). The politics of fiscal efforts in Ireland and Spain: Market credibility vs political legitimacy. In G. Karyotis & R. Gerodimos (Eds.), *The politics of extreme austerity: Greece in the Eurozone crisis* (pp. 198–221). Basingstoke: Palgrave Macmillan.

Dunphy, R. (2016). Struggling for coherence: Irish radical left and nationalist responses to the austerity crisis. In L. March & D. Keith (Eds.), *Europe's radical left: From marginality to the mainstream?* (pp. 191–209). London: Rowman and Littlefield.

Farrell, D. (2011). *Electoral systems: A comparative introduction* (2nd ed.). Basingstoke: Palgrave Macmillan.

Finn, D. (2015, September/October). Ireland's water wars. *New Left Review, 95*, 49–63.

Fitzgerald, L. (2015, July/August). Organised left force or disparate independents? *The Socialist, 93*.

Hearne, R. (2015). *The Irish water war, austerity and the 'risen people': An analysis of participant opinions, social and political impacts and transformative potential of the Irish anti-water charges movement*. Unpublished paper, Maynooth University.

Heilig, D. (2016). *Mapping the European left: Socialist parties in the EU*. Berlin: Rosa Luxemburg Stiftung.

Hughes, I., Clancy, P., Harris, C., & Beetham, D. (2007). *Power to the people? Assessing democracy in Ireland*. Dublin: TASC.

International Monetary Fund. (2011). *Staff country reports: Ireland*. Washington: Author.

Kirby, P., & Murphy, M. P. (2011). *Towards a second republic*. London: Pluto Press.

Komito, L. (1984). Irish clientelism: A reappraisal. *Economic and Social Review, 15*(3), 173–194.

Komito, L. (1992). Brokerage or friendship? Politics and networks in Ireland. *Economic and Social Review, 23*(2), 129–45.

Massey, D. (2015). European alternatives: A roundtable discussion with Marina Prentoulis, Sirio Canos and Simon Dubbins. *Soundings, 60,* 13–28.

McDaid, S. (2016, May). The crisis in Ireland: Where did it all go wrong? *Political Studies Review, 14*(2), 189–198.

Murphy, M. P. (2016). What do we need to a second republic? High energy democracy and a triple movement. *Études Irlandaises, 41*(2), 33–50.

Murphy, P. (2015, July/August). Why Syriza capitulated and the alternative road of 'rupture'. *The Socialist, 93.*

People Before Profit Alliance. (2016). *Share the wealth: An alternative vision for Ireland: A general election manifesto.* Dublin: Author.

Right 2 Change. (2015). *Policy principles for a progressive Irish government.* Dublin: Author.

Risse, T. (2010). *A community of Europeans? Transnational identities and public spheres.* Ithaca, NY: Cornell University Press.

Stopper, A. (2006). *Mondays at Gaj's: The story of the Irish women's liberation movement.* Dublin: Liffey Press.

United Left. (2015). *Submission [to the Right2Change discussions] from united left, Dublin south central.* Dublin: Author.

Weeks, L. (2009). We don't like (to) party: A typology of independents in Irish political life, 1922–2007. *Irish Political Studies, 24*(1), 1–27.

National Anti-austerity Protests in a European Crisis: Comparing the Europeanizing Impact of Protest in Greece and Germany During the Eurozone Crisis

Jochen Roose, Kostas Kanellopoulos ⓘ and Moritz Sommer

ABSTRACT
Protest and social movements are drivers for the Europeanization of national public spheres. This is suggested by the literature on the emergence of Europeanized public spheres and the Europeanization of social movements as well as the discussion about the politicization of the European polity. The article tests this assumption in a standardized content analysis for newspaper reporting on the Eurozone crisis in Greece and Germany. Focusing on the public attribution of responsibility, the analysis looks for horizontal Europeanization (senders/addressees from other EU countries), vertical Europeanization (senders/addressees from the EU level), and discursive Europeanization (similar topics discussed at the same time). The findings do not identify protest as a strong driving force towards vertical or horizontal Europeanization of the public spheres in Greece and Germany. There is a weak tendency towards discussing similar topics at the same time in German and Greek media reports on protest. Consequences for European democracy and crisis politics are discussed.

Introduction

In 2011, the world witnessed a dramatic series of huge protests: from the Arab Spring (Amin, 2012; Davis, 2016) to Occupy Wall Street and the British riots and from the Chilean student movement to the Israeli anti-austerity protests and Russian pro-democracy demonstrations. At the same time, hundreds of thousands of citizens, particularly in Southern Europe, marched, demonstrated, and occupied the central squares of their cities several times to protest against the structural reforms and austerity measures imposed on them by their governments and European Union (EU) authorities in the course of the Eurozone crisis. The sequence and the prominence of these events led many commentators to tag 2011 as a global revolutionary year and compare it with analogous global revolutionary years of the past like 1848 and 1968 (Mason, 2012).

When people turn to the streets and voice their discontent, they want to change politics by drawing attention to specific problems. They want to mobilize public opinion and put pressure on politicians or other decision takers. Thus, social movements intend to influence the public agenda, push their protest issue to the top and trigger a public debate supporting their aim (Gamson & Wolfsfeld, 1993; Koopmans, 2007; Koopmans & Rucht, 2002). These efforts can refer to a specific demand and therefore vanish from the public debate as soon as the issue is settled. However, we have seen multiple examples in which social movements led to a lasting change in the public discourse, infusing a permanent sensitivity for specific issue fields. The protest in the context of the Eurozone crisis could lead to such a permanent sensitivity for European matters.

The Eurozone crisis was heralded by the 'Great Recession', which started with the 2008 financial crash and led to severe economic and social problems in many countries (Reinhart & Rogoff, 2009). Especially in Europe, the banking crisis was soon transformed into a sovereign debt crisis for most peripheral EU member states (Lapavitsas, 2012; Patomaki, 2013). Countries like Ireland, Greece, Portugal, and Spain (all Eurozone members), as well as Hungary, Romania, and Latvia, were unable to re-finance their sovereign budgets on the financial markets and a special bailout mechanism had to be crafted at the transnational level to rescue these states from bankruptcy. To provide guarantees for further loans, the EU formed the European Financial Stability Facility (EFSF), later amended with the permanent European Stability Mechanism (ESM), which not only offered support to countries in severe difficulty but also oversaw the transposition of a strict conditionality, negotiated by the European Commission, the European Central Bank (ECB), and the International Monetary Fund (IMF), jointly called 'the Troika' or 'the institutions'. All countries receiving support from the EFSF/ESM had to commit to fundamental reforms and strict austerity measures.

The measures of the EFSF/ESM were agreed with and implemented by the governments of the respective countries. National and transnational institutions jointly decided on structural reforms and austerity measures from the very beginning of the Eurozone crisis. Transnational institutions, whose members are national governments, imposed structural reforms and austerity in agreement with the governments of the crisis countries. Thus, the locus of austerity governance was at the same time both transnational and national. Protest referring to the Eurozone crisis could thus also pick up the national as well as the European level, addressing national or European actors.

The crisis and the adjacent protests could have become a push towards intensified controversies around the European political system and its decisions (Statham & Trenz, 2012, 2015). The debate about the politicization of international and European institutions assumed that decisions and the European polity as such would become increasingly the issue of public controversy (Grande & Hutter, 2014; Hooghe & Marks, 2012; Hutter, 2014; Roose, 2015; Zürn, Binder, & Ecker-Ehrhardt, 2012). The social movements protesting in the context of the Eurozone crisis could be a driving force to shift the public's attention towards EU institutions and European decisions (Della Porta, 2015). Also, the role of other countries in these processes, particularly other EU member states, might be prone to become controversial in the context of the Eurozone crisis. Protest around the Eurozone crisis could enhance a public debate also referring to the European level and other member states. While for many political actors, loyalties or dependencies might prevent public controversies with their European counterparts, social movements are less restricted and free to articulate criticism and demands. Social movements might trigger a Europeanized debate.

In this article, we take up the discussion about the emergence of a European public sphere as one subtype of transnationalized public spheres, discussed in this special issue. We want to know whether the protest in the context of the Eurozone crisis is a driver towards the Europeanization of the public debate. In particular, we examine whether, in the context of protest as the primary public activity of social movements, the debate is more Europeanized than on other occasions. The assumption that social movements are driving forces of the politicization of international politics (Habermas, 2012), in this case primarily European politics and the formation of a Europeanized public sphere is tested.

Our research is focused in two ways. First, we concentrate on two countries, Greece and Germany. Second, we focus on the public and discursive attribution of responsibility as the basic unit of analysis.

Greece and Germany are the two countries with the most prominent positions in the Eurozone crisis – though in very different roles. Greece has been hit most severely by the crisis. The social consequences of the crisis are most pervasive, the political system has been shaken, and the need for credit support is largest. Germany on the other hand is not only providing guarantees for the largest share of the credits but has also been the strongest force pressing for crisis management with strict austerity measures and market liberalization. Both countries are not only the different extremes but they are also closely intertwined by the crisis. Policy measures pushed by the German government to overcome the crisis have had a tremendous effect in Greece; on the other hand, Greece's budgetary situation has direct implications for Germany's public budget because of the credit guarantees for Greece. Looking at Greece and Germany in the Eurozone crisis allows us to gain an impression of the developments in the public spheres in two highly involved countries from different angles.

Focusing on attributions of responsibility, we limit our analysis to a specific but crucial part of a public discourse. The attribution of responsibility, the discursive link between an actor and an issue, is a key element of discourses. It interprets potential or real situations as the result of action. It is this interpretation which introduces reality into the social world. With the linking of issues and actors, this interpretation already receives a specific spin. Blaming the crisis on the architecture of the Eurozone system puts the crisis in a completely different context than blaming it on a national government for overspending. Opting for one of these perspectives has fundamental implications for solutions to overcome the crisis and plausible demands addressed at one actor or another. Analysing the attribution of responsibility allows for systematically identifying a core aspect of interpretation. We do this in a standardized content analysis of newspaper reporting in the two countries.

The article evolves as follows. In the first section, we describe our conceptual approach, encompassing three aspects. First, we briefly introduce the concept of attribution of responsibility. Second, we refer to the debate on an emerging European public sphere, which elaborates on dimensions of a Europeanized public sphere, such as vertical and horizontal Europeanization (subdivided in weak and strong horizontal Europeanization on the one hand and top-down versus bottom-up vertical Europeanization on the other hand) and on discursive Europeanization as a more complex concept of a Europeanized discourse. Third, we briefly present arguments on the role of social movements and their protest activity in the Europeanization of public spheres. In the following section, we discuss the method of Discursive Actor Attribution Analysis, a standardized content analysis of newspaper reporting, to code the public attribution of responsibility. In the analysis section, we show that the degree of Europeanization of the public spheres in Greece and Germany is

Attributions, European public sphere, and social movements

Attributing responsibility

Attributions of responsibility are ubiquitous. The identification of something as the result of an action is already an attribution of responsibility. Most of these links are socially so well institutionalized that they are consensually taken for granted. However, this may change. Some actors maybe called to action, but their actions do not necessarily correspond to the initial call. It also changes if the combination of actor and action is evaluated. In this case, the possibly self-evident, possibly debatable link between actor and action becomes discursive in the way that it is part of a contestable claim with consequences for the actor's evaluation.

Especially the attribution of blame has attracted wide academic interest (Bovens, Schillemans, & Goodin, 2014; Hood, 2011, 2014; Vis, 2016), dating back to the seminal article by Weaver (1986) on blame avoidance. While this literature focused mostly on institutional design and policies, many social movement scholars took it up. The resulting framing approach asked how social movement actors interpret reality in order to convince bystanders of their cause (Snow, 2007; Snow, Benford, McCammon, Hewitt, & Fitzgerald, 2014; Snow, Burke Rochford, Worden, & Benford, 1986). A crucial part of this interpretation is the attribution of responsibility (Gerhards, 1995; Snow & Benford, 1988). These attributions include blaming as part of 'diagnostic framing' in a cause-effect logic. And they include calls for action as part of 'prognostic framing'. Unlike blame (or praise) these demands attribute responsibility to act.

The framing approach also made its career in media studies (Chong & Druckman, 2007; Scheufele, 1999) with the aim to understand the broader interpretative frameworks presented to the audience. Only recently, the more specific aspect of publicly attributing responsibility received attention (Gerhards, Offerhaus, & Roose, 2007; Greuter, 2014; Hasler, Kübler, & Marcinkowski, 2016). Especially in the European multi-level polity, European institutions and governments of other countries turned out to be viable scapegoats for blaming (Gerhards, Offerhaus, & Roose, 2009; Gerhards, Roose, & Offerhaus, 2013).

The discussion on the public attribution of responsibility has shown the relevance of the concept for understanding public discourses. Furthermore, we have learned that the European polity offers multiple opportunities for attributing responsibility, also across the national border towards actors in other countries or on the European level. Finally, standardized content analysis has proven to be an adequate method for systematically testing hypotheses about a discourse. Previous literature has taken up the 'blame game' that evolved in national and Europeanized public spheres regarding the financial crisis in Europe (Joris, d'Haenens, & Van Gorp, 2014; Mylonas, 2014; Vasilopoulou, Halikiopoulou, & Exadaktylos, 2014; Wodak & Angouri, 2014). These qualitative studies reconstruct parts of the discourse and focus on narratives, metaphors, and discursive images. They present thick descriptions of the discourse, but they do not allow systematic comparisons across countries or contexts.

EUROPEAN SOCIAL MOVEMENTS AND TRANSNATIONALIZATION

An emerging European public sphere?

Mass media systems are in respect to their outlets and audiences by and large nationally confined, not the least due to language barriers. Accordingly, a European media system is highly unlikely to emerge (Gerhards, 2000). It is more plausible to expect the transnationalization and more specifically the Europeanization of national public spheres in response to the increased importance of the European polity. This holds even more in the context of the Eurozone crisis with European institutional actors becoming even more powerful and more influential for the living situation of the people, especially in countries where programmes of the ESM/EFSF with their strict regulations are in force.

A transnationalization of national public spheres would be '[…] a process that enlarges the scope of public discourse beyond the territorial state' (Brüggemann, Sifft, Kleinen von Königslöw, Peters, & Wimmel, 2006, p. 5).[1] The scope of a public discourse can be assessed in different ways, depending on the concept of the public sphere. In a first step, a public sphere should represent what is (politically) relevant. Due to the close connections between the European countries, especially in the context of the Eurozone crisis, the coverage of events and contributions to debates also from Europe beyond the domestic borders seems indispensable. This is even more underlined by the democratic principle of informed citizens. Political actors must be held accountable for their actions. An informed electorate, able to judge politicians' actions and to choose competently between arguments and concepts, is a prerequisite for democracy.

Following Habermas' idea of the public sphere as an arena in which arguments are exchanged from a wide range of perspectives (Habermas, 1989, 1998; also Alexander, 2006), the speakers should not be confined to political actors but rather should represent actors of all kinds and origins. Europeanization in this sense would mean an increased inclusion of all kinds of actors, including those from beyond the national borders.

Within the EU, this Europeanization of public spheres could follow two directions (Gerhards, 1993, 2000; Koopmans & Erbe, 2004): horizontal and vertical. In relation to the media's role in the public sphere, the horizontal dimension means that journalists from one EU country not only pay attention to debates and actors from their own country but also cover the public discourse in other European countries as well (Brüggemann & Kleinen-von Königslöw, 2009, p. 29). This could happen by simply reporting on issues happening or being discussed in other countries or by interviewing or citing actors from another EU member state. The public sphere is extended horizontally across the national arena towards other European countries.

For horizontal Europeanization, Koopmans and Statham distinguish a weak and stronger form:

> In the weak variant, the media in one country cover debates and contestation in another country, but there is no communicative link in the structure of claim making between actors in different countries. In the stronger variant, there is such a communicative link, and actors from one country explicitly address or refer to actors or policies in another European country. (Koopmans & Statham, 2010, p. 10)

While the weak Europeanization is a form of merely observing another country from a distance, the strong version is the atom of a Europeanized discourse. Actors from different European countries interact; national discourses interweave in a broader European setting.

Next to horizontal Europeanization, there is vertical Europeanization. Vertical Europeanization means that nation state actors pay closer attention to what is happening in Brussels. The reporting links the national with the European level. Koopmans and Statham again distinguish two forms: 'a bottom-up one, in which national actors address European actors, make claims on European issues, or both; and a top-down one, in which European actors intervene in national public debates' (Koopmans & Statham, 2010, p. 38).

Empirical studies have shown overall little Europeanization, neither vertically nor horizontally (Brüggemann & Kleinen-von Königslöw, 2009; Brüggemann et al., 2006; Gerhards, 2000; Machill, Beiler, & Fischer, 2006, p. 4858; Roose, 2012). And there is no increase in these dimensions over time.

While the dimensions of vertical and horizontal Europeanization in its respective forms (weak vs. strong, top-down vs. bottom-up) focus on actors, Eder and Kantner (2000) referred to the content of the debate. Inspired by the idea of an ideal discourse proposed by Habermas (1981), they consider a discourse as European if it discusses the same issues at the same time under the same points of reference (Eder & Kantner, 2000, p. 315; see also Steeg & Risse, 2010, p. 7; similarly Díez Medrano, 2003, p. 193). We call this discursive Europeanization.

Discursive Europeanization is difficult to assess. Trenz (2005) claims to have found indications of a Europeanized discourse among five countries (Austria, France, Germany, Spain, UK). Díez Medrano (2003) finds for quality newspapers in Germany, UK, and Spain convergent interpretations of the European integration process itself. It is beyond the scope of this article to fully assess the similarity of discourses in its whole complexity. Notably the reconstruction of similar reference points is highly difficult. Here, we confine the analysis to the question of to what extent similar topics are discussed in our two countries – Greece and Germany – and whether this similarity increases in the context of protest. A discussion of the same topics at the same time is a precondition for the more encompassing idea of Eder and Kantner (2000), and therefore its assessment is already highly relevant for diagnosing discursive Europeanization.

The whole range of empirical studies mentioned here refers to an Europeanization of public spheres before the crisis. This concerns studies on all dimensions: horizontal Europeanization, vertical Europeanization, and discursive Europeanization. It is a very plausible assumption that the crisis and the policies linked to its management may have changed the picture. We cannot provide a comparison of the attribution patterns before and after the crisis. Rather we are interested in a possible driving force for Europeanization of national public spheres: protest of social movements.

Social movements as drivers of a European public sphere

The argument that social movements and protest are factors for accelerating the Europeanization of national public spheres can be deduced from three interrelated debates: the research on the European public sphere, the debate on the Europeanization of social movements, and that on the politicization of international and particularly European authority.

Research on the Europeanization of public spheres identified occasions when media reporting covered an increasing share of European issues and actors. Conflict about European topics has been identified as one driving force for a more Europeanized reporting

(Berkel, 2006; Roose, 2012; Schneider, 2008; Trenz & Statham, 2013). This is not overly surprising, considering the general effect of controversy on the likeliness of reporting (Eilders, 2006). Social movements contest political decisions by means of protest and other forms of contentious politics. They infuse controversy into the public debate. Based on that argument, one could suspect that social movements become the driving forces of a Europeanized debate, especially in the highly European setting of the Eurozone crisis.

This argument coincides with the debate addressing the Europeanization of contention (Della Porta & Caiani, 2009). Previous research documented the difficulties for civil society actors in adapting to the Europeanization of political systems (Imig & Tarrow, 2000; Uba & Uggla, 2011). But in recent years, the Global Justice Movement (GJM) became one of the major movements in Western Europe, with a strong transnational perspective and transnational links (Della Porta, 2007; Flesher Fominaya, 2014; Kanellopoulos, 2009). This may have provided fertile ground for a more Europeanized crisis-related mobilization. More recent work on reactions to the crisis-related EU and Troika policies identified some Europeanization tendencies among unions and social movements (Diani & Kousis, 2014; Kanellopoulos, Kostopoulos, Papanikolopoulos, & Rongas, 2017; Kouzis, 2014). Thus, a European perspective may be one of the contributions by social movements to the public discourse, triggering a more Europeanized public sphere.

Finally, the recent debate on the politicization of international and, more specifically, European authority argued that actors that were almost invisible in public debates now become focal points of controversies. They are politicized in the sense that their set up, their policies and actions are questioned and criticized by a wide range of societal actors (Hooghe & Marks, 2012; Roose, 2015; Zürn et al., 2012).

According to the theoretical assumptions, the process of politicization is driven by various factors. One of them is mobilization by protest and social movement actors. Civil society actors problematize international organizations and thereby they make them subject to political contestation (Beck & Grande, 2007; Grande & Hutter, 2014; Hutter, 2014). Social movements are seen as a crucial promoter of politicization. Habermas claimed, 'the things which are taken for granted in politics and culture, hence the parameters of public discussion, do not change without the dogged, subterranean work of social movements' (Habermas, 2012, p. 137).

Empirical studies are rather skeptical concerning an increase of the EU's politicization by social movements. Dolezal, Hutter, and Becker (2016) cannot find an increase of protest directed against EU institutions or their policies between the mid-1990s and late 2000s. The protest around the turn of the century was 'a rather short-lived peak' (Dolezal et al., 2016, p. 133).

The most recent developments may have changed the picture (Cinalli & Giugni, in press). Some authors suggest a 'wave' of global protests continuing the struggles that began in the GJM at the beginning of the century (Flesher Fominaya & Cox, 2013; Smith, 2012). Others argue for the development of two consecutive waves of global protests, separating the GJM from the ongoing anti-austerity protests whose main similarity is their mutual focus on 'another democracy' (Della Porta, 2013; Della Porta & Mattoni, 2014). Tejerina, Perugorría, Benski, and Langman (2013) have also argued for the emergence of a new global wave of protest that links the Arab Spring, Indignados, and Occupy. Hence, we may visit a new wave of protest linked to the Eurozone crisis. However, also these claims still await a more systematic check.

While these analyses look at the protests as a whole and focus on protest actors, the effect of Europeanized protest on the development of Europeanized public spheres has not been covered yet. A more focused look at the claims and addressees of protest is currently pursued by several empirical projects (Cinalli & Giugni, in press; Roose, Sommer, & Scholl, in press; Roose et al., in press). The following analysis contributes to this discussion.

What we are lacking is an assessment of the relative contribution of social movements to the public discourse with regard to Europeanization. Even if we find a Europeanized pattern of issues and actors addressed in the context of protest, this may simply mirror a turn in the overall discourse. In this case, we may see a change in the reporting around protest towards Europeanization. However, if this is just a part of a broader trend which affects all kinds of reporting, the claim of social movements as driving forces of Europeanizing the public sphere would not be justified. Possibly social movements just follow the general direction of the public discourse.

In this contribution, we bring together the theoretical assumptions from all three debates (European public sphere, Europeanization of social movements, politicization of Europe by mobilization) and test the core assumption of protest as a driving force for the Europeanization of the public debate.

Discursive actor attribution analysis

The discursive actor attribution analysis (DAAA) is a tool for the standardized measurement of the backbone of a controversial discourse: the attribution of responsibility. Its unit of analysis, an actor attribution, is the reconstructed answer to the question: Who makes whom responsible for what? The actor attribution consists of an attribution sender, an attribution issue and an attribution addressee (see Figure 1), as well as an evaluation. Only if these four elements (sender, addressee, issue, evaluation) are clearly identifiable, an attribution of responsibility (AoR) is coded.

The AoRs are reconstructed in newspaper reporting on the Eurozone crisis. Based on this material, we looked for actors who attribute responsibility to others, in direct or indirect quotes. Actors are not necessarily individuals; collective actors such as institutions and organizations can be senders or addressees, too. Journalists are only regarded as senders when they get actively involved in the debate by explicitly evaluating others.

We distinguish two basic forms of attributions: causal attributions and demand attributions. Causal attributions evaluate the causal effects of an action that was taken or is planned to be taken. Demand attributions call for an actor's action in response to a claim. This can be

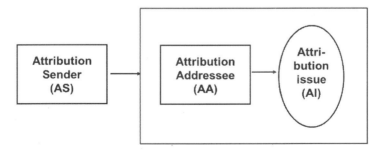

Figure 1. The attribution trias (adapted from Gerhards et al., 2007, p. 111).

a specific action at a specific time or the ascription of a general (formal) competence to take the necessary action in a field. These forms can be found with a positive or negative evaluation for causal attributions or the ascription versus rejection for demand attributions.[2]

Together with the individual attributions, our unit of analysis, we coded the context in which they appeared. While some attributions do not have a clear context and are just general contributions to the public debate, others are voiced in relation to specific events. Particularly we are interested in attributions voiced in the context of protests or demonstrations. Knowledge about the context in which the attribution is publicly presented allows us to distinguish between attributions linked to protest and other attributions.[3]

Data for this analysis stems from the research project *'The Greeks, the Germans and the Crisis (GGCRISI)'*, a joint Greek–German project, funded by the General Secretariat for Research and Technology (GSRT) of the Ministry of Education and Religious Affairs, Culture and Sports of Greece and the German Federal Ministry for Education and Research (BMBF).[4] The analysed material is taken from quality newspapers between September 2009 and March 2016.

The data for this paper is taken from the German *Süddeutsche Zeitung* and *Frankfurter Allgemeine Zeitung* as well as the Greek *Kathimerini, Eleftherotypia* and *Ta NEA* (for 2012, the year that *Eleftherotypia* stopped operating). We sampled every seventh issue resulting in a rotating week design with changing weekdays. Each newspaper covers the selected days in turn. Additionally, we covered articles referring to approx. 40 events, which were of major importance for the crisis development.[5] This sampling strategy made sure that reporting on major developments is not missed due to the systematic sampling covering only one seventh of all issues. Two weekly papers per country, namely the qualitative papers *Die Zeit* from Germany, and *ToVima* from Greece, and the tabloid style papers, *Bild am Sonntag* from Germany, and *ProtoThema* from Greece, supplement the sample.

For this analysis, we consider a total of 11,246 attributions. The coders were instructed to include only those articles and attributions containing relevant information immediately connected to the Eurozone crisis.[6]

The DAAA we have applied here is, of course, not meant to cover all the transformations regarding the Europeanization of public spheres. It only examines a mediated form of discourse from a specific perspective. The attribution of responsibility in and around the Eurozone crisis is one of the most heated topics of the debate, and DAAA offers a systematic way of examining a crucial part of it. We are well aware that political debates, social movement campaigns, and public spheres in contemporary societies are also produced and reproduced in the electronic media and in emerging social media (Earl & Kimport, 2011, Fuchs & Trottier, 2014; Michailidou & Barisione, 2017). But we also believe that in terms of influencing agenda setting and decision-making, the role of printed media remains indispensable. Politicians and other civil society actors frequently talk to the press and thus, what is reproduced in the press significantly influences the formation and the transformation of the public sphere.

Analysis

In our analysis, we proceed in two steps. First, we analyse the horizontal and vertical dimension of the public sphere's Europeanization, and then we turn to the discursive

Europeanization. We compare the Greek and the German public spheres, represented by the newspaper reporting from each country.

Vertical and horizontal Europeanization in the context of protest

In the sample, the systematic content analysis identified a total of 151 protest events in the Greek newspapers and 45 protest events in German newspapers. These were supplemented by 14 major protest events around which reporting was sampled. As these 14 sampling dates were linked to protests at various places and thus resulted in the coding of multiple protest events, the total number of coded protest events for Greek newspapers were 233 and for German newspapers 91.

The protests covered in the newspapers are not necessarily protests from the newspaper's own country. Also protest from abroad is covered. In Greek newspapers, the covered protest events are predominantly in Greece (78% of the protest events reported took place in Greece). The only other country, from which a sizeable number of protests with relation to the Eurozone crisis is covered, is Germany. Fifteen protest events in Germany (11% of all protest events) are found in Greek sources. For German newspapers, protest events in Germany are not very well covered. Three protest events with relation to the Eurozone crisis are recorded, amounting to seven per cent of all protest events covered in German sources. Thus, the German newspapers cover protest events connected to the Eurozone crisis in Germany less than Greek newspapers do. Similar to the Greek newspapers, the largest share of reported protest events in German newspapers took place in Greece (66% of all crisis-related protest events found in German newspapers). The share is nearly as high as for the Greek newspapers, though the absolute number is considerably smaller (27 protest events). Additionally, German newspapers pay attention to protest events in France (15%), while other countries appear each only once.

In the course of protest events, various claims are voiced. Demands are made but also interpretations of the situation are offered including causal attributions. The protesters themselves do not only make these attributions. Protest is rather an opportunity for protesters as well as others to appear in the media, to voice demands or react to them or use the opportunity for spreading different interpretations. All these interpretations and particularly attributions of responsibility are thus linked to the protest, even if they do not necessarily share the views of the protesters. Overall, in the Greek newspapers, 517 AoR are reported in the context of protest and for German newspapers, the respective number is 150.

Our first analytical interest concerns the speakers (or senders) appearing in the reporting. Are speakers that are covered by the newspapers in the context of protest events more horizontally or vertically Europeanized than speakers in the rest of the reporting?

In the Greek sources, domestic senders of attributions dominate. Overall in nearly two thirds of all cases the sender of an attribution is a Greek actor (Table 1). Actors on the European or transnational level appear in 16% of the cases, while senders from other EU member states are about as frequent (15%). The overall Europeanization of the senders in the Greek debate is not overly large. Senders from the European level (vertical Europeanization) as well as senders from other European member states (horizontal Europeanization) each make up only roughly one-fifth of all attribution senders.

Table 1. Senders of attributions – Greek (GR) sources.

Senders	Protest context	No protest context	Total
GR government and coalition parties	5.0%	19.6%	18.6%
GR opposition	12.0%	14.2%	14.0%
GR Civil Society + Science	26.1%	5.1%	6.6%
GR media	7.7%	19.9%	19.0%
GR, other actors	23.8%	7.3%	8.4%
Domestic total	*74.6%*	*66.1%*	*66.6%*
EU governance + Troika	0.2%	10.2%	9.5%
Other EU level actors	3.7%	0.7%	0.9%
Transnational actors	7.4%	5.2%	5.4%
Vertically transnationalized total	*11.3%*	*16.1%*	*15.8%*
Actors, other EU member states	13.0%	14.8%	14.6%
Horizontally Europeanized total	*13.0%*	*14.8%*	*14.6%*
Other actors	1.2%	3.0%	2.9%
N	517	6991	7508

Source: GGCRISI.

Protest does not change the picture of the overall debate in Greece. Domestic senders are even more frequent in Greece in the context of protest events; 75% of all senders in the context of protest are Greek, compared to 66% of the senders in other reporting. While actors from other EU member states appear in the context of protest with 13% of all senders to a similar share than in the rest of the reporting (15%), the vertical transnationalization is weaker in the context of protest with respect to the senders. Reporting in the context of protest covers actors from the EU and beyond (global level, other continental organizations) with a share of 11% of all attribution senders, while it is 16% for the rest of the reporting. Thus, in Greece protest is not a driver for the Europeanization of attribution senders, neither horizontally nor vertically.

Turning to Germany, the picture changes completely (Table 2). The overall share of domestic senders in German sources is considerably lower than in Greece. While in the Greek media, domestic senders account for 66% of all senders, in Germany the share of domestic senders is 53%. Especially senders from other EU member states appear more often in German reporting (21%) than in Greek reporting (14%).

The difference between reporting in the context of protest and all other reporting in German media is huge. In protest-related reporting domestic senders make up a minority of 19%, compared to the 54% in the rest of the reporting. Vertically transnationalized

Table 2. Senders of attributions – German (DE) sources.

Senders	Protest context	No protest context	Total
DE government and coalition parties	0.7%	13.0%	12.7%
DE opposition	4.0%	6.7%	6.7%
DE Civil Society + Science	2.0%	5.4%	5.3%
DE media	6.7%	22.6%	22.1%
DE, other actors	5.3%	6.0%	5.9%
Domestic total	*18.7%*	*53.7%*	*52.7%*
EU governance + Troika	0.0%	14.1%	13.7%
Other EU level actors	0.0%	0.6%	0.6%
Transnational actors	0.7%	5.6%	5.4%
Vertically transnationalized total	*0.7%*	*20.3%*	*19.7%*
Actors, other EU member states	80.6%	19.1%	21.1%
Horizontally Europeanized total	*80.6%*	*19.1%*	*21.1%*
Other actors	0.0%	3.1%	3.0%
N	150	4644	4794

Source: GGCRISI.

senders are negligible. It is actors from other EU member states that are dominantly covered as senders of attributions in the context of protest; 81% of all senders of attributions in the context of protest come from other EU member states. In German newspapers, the horizontal Europeanization of attribution senders is much stronger in the context of protests than in the rest of the reporting. This is primarily due to the location of the protests. The coverage of protests outside of Germany consequentially leads to the coverage of attribution senders from other countries. Attributions voiced in the reporting around protest events outside Germany are sent dominantly by actors from other EU member states (80%), with Greek actors alone accounting for a third. Thus, regarding senders, protest events are a strong driver for horizontal though not vertical Europeanization in the German reporting.

While the analysis of senders tells us who made her or his voice heard, the analysis of addressees gives us hints about the interpretation of the crisis constellation.

In Greek media, also the addressees are predominantly Greek (Table 3). The most important addressee accounting for half of the attributions is the national government with the governing parties. As also other Greek actors are frequently addressed, 71% of all attributions are addressed at domestic actors. European and transnational actors (vertical transnationalization) and actors from other EU countries (horizontal Europeanization) account for 15% and 13%, respectively.

The distributions of addressees for reporting around protests and reporting on other occasions in Greece are remarkably similar. The respective shares differ by only one percentage point. Thus, in the Greek media, there is no visible Europeanization effect in respect to addressees.

The picture changes again for the German newspapers (Table 4). First of all, domestic addressees are much less frequent than in Greece. A quarter of the addressees in German reporting are German. Much more present (42%) are actors from other member states; 16% of the attributions are addressed to Greek actors alone, another 26% to actors from various other EU member states. European and transnational actors, too, are addressed frequently, amounting to 28% of all addressees.

Reporting around protest events again differs considerably from other reporting in the German media. In the context of protest, domestic actors are addressed even less. Only every sixth attribution is addressed towards a German actor in the context of protest.

Table 3. Addressees of attributions – Greek (GR) sources.

Addressees	Protest context	No protest context	Total
GR government and coalition parties	50.7%	51.4%	51.4%
GR opposition	2.5%	5.7%	5.5%
GR Civil Society + Science	11.8%	6.4%	6.8%
GR media	0.6%	0.6%	0.6%
GR, other actors	7,7%	6.7%	6.8%
Domestic total	73.3%	70.8%	71.1%
EU governance + Troika	7.4%	11.5%	11.2%
Other EU level actors	4.1%	1.1%	1.3%
Transnational actors	4.1%	2.0%	2.1%
Vertically transnationalized total	15.6%	14.6%	14.6%
Actors, other EU member states	10.5%	12.6%	12.5%
Horizontally Europeanized total	10.5%	12.6%	12.5%
Other actors	0.8%	2.0%	1.9%
N	430	6022	6452

Source: GGCRISI.

Table 4. Addressees of attributions – German (DE) sources.

Addressees	Protest context	No protest context	Total
DE government and coalition parties	11.3%	18.6%	18.3%
DE opposition	0.0%	1.1%	1.0%
DE Civil Society + Science	4.7%	0.9%	1.1%
DE media	0.0%	0.2%	0.1%
DE, other actors	0.7%	5.4%	5.3%
Domestic total	*16.7%*	*26.2%*	*25.8%*
EU governance + Troika	6.0%	24.0%	23.4%
Other EU level actors	0.7%	1.5%	1.5%
Transnational actors	4.7%	3.5%	3.5%
Vertically transnationalized total	*11.4%*	*29.0%*	*28.4%*
Actors, other EU member states	69.3%	41.5%	42.3%
Horizontally Europeanized total	*69.3%*	*41.5%*	*42.3%*
Other actors	2.7%	3.4%	3.3%
N	150	4644	4794

Source: GGCRISI.

The largest share of attributions in the context of protest is addressed towards actors from other EU countries. These attributions account for 69%. Thus, the horizontal Europeanization is considerably stronger in the context of protest than in other reporting. For vertical Europeanization, the picture looks different. While in the general reporting 29% of the addressees are found on the European or transnational level, this applies only to 11% of the addressees in the context of protests. Vertical Europeanization is considerably weaker in the protest-related reporting than in other constellations.

The first conclusion for our research question concerning protest as a driver for Europeanization of the public sphere is mixed. In Greece, reporting around protest is as (little) Europeanized as the rest of the reporting. Protests do not affect the overall pattern of the debate. In the German media, the situation is different. Vertical as well as horizontal Europeanization in the reporting is much more frequent in general. In the context of protest, especially horizontal Europeanization increases considerably. If reporting is linked to protest, senders as well as addressees are predominantly from other EU member states. As the covered protest events mostly take place abroad we may suspect a high share of weak horizontal Europeanization, covering attributions made by foreign actors addressed to other actors from the sender's country. This is a plausible assumption, which will be addressed in the next subsection.

Forms of vertical and horizontal Europeanization

For horizontally Europeanized attributions, we distinguished weak and strong Europeanization. In the weak case, sender and addressee are both in the same country, different to the place where the newspaper is issued. In the strong case, sender and addressee are in different countries and thus communicate across a border. For vertically Europeanized attributions, we distinguish bottom-up and top-down attributions. In the following, we will inspect the forms of Europeanized attributions more closely.

The strong domestic focus is underlined by the sender–addressee constellations we find among attributions in the Greek newspapers (Table 5). Half of the attributions are internal domestic attributions with Greek senders addressing Greek addressees. This constellation is even more frequent in protest-related reporting than in other reporting.

In protest-related reporting, the weak horizontally Europeanized attributions with sender and addressee both coming from one other EU member state is relatively more frequent than in the usual reporting; 25% of the attributions in protest-related reporting are weak horizontally Europeanized while this applies to only 13% of the attributions in the rest of the reporting. The other forms of Europeanized attributions are less frequent in protest-related reporting than in the rest of the reporting.

Surprisingly, also attributions directed at the European level from the bottom up are less frequent in the context of protests. Protesters seem to attribute blame domestically rather than to the European or transnational level and demands are also rather directed at the national level. At the same time EU actors, who are not very active in the public anyway, seem not to comment or interfere in protest constellations. The top-down constellation with attributions sent from the EU level to domestic actors is completely absent in protest contexts.

The German newspapers are, as we have seen already for senders and addressees, more Europeanized in their reporting (Table 6). In particular, this applies to protest-related reporting. However, this is again predominantly horizontal Europeanization in its weak form. German newspapers cover protest and related attributions in other countries mainly as reports on what happens abroad. It does not involve domestic actors directly.

However, this general finding has to be qualified in two ways: first, in protest-related reports attributions sent bottom-up from other countries to the EU are slightly overrepresented. In protest-related reporting, foreign bottom-up attributions account for 9% instead of 7% in the remaining reporting. This difference is not overly large but considering the relatively low share in the Greek media where many of the protests take place, this difference is highly remarkable. Second, for assessing the German pattern we have to keep in mind that practically all protest events that triggered the reporting happened abroad. Considering that the initial protest event is (mostly) abroad, the number of attributions involving German actors is not that low.

Overall, considering the forms of Europeanized discourse, protest events seem to trigger specifically the more complex forms of Europeanized attributions. In both countries, the weak form of horizontally Europeanized reporting, which covers developments in another country without communicative links across borders, dominates.

Table 5. Forms of Europeanized attributions – Greek sources.

	Protest context	No protest context	Total
Inner domestic	55.7%	49.0%	49.4%
Weak horizontal: inner other EU MS	25.3%	13.2%	14.0%
Strong horizontal: domestic-other EU MS	1.7%	7.3%	6.9%
Bottom-up: domestic → EU	2.7%	5.1%	4.9%
Top-down: EU → domestic	0.0%	7.8%	7.3%
Foreign bottom-up: other EU MS → EU	3.3%	4.4%	4.4%
Foreign top-down: EU → other EU MS	0.4%	2.1%	2.0%
Other[a]	10.8%	11.2%	11.1%
N	517	6991	7508

Note: EU MS: European Union member state.
Source: GGCRISI.
[a]Other includes mainly strong attributions involving non-EU countries (primarily USA) and attributions within the EU level. Attributions between different, other EU MS are infrequent, but also included in 'other'.

Table 6. Forms of Europeanized attributions – German sources.

	Protest context	No protest context	Total
Inner domestic	12.0%	20.1%	19.8%
Weak horizontal: inner other EU MS	66.0%	14.8%	16.4%
Strong horizontal: domestic-other EU MS	6.0%	17.2%	16.9%
Bottom-up: domestic → EU	2.7%	14.9%	14.5%
Top-down: EU → domestic	0.0%	2.2%	2.1%
Foreign bottom-up: other EU MS → EU	8.7%	7.2%	7.2%
Foreign top-down: EU → other EU MS	0.0%	6.7%	6.5%
Other*	4.7%	16.9%	16.5%
N	150	4644	4794

Note: See Table 5.
Source: GGCRISI.
*Other includes mainly strong attributions involving non-EU countries (primarily USA) and attributions within the EU level. Attributions between different, other EU MS are infrequent, but also included in 'other'.

Discursive Europeanization of the debate?

The assessment of discursive Europeanization, that is, the similarity of topics at a given time, is highly difficult. It requires definitions of a time span and the similarity of topics. Furthermore, we have to choose comparisons, in our case of discourse sequences inspired by protest demands and other sequences.

To accomplish these goals, we have identified a number of larger protests spread out across the time under investigation (2009–2016). These protests differ in time and place. In accordance with our understanding of the character of the crisis, we not only refer to protest in Germany and Greece but in the whole Eurozone. This set of protest events was compared with nine other, mostly political events, which are relatively close (in terms of issues and topics) to the respective protests. To assess the similarity of issues, we categorized all issues in eleven groups, which are formed along a distinction of policy areas and political levels.[7] Similarity of the topics discussed around an event in Greece and Germany is defined for this purpose as the sum of percentage point differences for each issue category between the two countries.[8] Thus the measure can have values between 0 for a totally equal distribution of attribution issues in both countries and 200 for absolutely no overlap of issues between the two countries; 100 would mean that half of the attributions have identical issues and the other half differs.

Overall, the protest events were not able to synchronize the debate more than other events. The measure for issue similarity is on average 133 for the protest events and 103 for the other events. The various political and economic events around the Eurozone crisis seem to coordinate the discourse more than the protest events.

This general finding, however, tells only part of the story. Looking at the similarities in more detail unveils a rather different picture. The similarity of discourses around protest events is relatively high at the beginning (Figure 2). This similarity is not due to a common focus on specific issues but rather the discourses cover the whole range of issues in both countries. For the protest events in 2010, the difference between the discourses in Greece and Germany increases with reporting around protest focusing on different issues. However, from mid-2011 the issues covered become considerably more similar again. In this phase attributions refer more to criticism of the EU and crisis management institutions and austerity, as well as discussions about the role of protest itself. In this period,

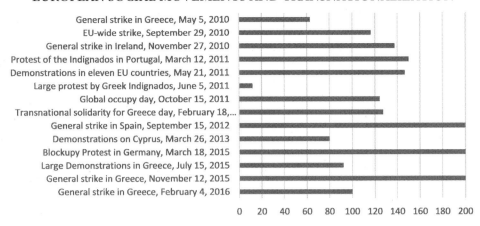

Figure 2. Similarity of discourses in GR and DE (protest events).

the interpretation of the Eurozone crisis from the protest part becomes more similar in the two countries.

This picture is distorted by a number of cases with extreme dissimilarity (general strike in Spain in September 2012, Blockupy protest in Germany in March 2015, and general strike in Greece in November 2015). These strong differences appear because in one country there are no or practically no attributions linked to the respective event due to extremely limited or absent reporting. If we leave these cases aside, we do find a tendency towards more similar issues discussed in both countries around protest. We consider this as an empirical indication for a common anti-austerity frame, a development also suggested in the relevant literature (Diani & Kousis, 2014; Kanellopoulos & Kousis, in press).

The other political and economic events produce by and large a more similar reporting in the two countries (Figure 3). However, this may be due to the fact that the respective events were focused on very specific questions. The more general EU summits or the annual meeting of the IMF did not lead to overly synchronized reporting in the two countries. Only specific decisions and meetings linked to specific decisions led to quite similar reporting in both countries.

Figure 3. Similarity of discourses in GR and DE (other events).

Overall, we do see indications that protest makes discursive Europeanization in the form of discussing similar topics at the same time in the two countries' public spheres more increasingly likely. While such an effect was practically absent at the beginning of the crisis, protest tends to focus and mutually inspire the discourses in the two countries over the years. However, this is dependent on the fact that the protest attracts sufficient attention in the first place. This effect is not overly strong and focused political events are stronger in coordinating the discourses in the two countries, but still protest has an effect.

Conclusion

Social movements and their protest activity lead to a more Europeanized public discourse with more mutual references across borders, more discursive links across borders and political levels, and more European debates discussing the same issues at the same time. This was the starting hypothesis. The idea is well elaborated in the literature on the European public sphere and the Europeanization of social movements as well as the debate on politicization of European politics. Findings supporting this idea would not come as a surprise. Especially with the Eurozone crisis as a strong factor pushing towards a more Europeanized public sphere, protest should enforce the Europeanized character of public debates.

We tested these assumptions with a broad content analysis of newspaper reporting in Greece and Germany. Our data covers a long time span from 2009, the beginning of the crisis, until March 2016. For our systematic analysis, we focused on attributions of responsibility as the core of the interpretation process. With a total of more than 16,000 cases, we should receive a clear picture of whether and how protest triggers a European character of reporting.

Unfortunately, reality is somewhat more complicated. For Greece, we found neither more horizontally nor more vertically Europeanized reporting around protest than in the rest of the crisis reporting. The debate is overall dominantly focused on the domestic realm. Attributions addressed to actors in other European countries or at the European level are relatively scarce. Also, senders from abroad or the European level, voicing their interpretation in the Greek media, are relatively seldom. In particular, the level of Europeanization does not differ between reporting around protest events and the remaining reporting. In German media, the picture is quite different. Here we have larger shares of addressees and also senders in other EU countries or on the European level. Reporting around protest is considerably more Europeanized than the usual crisis reporting. This applies predominantly to horizontal Europeanization.

Looking at the forms of vertically and especially horizontally Europeanized reporting, we discover only the weak tendencies of Europeanization. In cases when senders or addressees from other countries appear, it is mainly senders from another country addressing actors of their same country. The weak form of horizontal Europeanization is most frequent, sidelining the more demanding forms of strong Europeanization. This applies even more to reporting around protests than to the rest of the crisis reporting.

A Europeanized discourse with the media in different countries debating the same issues at the same time is the most complex concept of a European public sphere. Protest could be a strong driver of such a process by bringing specific issues in and changing the public agenda. A more Europeanized movement sphere with strong interaction and coordination of social movement organizations from various countries might be able to equally influence the public agenda in the respective countries at the same time. At the beginning of the Eurozone crisis, this was hardly the case. The discourses in both countries were broad and unfocused. Overlap appeared mainly due to the wide array of attributions made. Over time we found more similarity of attribution issues around protests. There are indications, though not overly strong ones, that protests inspired a discourse around the role of EU institutions, austerity policy and the socio-economic consequences of the crisis response policies. At the same time, it remains difficult for protest actors to make their voices heard in several EU countries; in some cases, even large protest events such as general strikes are not even reported in other countries' print media.

This finding is disconcerting from various perspectives. Social movements have considerably increased their transnational links in Europe. The crisis should have further strengthened these ties. Nevertheless, social movements find it still difficult to make their voices heard and to get a European perspective across. They still do not inhabit the European public sphere.

For the prospects of democracy in Europe, the absence of a strong social movement voice is bad news. While institutional changes have improved the democratic character of the EU, the public sphere and a European civil society contributing to a political discourse in a European arena remains the Achilles' heel of European democracy. In the Eurozone crisis, social movements were unable to compensate for this general weakness.

Finally, the crisis linked the European countries more closely and so does the crisis response policy. The problems at stake are dramatic. This concerns the socio-economic effects of austerity programmes as well as the potential instability of the common currency. The crisis brought up tremendously important issues. Therefore, a European discourse about policy measures and consequences is even more important and a strong Europeanized voice of social movements in a strongly and multi-dimensionally Europeanized public discourse is needed. However, we found only weak indications in this direction. We may continue to put hopes on social movements and their contribution to more Europeanized public spheres, but we should not be overly optimistic.

Notes

1. For a broader presentation and discussion of the literature on a European public sphere, see the contribution by Bourne (2017).
2. Additionally, ambivalent forms weighing positive and negative aspects may occur for causal attributions. These are very seldom and depending on the analysis they might be left out.
3. With this information, the method profits from experiences by protest event analysis (Koopmans & Rucht, 2002). Though the data set itself contains more detailed information on the protests, this is not relevant for the presented analysis.
4. The project is co-coordinated by Jochen Roose (for Germany) and Maria Kousis (for Greece) and conducted by two groups of researchers, one in Germany and one in Greece. We gratefully acknowledge Martin Wettstein's (University Zürich) very helpful coding tool 'angrist' which has facilitated the coding process.
5. For the analysis of the four most recent events between 2015 and 2016 in Greece we rely on reporting from *Efimerida ton Syntakton* (EfSyn).
6. Further methodological considerations can be found in Roose, Kousis, and Sommer (2014) and on the project website: www.ggcrisi.org. This includes the codebook with the detailed coding instructions.

7. For details, see the codebook on www.ggcrisi.org.
8. For example, in the context of the strike in Greece on 5 May 2010, the attributions voiced in the Greek newspapers dealt with EU crisis management and crisis institutions in 1.8% of all attributions, while in Germany around the same event 2.1% of all attributions discussed this issue. This contributes a percentage point difference of only 0.3 to the sum of percentage point differences for this event. Socio-economic policies and measures of redistribution were discussed in 5.4% of all attributions in Greece, but in 14.9% of all attributions in Germany, contributing a difference of 9.5 percentage points to the sum. The differences for these and all other issue categories result in a total sum of percentage point differences of 63 for this event. Around the global occupy day, the public attributions in Greece focused on budget policy and austerity (66.7% of all attributions in Greek newspapers) while the attributions in Germany focused on fiscal market regulation (50% of all attributions in German newspapers). The overall sum of percentage point differences for this event is 124.

Disclosure statement

No potential conflict of interest was reported by the authors.

ORCID

Kostas Kanellopoulos http://orcid.org/0000-0001-8869-6943

References

Alexander, J. (2006). *The civil sphere*. New York, NY: Oxford University Press.
Amin, S. (2012). The Arab revolutions: A year after. *Interface: A Journal for and about Social Movements*, 4(1), 33–42.
Beck, U., & Grande, E. (2007). *Cosmopolitan Europe*. Cambridge: Polity Press.
Berkel, B. (2006). *Konflikt Als Motor Europäischer Öffentlichkeit. Eine Inhaltsanalyse Von Tageszeitungen in Deutschland, Frankreich, Großbritannien Und Österreich*. Wiesbaden: VS Verlag für Sozialwissenschaften.
Bourne, A. (2017). Social movements and the transnational transformation of public spheres. *Journal of Civil Society*, 13(3), 231–246.
Bovens, M., Schillemans, T., & Goodin, R. (2014). Public accountability. In M. Bovens, R. Goodin, & T. Schillemans (Eds.), *The oxford handbook of public accountability* (pp. 1–22). Oxford: Oxford University Press.
Brüggemann, M., & Kleinen-von Königslöw, K. (2009). `Let's talk about Europe'. Why Europeanization shows a different face in different newspapers. *European Journal of Communication*, 24(1), 27–48.
Brüggemann, M., Sifft, S., Kleinen von Königslöw, K., Peters, B., & Wimmel, A. (2006). *Segmented Europeanization. The Transnationalization of Public Spheres, in Europe: Trends and Patterns* (Transtate Working Papers 37). Bremen: Universität Bremen.
Chong, D., & Druckman, J. (2007). Framing theory. *Annual Review of Political Science*, 10(1), 103–26.
Cinalli, M., & Giugni, M. (in press). How did European citizens respond to the great recession? A comparison of claims making in nine European countries, 2008–2014. In J. Roose, M. Sommer, & F. Scholl (Eds.), *Protest, Resilienz Und Transnationale Solidarität*. Wiesbaden: Springer VS.
Davis, J. (2016). *The Arab spring and Arab thaw: Unfinished revolutions and the quest for democracy*. London: Routledge.
Della Porta, D. (Ed.). (2007). *The global justice movement. Cross-National and transnational perspectives*. Boulder, CO: Paradigm.

Della Porta, D. (2013). Social movements and the public sphere. In A. Salvatore, O. Schmidtke, & H-J Trenz (Eds.), *Rethinking the public sphere through transnationalizing processes: Europe and beyond* (pp. 107–135). Houndsmills: Palgrave Macmillan.

Della Porta, D. (2015). Kritisches Vertrauen: Soziale Bewegungen Und Demokratie in Krisenzeiten. In J. Rössel & J. Roose (Eds.), *Empirische Kultursoziologie. Festschrift Für Jürgen Gerhards Zum 60. Geburtstag* (pp. 221–241). Wiesbaden: VS Verlag für Sozialwissenschaften.

Della Porta, D., & Caiani, M. (2009). *Social movements and Europeanization*. Oxford: Oxford University Press.

Della Porta, D., & Mattoni, A. (Eds.). (2014). *Spreading protests: Social movements in times of crisis*. Colchester: ECPR Press.

Diani, M., & Kousis, M. (2014). The duality of claims and events: The Greek campaign against the Troika's memoranda and austerity, 2010–2012. *Mobilization, 19*(4), 387–404.

Díez Medrano, J. (2003). Qualitätspresse und Europäische integration. In A. Klein, R. Koopmans, H-J. Trenz, L. Klein, C. Lahusen, & D. Rucht (Eds.), *Bürgerschaft, Öffentlichkeit Und Demokratie in Europa* (pp. 193–214). Opladen: Leske + Budrich.

Dolezal, M., Hutter, S., & Becker, R. (2016). Protesting European integration. Politicisation from below? In S. Hutter, E. Grande, & H. Kriesi (Eds.), *Politicising Europe. Integration and mass politics* (pp. 137–155). Cambridge: Cambridge University Press.

Earl, J., & Kimport, K. (2011). Movement societies and digital protest. Fan activism and other non-political protest online. *Sociological Theory, 27*(3), 220–243.

Eder, K., & Kantner, C. (2000). Transnationale Resonanzstrukturen in Europa. Eine Kritik Der Rede Vom Öffentlichkeitsdefizit. In M. Bach (Ed.), *Die Europäisierung Nationaler Gesellschaften. Sonderheft 40 Der Kölner Zeitschrift Für Soziologie Und Sozialpsychologie* (pp. 306–331). Opladen: Westdeutscher Verlag.

Eilders, C. (2006). News factors and news decisions. Theoretical and methodological advances in Germany. *Communications, 31*(1), 5–24.

Flesher Fominaya, C. (2014). *Social movements and globalization. How protests, occupations, and uprisings are changing the world*. Basingstoke: Palgrave Macmillan.

Flesher Fominaya, C., & Cox, L. (2013). Introduction: Rethinking social movements and social theory. A richer narrative? In C. Flesher Fominaya & L. Cox (Eds.), *Understanding European movements. New social movements, global justice struggles, anti-austerity protest* (pp. 7–29). London: Routledge.

Fuchs, C., & Trottier, D. (Eds.). (2014). *Social media, politics and the state: Protests, revolutions, riots, crime and policing in the age of Facebook, twitter and Youtube*. London: Routledge.

Gamson, W., & Wolfsfeld, G. (1993). Movements and media as interacting systems. *The ANNALS of the American Academy of Political and Social Science, 528*, 114–125.

Gerhards, J. (1993). Westeuropäische Integration Und Die Schwierigkeiten Der Entstehung Einer Europäischen Öffentlichkeit. *Zeitschrift für Soziologie, 22*(2), 96–110.

Gerhards, J. (1995). Framing dimensions and framing strategies: Contrasting ideal- and real-type frames. *Social Science Information, 34*(2), 225–248.

Gerhards, J. (2000). Europäisierung Von Ökonomie Und Politik Und Die Trägheit Der Entstehung Einer Europäischen Öffentlichkeit. In M. Bach (Ed.), *Die Europäisierung Nationaler Gesellschaften. Sonderheft 40 Der Kölner Zeitschrift Für Soziologie Und Sozialpsychologie* (pp. 277–305). Wiesbaden: Westdeutscher Verlag.

Gerhards, J., Offerhaus, A., & Roose, J. (2007). Die Öffentliche Zuschreibung Von Verantwortung. Zur Entwicklung Eines Inhaltsanalytischen Instrumentariums. *Kölner Zeitschrift für Soziologie und Sozialpsychologie, 59*(1), 105–124.

Gerhards, J., Offerhaus, A., & Roose, J. (2009). Wer Ist Verantwortlich? Die Europäische Union, Ihre Nationalstaaten Und Die Massenmediale Attribution Von Verantwortung Für Erfolge Und Misserfolge. In B. Pfetsch & F. Marcinkowski (Eds.), *Politik in Der Mediendemokratie. Sonderheft 42 Der Politischen Vierteljahresschrift* (pp. 529–558). Wiesbaden: VS Verlag für Sozialwissenschaften.

Gerhards, J., Roose, J., & Offerhaus, A. (2013). Die Rekonfiguration Von Politischer Verantwortungszuschreibung Im Rahmen Staatlichen Wandels. In M. Zürn & M. Ecker-Ehrhardt (Eds.), *Die Politisierung Der Weltpolitik* (pp. 109–133). Frankfurt/M.: Suhrkamp.

Grande, E., & Hutter, S. (2014). Politicizing Europe in the national electoral arena. A comparative analysis of five West European Countries, 1970–2010. *Journal of Common Market Studies, 52*(5), 1002–1018.

Greuter, N. (2014). *Accountability without election*. Baden-Baden: Nomos.

Habermas, J. (1981). *Theorie Des Kommunikativen Handelns. Zwei Bände*. Frankfurt/M.: Suhrkamp.

Habermas, J. (1989). *The structural transformation of the public sphere*. Cambridge: Polity Press.

Habermas, J. (1998). *Between facts and norms*. Cambridge: MIT Press.

Habermas, J. (2012). *The crisis of the European Union. A response*. Cambridge: Polity Press.

Hasler, K., Kübler, D., & Marcinkowski, F. (2016). Over-Responsibilised and over-blamed: Elected actors in media reporting on network governance. A comparative analysis in eight European metropolitan areas. *Media and Governance, 44*(1), 135–152.

Hood, C. (2011). *The blame game. Spin, bureaucracy, and self-presentation in government*. Oxford: Princeton University Press.

Hood, C. (2014). Accountability and blame-avoidance. In M. Bovens, R. Goodin, & T. Schillemans (Eds.), *The oxford handbook of public accountability* (pp. 603–616). Oxford: Oxford University Press.

Hooghe, L., & Marks, G. (2012). Politicization. In E. Jones, A. Menon, & S. Weatherill (Eds.), *The oxford handbook of the European Union* (pp. 841–849). Oxford: Oxford University Press.

Hutter, S. (2014). *Protesting culture and economics in Western Europe. New cleavages in left and right politics*. Minneapolis: University of Minnesota Press.

Imig, D., & Tarrow, S. (2000). Political contention in a Europeanising polity. *West European Politics, 23*(4), 73–93.

Joris, W., d'Haenens, L., & Van Gorp, B. (2014). The Euro crisis in metaphors and frames: Focus on the press in the low countries. *European Journal of Communication, 29*(5), 608–617.

Kanellopoulos, K. (2009). *Constitution processes and theoretical issues on social movements: The movement against neoliberal globalization* (Doctoral dissertation). Panteion University of Political and Social Sciences, Athens.

Kanellopoulos, K., Kostopoulos, K., Papanikolopoulos, D., & Rongas, V. (2017). Competing modes of coordination in the Greek anti-austerity campaign, 2010–2012. *Social Movement Studies, 16*(1), 101–118.

Kanellopoulos, K., & Kousis, M. (in press). Protest, elections and austerity politics in Greece. In D. Doxiadis & A. Placas (Eds.), *Living under austerity: Greek society in crisis*. New York, NY: Berghan Books.

Koopmans, R. (2007). Who inhabits the European public sphere? Winners and losers, supporters and opponents in Europeanised political debates. *European Journal of Political Research, 46*(2), 183–210.

Koopmans, R., & Erbe, J. (2004). Towards a European public sphere? Vertical and horizontal dimensions of Europeanized political communication. *Innovation: The European Journal of Social Sciences, 17*(2), 97–118.

Koopmans, R., & Rucht, D. (2002). Protest event analysis. In B. Klandermans & S. Staggenborg (Eds.), *Methods of social movement research* (pp. 231–259). Minneapolis: University of Minnesota Press.

Koopmans, R., & Statham, P. (2010). Theoretical framework, research design, and methods. In R. Koopmans & P. Statham (Eds.), *The making of a European public sphere. Media discourse and political contention* (pp. 34–62). Cambridge: Cambridge University Press.

Kouzis, G. (2014). Labor amidst the economic crisis and the memoranda. In S. Zambarloukou & M. Kousis (Eds.), *Social aspects of the crisis in Greece* (pp. 231–246). Athens: Pedio Publisher.

Lapavitsas, C. (2012). *Crisis in the Eurozone*. London: Verso.

Machill, M., Beiler, M., & Fischer, C. (2006). Europe-Topics in Europe's media. The debate about the European public sphere: A meta-analysis of media content analyses. *European Journal of Communication, 21*(1), 57–88.

Mason, P. (2012). *Why it's kicking off everywhere: The new global revolutions.* London: Verso.

Michailidou, A., & Barisione, M. (Eds.). (2017). *Social media and European politics. Rethinking power and legitimacy in the digital era.* Basingstoke: Palgrave MacMillan.

Mylonas, Y. (2014). Crisis, austerity and opposition in mainstream media discourse of Greece. *Critical Discourse Studies, 11*(3), 305–321.

Patomaki, H. (2013). *The great Eurozone disaster. From crisis to global new deal.* London: Zed Books.

Reinhart, C., & Rogoff, K. (2009). *This time is different. Eight centuries of financial folly.* Princeton, NJ: Princeton University Press.

Roose, J. (2012). Was Wir Von Simmel Über die Chancen Einer Sozialen Integration Europas Lernen Können. Integration Durch Konflikt Als Weg Für Die Eu - Eine Diagnose. In H-G. Soeffner (Ed.), *Transnationale Vergesellschaftungen. Verhandlungen Des 35. Dgs-Kongresses 2010* (pp. 215–229). Wiesbaden: VS Verlag für Sozialwissenschaften.

Roose, J. (2015). Politisiert Die Krise? Veränderungen Bei Der Diskussion Eu-Politischer Fragen in Der Bevölkerung. In J. Rössel & J. Roose (Eds.), *Empirische Kultursoziologie. Festschrift Für Jürgen Gerhards Zum 60. Geburtstag* (pp. 425–454). Wiesbaden: Springer VS.

Roose, J., Kousis, M., & Sommer, M. (2014, September). *Discursive actor attribution analysis. A tool to analyze how people make sense of the Eurozone crisis.* Paper presented at the 8th ECPR General Conference, Glasgow.

Roose, J., Kousis, M., Sommer, M., Scholl, F., Kanellopoulos, K., Loukakis, A., & Papanikolopoulos, D. (in press). New rage, new perspectives? Protest in the Eurozone crisis in Greece and Germany. In J. Beyer & C. Trampusch (Eds.), *Finanzmarkt, Demokratie Und Gesellschaft. Sonderheft Der Kölner Zeitschrift Für Soziolgie Und Sozialpsychologie.* Wiesbaden: Springer VS.

Roose, J., Sommer, M., & Scholl, F. (in press). Verantwortungszuschreibungen in der Eurozonen-Krise. Das Kommunikationsverhalten von Politik und Zivilgesellschaft im Deutsch-Griechischen Vergleich. In J. Roose, M. Sommer, & F. Scholl (Eds.), *Protest, Resilienz und Transnationale Solidarität.* Wiesbaden: Springer VS.

Scheufele, D. (1999). Framing as a theory of media effects. *Journal of Communication, 49*(4), 103–122.

Schneider, S. (2008). United in protest? The European struggle over genetically modified food. In H. Wessler, B. Peters, M. Brüggemann, K. Kleinen-von Königslöw, & S. Sifft (Eds.), *Transnationalization of public spheres* (pp. 131–167). Basingstoke: Palgrave.

Smith, J. (2012). Connecting social movements and political movements: Bringing movement building tools from global justice to occupy wall street activism. *Interface: A Journal for and about Social Movements, 4*(2), 369–382.

Snow, D. (2007). Framing processes, ideology, and discursive fields. In D. Snow, S. Soule, & H. Kriesi (Eds.), *The Blackwell companion to social movements* (pp. 380–412). Malden, MA: Blackwell.

Snow, D., & Benford, R. (1988). Ideology, frame resonance and participant mobilization. In B. Klandermans, H. Kriesi, & S. Tarrow (Eds.), *From structure to action: Comparing social movement across cultures* (pp. 197–218). London: JAI Press.

Snow, D., Benford, R., McCammon, H., Hewitt, L., & Fitzgerald, S. (2014). The emergence, development, and future of the framing perspective: 25+ years since "frame alignment". *Mobilization, 19*(1), 23–46.

Snow, D., Burke Rochford, E., Worden, S., & Benford, R. (1986). Frame alignment processes, micromobilization and movement participation. *American Sociological Review, 51*(4), 464–481.

Statham, P., & Trenz, H.-J. (2012). *The politicization of Europe. Contesting the constitution in the mass media.* Hinsdale, IL: Dryden Press.

Statham, P., & Trenz, H.-J. (2015). Understanding the mechanisms of EU politicization. Lessons from the Eurozone crisis. *Comparative European Politics, 13*, 287–306.

Steeg, M., & Risse, T. (2010). *The emergence of a European community of communication: Insights from empirical research on the Europeanization of public spheres* (Kfg working paper series, no. 15). Kolleg-Forschergruppe "The transformative power of Europe". Berlin: Freie Universität Berlin.

Tejerina, B., Perugorría, I., Benski, T., & Langman, L. (2013). From indignation to occupation: A new wave of global mobilization. *Current Sociology, 61*(4), 377–392.

Trenz, H.-J. (2005). Die Mediale Ordnung Des Politischen Europas. Formen Und Dynamiken Der Europäisierung Politischer Kommunikation in Der Qualitätspresse. *Zeitschrift für Soziologie, 34*(3), 188–206.

Trenz, H.-J., & Statham, P. (2013). How European Union politicization can emerge through contestation: The constitution case. *Journal of Common Market Studies, 51*(5), 965–980.

Uba, K., & Uggla, F. (2011). Protest actions against the European Union, 1992–2007. *West European Politcs, 34*(2), 384–393.

Vasilopoulou, S., Halikiopoulou, D., & Exadaktylos, T. (2014). Greece in crisis: Austerity, populism and the politics of blame. *Journal of Common Market Studies, 52*(2), 388–402.

Vis, B. (2016). Taking stock of the comparative literature on the role of blame avoidance strategies in social policy reform. *Journal of Comparative Policy Analysis, 18*(2), 122–137.

Weaver, K. (1986). The politics of blame avoidance. *Journal of Public Policy, 6*(4), 371–398.

Wodak, R., & Angouri, J. (2014). From Grexit to Grecovery: Euro/crisis discourses. *Discourse & Society, 25*(4), 417–423.

Zürn, M., Binder, M., & Ecker-Ehrhardt, M. (2012). International authority and its politicization. *International Theory, 4*(1), 69–106.

The Gezi Protests and the Europeanization of the Turkish Public Sphere

Isabel David and Gabriela Anouck Côrte-Real Pinto

ABSTRACT
This article investigates the extent to which Turkish civil society organizations (CSOs) represented at the 2013 Gezi Park protests reflect a Europeanization of the Turkish public sphere. The methodology consists of 14 semi-structured interviews conducted with leaders of CSOs that participated in the protests and one questionnaire sent to a member of the Justice and Development Party (AKP) Istanbul Youth board (and member of the Istanbul Bar Association). The findings of our research reveal differentiated patterns of Europeanization of the Turkish public sphere, depending on CSOs' history, ideology, and multi-level relations with the European Union and the Turkish state. Conversely, pro- and anti-AKP CSOs converge on growing criticism of EU institutions.

Introduction

The 2013 Gezi Park protests in Turkey started as an environmental protest against the destruction of one of the few remaining green spaces in Istanbul in order to build a shopping mall and rebuild Ottoman army barracks. Following police brutality in evicting the original peaceful activists, the protest turned against the ruling Justice and Development Party (AKP), mobilizing between 2.5 and 3 million people in 79 (of 81) cities around the country (İnsan Hakları Derneği, 2013). Gezi Park was subsequently occupied by activists and supporters, who transformed it into a commune with libraries, kitchens, seminars, concerts, yoga, and math classes, amid clashes with the police (David & Toktamış, 2015, p. 18). During those weeks, the park witnessed an otherwise impossible peaceful coexistence and interaction among football fans, religious, and ethnic minorities (Alevis, Armenians, and Kurds), feminists, Ülkücü (far-right nationalists), Kemalists, pious Muslims, environmentalists, and LGBTI groups. The protests constituted the widest form of dissent against the 14-year rule of AKP and a landmark in political participation from below.

The Gezi protests were a branch of the wider global and particularly European wave of contestation following the 2008 Great Recession (Atak, 2014; Tuğal, 2013). The similarities between the Gezi and European mobilizations are twofold. First, the perceived retrenchment of democracy constituted the main cause of protests (KONDA, 2014; Roos &

Oikonomakis, 2014). Second, they shared common repertoires of protest, including occupations, and the use of social media, humour, graffiti, or art (cf. Della Porta & Mattoni, 2014; Flesher Fominaya, 2014).

Another important element of linkage to European mobilizations pertains to the fact that Turkey has been undergoing a process of formal Europeanization (EU-ization) since the country applied for European Union (EU now; at the time, the European Economic Community [EEC]) membership in 1987 and particularly after gaining official candidate status in 1999. In order to meet the EU conditions embodied in the Copenhagen criteria (democracy, market economy and the ability to assume the obligations of membership), Turkey and its civil society have been making multiple changes. EU action relating to civil society centres on funding, legislative changes, creation of networks with European civil society organizations (CSOs) and strengthening dialogue between Turkish civil society and the Turkish government.

Given this interaction with fellow European CSOs and EU institutions, the simultaneity of protests in EU countries and geographical proximity, it might be expected that Turkish CSOs that participated in the Gezi protests would reproduce European discourses and frames and highlight EU leverage and linkage. This article addresses precisely the absence of studies on this matter by trying to answer the following research questions: Did CSOs at Gezi formulate their claims in wider European terms? How Europeanized is Turkish civil society represented at Gezi? Are candidate states' civil societies part of a European public sphere and what are the mechanisms through which they participate in this European public sphere? The main aim is to assess to what extent Turkish civil society represented at Gezi reflects a Europeanization of the Turkish public sphere.

The article is organized as follows. The first section addresses the theoretical framework underlining our research. The second section then presents an account of the evolution of Turkish civil society and how the EU has promoted its Europeanization. Next, we describe the methodological frame of our research. The fourth section presents the main findings of the interviews we conducted with pro and anti-Gezi activists. The article concludes by linking findings to the theoretical framework and presenting directions for future research.

Europeanization and the creation of a European public sphere

The article takes as its starting point the premise that processes of Europeanization of candidate states contribute to the enlargement of the European public sphere to incorporate these states. Europeanization has been defined in multiple ways. Featherstone (2003, pp. 5–12), for example, identifies four understandings: As a historical phenomenon (through colonization), as transnational cultural diffusion, as institutional adaptation, and as adaptation of policies and political processes. Börzel and Risse (2000) define Europeanization as the adaptation of national processes, policies, and institutions to EU rules and norms. Diez, Agnantopoulos, and Kaliber (2005) mention four domains of Europeanization: Policies, political processes, identities, and public discourses.

We adopt Radaelli's (2003, p. 30) definition, which captures the multiple dimensions referred to by the previous authors:

> Europeanisation consists in processes of construction, diffusion and institutionalization of formal and informal rules, procedures, policy paradigms, styles, 'ways of doing things' and

shared beliefs and norms which are first defined and consolidated in the making of EU public policy and politics and then incorporated in the logic of domestic discourse, identities, political structures and public policies.

The definition is sufficiently broad to encompass macro, meso, and micro dimensions of society and politics and thus CSOs. According to this understanding, we follow the sociological institutionalist approach to Europeanization (March & Olsen, 1989): The domestic impact of the EU constitutes a socialization process, in which European institutions represent new rules, norms, practices, and structures of meaning that states should incorporate.

Europeanization involves a discursive component (Radaelli, 2004, p. 10): National actors make claims and references to the EU, its actors, and policies, instead of operating only on a national frame. This process is decisive for the constitution of a European public sphere. The public sphere can be conceptualized as rational public discourse that creates a communicative link between autonomous individuals as 'citizens', unifies them as 'the people' and integrates them into a form of collective self-government (Salvatore, Schmidtke, & Trenz, 2013, p. 1). The concept is intimately linked with the development of democracy and the necessary creation of solidarity bonds among citizens who do not know each other (Eder, 2006). This is the reason that the process of socialization inherent in Europeanization is fundamental for the creation of a European public sphere. In fact, a European public sphere should ideally involve not only a community of communication but also a common overarching European identity constructed discursively (Risse, 2003, pp. 4, 8). In this sense, the subjects under discussion should be addressed from a perspective extending beyond a particular country and its interests, involving similar meaning structures across national public spheres of both member states and candidate states (Díez Medrano & Gray, 2010, p. 195; Risse, 2003). Since the notion of the 'common good' is constitutively linked to the way in which citizens engage in public deliberation (Salvatore et al., 2013, p. 1), ideally, the idea of a European 'common good' should also stand behind public deliberation in the EU. This echoes the understanding of Habermas (1996, pp. 492–507), who views the European public sphere as an enlarged version of the Westphalian nation-state with a common political culture.

However, as a supranational community in the making composed of nation-states, this endeavour entails multiple difficulties. This is why, in the study of the creation of a European public sphere, debates have centred on three possible ways to achieve this (Koopmans & Erbe, 2004, quoted in Koopmans & Statham, 2010, p. 38):

- First, a supranational European public sphere, marked by the interaction among European-level institutions and collective actors around European themes, including European-wide mass media.
- Second, vertical Europeanization, that is, communicative linkages between the national and the European level, including a bottom-up variant (when national actors address European actors, make claims on European issues, or both) and a top-down variant (when European actors intervene in national public debates in the name of European regulations and common interests).
- Third, horizontal Europeanization, that is, communicative linkages between different European countries, with a weak variant (the media from one country report on

contestation and debate in another country, although there is no communicative link in the structure of claim-making between actors in different countries) and a strong variant (the communicative link exists and actors from one country explicitly address or mention actors and policies in another European country).

Our article corresponds to the third possibility. We believe that the creation of a European public sphere is a contentious process continuously being redefined since it is generated by heterogeneous, national public sphere actors and their histories as a response to processes of socialization promoted by EU norms, ideas, beliefs, and institutions. As Benhabib (1992, p. 105) mentions, the public sphere emerges when all people affected by general social and political norms of action engage in a practical discourse, evaluating their validity. This means that there are as many publics and, consequently, autonomous public spheres, as there are controversial debates regarding the validity of those norms (Benhabib, 1992). This aims at avoiding normative constraints to public discourse. In a democracy, the rules of the game, their interpretation, and the umpire are always contestable (Benhabib, 1992, pp. 106–107). As Risse (2003, pp. 4–5) argues, contestation and mobilization are fundamental pre-conditions for the emergence of a European public sphere in order to raise the salience of Europe and enlarge the sphere of participants. In this sense, public spheres are social constructions emerging through social and discursive practices.

The public sphere is operationalized by civil society. On the one hand, civil society actors can be promoted as an arena and instrument of democratization from below. These actors are seen as independent from state structures in terms of interests and experiences and exchange ideas and opinions (Splichal, 2010, pp. 29–31) with the goal of changing domination, which will thus be subjected to the needs of society (Habermas, 1989, p. 28). On the other, civil society can be considered as the area of state and market domination and indirect governing (Foucault, 2004, p. 307). As a result, civil society is located at the heart of state (de)legitimization and questions both the frontiers of state and market power and the conflictual relations between economic and social integration.

The EU's vision of civil society as an arena of deliberation and participation converges with the first definition. The EU defines CSOs as the structures of society outside of government and public administration, including economic agents not generally considered to be 'third sector' or non-governmental organizations (NGOs). Civil society may include trade unions, employers' organizations, consumer organizations, NGOs, community-based organizations, and religious communities (European Commission, 2002, p. 6). Further 'participation of civil society' is considered since the 2001 White Paper on European Governance as a key condition for promoting citizen participation in EU policy and legitimacy (Dakowska, 2003; Michel, 2007). Although it has the effect of diversifying EU private interlocutors, this civil society dialogue has been criticized for penalizing EU social partners and promoting lobbying instead of activism and social movements (Michel, 2007).

To take into account the ambivalence of civil society in terms of power effects we exclude neither the economy nor indirect state power, opting for a Gramsci (1999, pp. 145, 202, 531) definition of civil society: The set of organisms called 'private' or subaltern groups. These subaltern groups are in dialectical relation with dominant political formations, attempting to influence their programmes in order to advance their claims. State power is located within both 'political society', which is regulated by coercion and includes political institutions, army and police forces, and 'civil society', through cultural institutions which diffuse state ideology to promote consent (Gramsci, 1977, p. 565). This is because civil society is the locus where hegemony is disputed, as the dominant fundamental group seeks to extract consent.

In our article, we attempt to evaluate to what extent pro and anti-Gezi CSOs were socialized by the EU and subsequently developed common values, discourses, frames, themes, and identities with their European counterparts.

Turkish civil society in context

The EU sees Turkish civil society as an arena and actor of democratization, constituting a check on national state power,[1] and as a tool to legitimize the European hegemonic project. There are two periods in the history of Turkish civil society (TÜSEV, 2006). First, a long Ottoman past of 'associational life' outside the state, including religious foundations, and, after 1923, when the Republic was officially declared by Atatürk, associations in close relation with the state were favoured. The advent of the Republic and the subsequent exclusion of religion from the public sphere favoured secularist associations, while non-secularist associations and foundations, amputated from state support, were marginalized, closed, or nationalized (Côrte-Real Pinto, 2015; Ketola, 2013, p. 60). Under the Republic, Turkish civil society has been characterized by a corporatist mindset that has legitimized the state's developmentalist, nationalist, and securitarian ideology (Bora, 2000). Citizens did not have individual rights or freedoms, but only obligations towards the state (TÜSEV, 2006, p. 36).

From the 1960s, after the political opening, autonomous CSOs emerged, including leftist trade unions and the first private business associations (e.g., TÜSİAD, Turkish Industry and Business Association). However, social polarization and violence involving groups of students, trade unions, nationalists, and Islamists engulfed Turkey, leading to the 1980 military coup (see Ahmad, 1993). This restrictive tradition was continued by the framework of article 13 of the 1982 Constitution (which subjected fundamental rights and freedoms to national security criteria) and by the 1983 Law on Associations, which prohibited associations from engaging in political activities or from having a regional, ethnic, religious, sectarian, or class-based nature. Turkish associations could not engage with foreign associations, make public declarations or organize any kind of activity outside their premises without previous authorization from the competent authorities. The same applied, to some extent, to trade unions. Prime Minister Turgut Özal's opening, in the 1980s, created space for that fraction of Turkish civil society compatible with his neoliberal hegemonic project, particularly Islamic civil society, charities, and business associations (Ahmad, 1993). Simultaneously, pro-Kurdish organizations became more visible.

The second period in the history of Turkish civil society began in the post-Cold War era, with the emergence of a civil society engaged in public participation and democratization on a voluntary basis, illustrated by environmentalists, feminists, and human rights organizations. The EU accession process (started in 1987 when Turkey applied for EEC membership, followed by Customs Union in 1996, official candidate status in 1999, and opening of accession negotiations in 2005) brought renewed possibilities for Turkish civil society, through the transfer of norms, concepts, values, and technical and financial tools (see Zihnioğlu, 2013, pp. 42–49).

EU action has promoted four types of transformations of CSOs (Rumelili & Boşnak, 2015, pp. 131–139). Firstly, the legal framework was changed in order to comply with the Copenhagen criteria, namely lifting restrictions (including penal consequences) on the operation of CSOs. The 2004 new Law on Associations illustrates this. Secondly, funding provided to CSOs by the EU enabled a relative autonomization vis-à-vis the Turkish state, viability and professionalization of these organizations, and the reorganization of their agenda according to EU priorities. Thirdly, networks were formed with European CSOs (fostering the diffusion of European norms and practices to Turkish NGOs), and the visibility of Turkish NGOs' issues in the EU agenda was raised. Networking also includes linkages between Turkish NGOs and Turkish policy-makers (mainly ministries and municipalities), allowing Turkish CSOs to gain some leverage against the government. Fourthly, Turkish NGOs' ideas and activities were legitimized in the eyes of Turkish society, mostly until 2007, when EU credibility started to decline.

Scholarship has also analysed the shortcomings of EU action. The bureaucracy attached to EU funding and projects tends to exclude smaller, non-professional CSOs from access to those resources (Ketola, 2013; Kuzmanovic, 2012; Zihnioğlu, 2013), and it indirectly encourages professionalization, which hinders contact with grassroots members (Zihnioğlu, 2013). The EU has developed a project culture that fostered fierce competition among Turkish CSOs for resources, dominance, and legitimacy (Ketola, 2013; Kuzmanovic, 2012). Zihnioğlu (2013) also discovered that EU-funded projects have limited impact beyond the target group and do not help increase knowledge about or support for the EU. This may be linked to the fact that EU institutions do not interact with Turkish CSOs systematically but rather on an ad hoc basis. Secularist CSOs fear that EU accession helped to empower AKP and the CSOs supporting the party, hence the growing polarization and hostility among Turkish CSOs (Ketola, 2013; Kuzmanovic, 2012; Zihnioğlu, 2013). A common finding of these authors is the perception among the population that Turkish CSOs are at the service of foreign powers, reflecting the Turkish obsessive social imaginary and ambivalence towards the EU (the so-called Sèvres Syndrome[2]).

Methodology

This article draws on 14 semi-structured in-depth interviews and one written response to a modified questionnaire conducted in December 2016 and January and May 2017 in Turkish and in English with 13 pro-Gezi activists and 2 anti-Gezi activists. Interviews were granted on the condition that interviewees (and some CSOs) remain anonymous. Questions were structured keeping in mind the indicators for empirical analysis of the role of CSOs as agents in the transnational transformation of public spheres summarized in Table 1 (see Bourne's (2017) second article in this issue, in which such indicators were introduced with social movements as the unit of analysis). Though CSOs represented only one-fifth of Gezi participants (Konda, 2014), CSO affiliation enables us to question the articulation between organizational and individual levels and identity. In fact, membership in an organization does not annul the individual values and options of its activists (Della Porta & Diani, 2006). Heterogeneous personal experiences vis-à-vis the EU outside of the respondents' organizational affiliation (e.g., Erasmus programme, political asylum, diaspora family living in EU, double Turkish–EU citizenship) had an impact on at least eleven pro- and anti-Gezi interviewees' visions of the EU.

Table 1. Indicators for empirical analysis of the role of CSOs as agents in the transnational transformation of public spheres.

	Focus of analysis	Research questions
CSOs as actors	Territorial scope of claim-making	At what territorial levels is a CSO's claim-making directed?
		What is the territorial scope of the interest they claim to represent?
	Simultaneous claim-making	To what extent do CSOs of similar types in different countries focus attention on similar issues at the same time?
	Criteria of relevance/discourse convergence	To what extent do CSOs in different countries use similar frames of reference and meaning structure?
		To what extent do discourse coalitions in different countries contain similar types of political actors?
CSOs as arenas	Weak horizontal communication/ monitoring governance	To what extent do CSOs report on what happens within the national spaces of other European countries?
	Strong horizontal communication	To what extent do CSOs evaluate political developments in other countries?
		To what extent do CSOs frame claims in a comparative manner?
	Community of communication/ collective identities	To what extent do European or other national speakers regularly participate in cross-border debates?
		To what extent do speakers and listeners recognize each other as legitimate participants in transnational discourses?
		To what extent are ideas diffused across national spheres?
		To what extent are issues framed as common European problems?
		To what extent do CSOs include themselves in transnational communities?

Each pro-Gezi interviewee was affiliated with at least one Turkish CSO. We interviewed feminist and LGBTI associations, Green[3] organizations (Greens and the Left Party of the Future [*Yeşil ve Sol Gelecek Partisi*, YSGP] and Green House [*Yeşil Ev*, an association]), a human rights organization (Helsinki Citizens Assembly [*Helsinki Yurttaşlar Derneği*], HYD), three professional chambers (Union of Chambers of Turkish Engineers and Architects [*Türk Mühendis ve Mimar Odaları Birliği*, TMMOB], Istanbul Chamber of Urbanists and Istanbul Bar Association), a left-wing trade union (Confederation of Progressive Trade Unions of Turkey, *Türkiye Devrimci İşçi Sendikaları Konfederasyonu*, DİSK), a Kemalist NGO, Caferağa Dayanışması (a forum in the Kadıköy neighbourhood), a Marxist organization, and a Pro-Kurdish TV group (IMC TV). Many of these CSOs were part of various informal and multi-sectorial initiatives and platforms related to Gezi protests, including Taksim Solidarity Platform, Joint Human Rights Platform, and Work and Justice Platform. In order to consider discourses critical of Gezi, our fieldwork includes a representative from Mazlumder (an Islamic human rights organization) and a member of the AKP Istanbul Youth board. The latter responded in writing to a questionnaire that was adapted from the original. Time constraints, in part related with AKP's highly centralized organizational structure, prevented us from conducting face-to-face interviews with rank and file members of AKP Youth. Instead, we were given written answers from the AKP Youth board.

To ensure gender balance, half of the interviewees were women. Interviewees were either students or persons who were employed or self-employed during the Gezi protests. Except for 3, all were aged between 23 and 24 at the time of the protests. All had graduated from university. These profiles correspond to the characteristics of a majority of Gezi participants (KONDA, 2014). We only interviewed activists based in Istanbul (Gezi Park and Kadıköy). We acknowledge the limitations involved in interviewing 15 activists, namely the representativeness of their response; however, we considered their particular prominence, selecting key actors, that is, leaders of CSOs and of AKP Youth. The commonality of most of the pro-Gezi interviewees was also their membership in Taksim Solidarity Platform, the largest ad hoc intersectorial formation that aimed to rationalize pro-Gezi demands and to 'represent' all Gezi activists before the Turkish government and foreign media.

We encountered five major obstacles during our interviews. The first was the subjectivity of affiliation to a CSO (many of those organizations are ad hoc, volunteer-based, or compulsory). Second, the focus on formal and institutionalized CSOs prevents us from understanding the dynamics and interdependencies with informal civil society activism, hence our particular attention to Taksim Solidarity Platform and the multi-positionality of the interviewees (e.g., the interviewee from the Kemalist CSO was also Kurdish, while the member from AKP Youth board was also a member of the Istanbul Bar Association). Third, the timing of our research – three years after Gezi – ensured more distance regarding the events, but the post-Gezi authoritarian turn in Turkey and related worrying signs in some EU member states may have retroactively negatively influenced their perceptions on the EU. Fourth, the official discourses of AKP representatives framing Gezi as a foreign conspiracy impacted our research due to our subject, profession, and foreign nationalities. As a consequence, and fifth, four of the six pro-AKP CSOs opposing Gezi that we contacted did not respond to our interview requests.

Gezi Park and the Europeanization of the Turkish public sphere

In order to better analyse the modalities and degree of Europeanization of Turkish CSOs represented at Gezi, we tried to understand: (1) To what extent CSOs' historical trajectories – along with their level of dependence on EU political, symbolic, and financial resources – impacted their framing of the EU; (2) How they framed Gezi protests and how they articulated them with EU linkage and leverage.

Among the pro-Gezi activists, we find three different types of CSOs to which they are affiliated. The first type, which emerged after 1989, can be considered as post-national, pro-EU and part of a Europeanized Turkish public sphere. It includes feminist, Green, LGBTI and human rights organizations. These CSOs benefit from EU funds. As acknowledged by the two interviewees from a feminist CSO, the interviewee from an LGBTI association and the interviewees from the Green organizations, their CSOs lack grassroots ties, so their institutional existence depends to some extent on the EU. They also stated that this funding generates distrust among Turkish society. The Yeşil Ev interviewee gave as an example the Bergama Case,[4] in which the German foundation Heinrich Böll was accused by Turkish Nationalists of acting as a foreign agent to destabilize the country.

These post-national CSOs view the EU as a point of leverage to promote fundamental rights in Turkey. The two feminist activists acknowledged the impact of the EU on making the AKP government adopt legislation to fight violence against women, but they also insisted on EU's limits in terms of law implementation. The two interviewees from the Green organizations emphasized how the EU anchor was used to improve democracy and environmental issues in Turkey. While YSGP's member mentioned the recent retrenchment of EU legitimacy and transformative power in Turkey, the other interviewee considers that 'since 2011 [AKP victory in legislative elections] criticizing the EU has unfortunately become a luxury in Turkey due to the growing authoritarianism of the regime'. According to this interviewee, maintaining EU leverage is essential for protecting Turkish civil society from the government, to legitimize it and to fund it. The HYD interviewee stated that the 'EU provides an important leverage to keep Turkey on track in terms of rule of law'.

The interviewees of this first group mentioned their socialization with EU counterparts and membership in EU transnational activist networks. Feminist interviewees stated that this was done through transnational membership of the CSOs, various programmes, conferences, and visa facilitation. The YSGP interviewee mentioned the organization's membership in the European Green Party and Dutch 'East–West Dialogues' and their deep and historical relations with German and Dutch Green parties and their representatives, due to 'the presence of a large Turkish diaspora living in those countries', 'law makers of Turkish descent' and 'personal affinities'. According to the *Yeşil Ev* interviewee, besides European Greens' solidarity, EU-funded projects and actions have contributed to developing their EU contacts 'superficially, more in terms of exchange of information'. Despite this, during the Gezi protests, their links with EU counterparts were seen as not very helpful (feminist, *Yeşil Ev*, YSPG interviewees), as the Turkish activists were focused on direct action. Accordingly, Gezi protests revealed that the 'EU has not managed to develop linkages or transnational activism, but rather helped shape a common political discourse on human rights, environmental issues and women, and created communities' (HYD interviewee).

These CSOs frame their battles beyond the national arena. They acknowledge sharing common values and discourses with EU counterparts 'on environmental issues and democracy' (YSPG interviewee), fighting violence against women, ensuring transgenders' rights, and fighting prejudice and discrimination 'while taking care not to nurture EU prejudices against Islam' (LGBTI and feminist interviewees). These are neither national issues (YSPG interviewee), nor are they monopolized by the EU, but rather universal values (feminist interviewee). The Gezi protests were the expression of those common transnational pluralist norms but were, at the same time, very local and national: Gezi happened 'because Istanbul life was at risk; it started as a very local revolt which became national due to Taksim's history and symbolic power' (HYD interviewee).

Concerning the sociology and divisions among Turkish CSOs that participated in the protests, 'Gezi's initiators had nothing to do with EU liberal circles'; they were either 'hostile to or at least not aware of EU impact on their daily life' (HYD interviewee).

Among the pro-Gezi institutions and prominent members of Taksim Solidarity Platform, we find a second category of CSOs, which are more nationalist and sceptical/ambivalent towards the EU. Nevertheless, they can be considered part of a Europeanized public sphere, for they share common lifestyles, norms, and discourses with European counterparts. Most were created before 1989 and some were very influenced by developmentalism and Kemalist ideology, which supports Turkey's Europeanization while echoing the Sèvres Syndrome. A majority of those CSOs suffered under past military coups and state repression. They include semi-public, left-wing professional chambers and trade unions, Marxist organizations, and Kemalist associations. They favour social protests and public declarations over dialogue with the AKP government, which they consider illegitimate. Those organizations focus on social rights and secularism. They share anti-imperialist, anti-capitalist and, to some extent, nationalist discourses. The interviewee from the Istanbul Chamber of Urbanists (affiliated with TMMOB) stated that

Turkish liberals and the EU have reinforced the power of this Islamist and neoliberal government, thinking it would be the perfect solution for Turkey to catch up with democratisation (…). There is no link between EU accession and the rule of law. The law has been continuously manipulated.

This sentiment was echoed by the interviewee from a Marxist organization. This is why, to ensure their autonomy, TMMOB and the Marxist organization refuse foreign funds, including EU funds, even though the Istanbul Chamber of Urbanists is a member of the European Council of Town Planners.

Left-wing trade unions are more ambivalent, acknowledging the EU's positive leverage and linkage, in part due to their history and EU financial and political support. The DİSK interviewee criticized the priority given by the European Commission to the economy over social rights. This fact undermines DİSK's position as an official social partner. DİSK, which has been a member of the European Trade Union Confederation since the 1990s, benefited from EEC solidarity when they were closed down after the 1980 military coup and afterwards.[5] According to the interviewee, DİSK participates in a large number of EU-funded projects. DİSK leaders are pro-European, while its membership base is more 'conservative and nationalist' (DİSK interviewee).

This second group of CSOs were very influential during the Gezi protests due to their past and rich experiences in coordinating social movements, opposing major infrastructure projects and resisting police violence and legal harassment (Uysal, 2017). This is why, according to TMMOB and DİSK interviewees, both organizations did not need foreign inspiration or logistical support. Except for the Marxist organization, these CSOs were not in contact with their EU counterparts during the Gezi protests. They either regretted it (DİSK interviewee) or claimed it was proof of their national organizational autonomy. The role of foreign media was however seen as important, in order to reach out to world opinion and indirectly to Turkish society (Istanbul Bar Association and TMMOB interviewees) because of the (self-)censorship of Turkish media. During the Gezi protests, 'we had plenty of reporters from EU and European Commission representatives who came to talk to us to gather information' (TMMOB interviewee). Gezi activists were 'following foreign comments, ideas and support in social media', giving them an impression of 'global invisible unity' (Kemalist NGO interviewee). Also, the Istanbul Bar Association applied to the European Court of Human Rights after the Gezi protests ended.

A third category of actors that participated in the Gezi protests were identity-based CSOs, namely pro-Kurdish institutions and activists. Pro-EU and part of a Europeanized public sphere, their vision of the Gezi protests remains ambivalent (IMC interviewee). Heirs of leftist social mobilizations in the 1960s, Kurdish activists became autonomous from their Turkish leftist counterparts in the 1970s. They launched afterwards a 'minority socialism' before integrating, in the 2000s, feminist and environmentalist values (IMC interviewee). Even if the EU has not directly financed pro-Kurdish organizations, it has helped the Kurdish social movement in many ways, including the creation of Kurdish satellite TV channels in 1995 that helped to bypass Turkish state control – at least until 2010 – contributing to the enlargement and formation of a transnational Kurdish identity. According to the interviewee, EU funds for Turkish civil society have been misused, benefitting either CSOs lacking a grassroots base (leading to their marketization) or pro-government CSOs. Based on his own trajectory, he stated that Kurdish activists' relations with the EU are less institutional and more personal than other Turkish activists' relations with the EU due to the large number of political exiles and the existence of a huge Kurdish diaspora in EU countries. If IMC TV was one of the only Turkish TV channels to live broadcast the Gezi protests from the beginning, the interviewee stated that it was mainly social media that promoted a 'world social forum' in favour of Gezi protests and even its global 'interactivity', as illustrated by numerous 'EU high school visits to Turkey and solidarity protests' with Gezi activists.

The Islamic-based CSO we contacted exemplifies a fourth category of actors. They are more sceptical towards the Gezi protests and the EU and closer to the government. Created in 1991 during the surge of political Islam in Turkey, Mazlumder is the only Turkish human rights association with a large grassroots base and without EU funding. It promotes minority rights, including Kurdish and Alevi rights. According to the Maslumder interviewee, CSOs should remain 'apolitical' and financially autonomous by relying 'exclusively on membership fees and donations' and promoting 'equal distance and dialogue between government and opposition'. As for human rights framing, the 'EU is not our (Mazlumder's) reference' because it is a rather 'universal concept'. This absence of EU framing also results from the 'EU's numerous violations of human rights such as racism against refugees and discrimination against Muslims'. The

> EU's concept of human rights is also more secular than the one promoted by Mazlumder (…). We are against abortion and euthanasia. We fight for all the oppressed (*mazlum*) regardless of religion (…) [F]or us Muhammad was the first defender of human rights.

Mazlumder does not refuse cooperation with Westernized CSOs, he stated, while ignoring whether there had been previous contacts. By publishing communiqués criticizing both (Gezi) 'vandals' and 'excessive use of police force', Mazlumder remained 'neutral' during the Gezi protests, according to the interviewee, while regretting 'individual politicization' of Mazlumder leaders in favour of Gezi, which he considers an 'elitist' protest.

According to the questionnaire filled by the member of AKP Youth board (who is also member of the Istanbul Bar Association), the EU has lost leverage on AKP because 'it applies double standards' in terms of democracy towards Turkey, since it does 'not respect our votes, our national will and our democracy (…) and does not help (Syrian) refugees to live humanely'. In his view, 'the EU supported Gezi vandals. EU news reports were biased' and influenced mainly by 'the secular Turkish party CHP [People's Republican Party] or by the terrorist party HDP/PKK's [People's Democratic Party/Kurdistan Workers' Party] sources', who 'shared lots of inaccurate tweets and posts' while 'we (AKP) gave exact information to society'. For this interviewee, the Gezi protests had nothing to do with EU social protests, as 'it was a lie', exclusively meant for 'subversion'; it was staged by 'terrorists' while '*we* (AKP) respect people's lifestyle, their freedoms and rights'.

In terms of international framing of Gezi, pro-Gezi interviewees mentioned numerous potential comparisons with mobilizations associated with democratic demands: Occupy Wall Street, the Arab Spring, EU-based environmental protests, Ukraine, the Paris Commune and May 68. For interviewees critical of Gezi, the interpretation was different: Gezi was 'instrumentalized by opposition parties in order to make a Turkish Arab Spring' (Mazlumder interviewee); rather, 'similar to the Egyptian coup against Morsi (…) they tried to make a military coup in Turkey' (AKP Youth board member). While the AKP

Youth board member claimed that the EU supported Gezi, pro-Gezi interviewees denied any institutional linkage, as it was time for 'direct action': 'we were too busy avoiding pepper gas and police violence' (HYD interviewee). Three expressions of EU and transnational solidarity were, however, acknowledged by the pro-Gezi interviewees: Erasmus students at Gezi and more generally the presence of some 'foreigners living in Turkey who participated in Gezi and as such members of Turkish society' (Caferağa Dayanışması, IMC, and TMMOB interviewees); solidarity protests in EU countries; and the key role of foreign media in creating an imaginary pro-Gezi transnational community.

All interviewees insisted on the historical specificities of the Gezi protests and political violence in Turkey, however differently. The AKP Youth board member interpreted the Gezi protests as a staged movement 'used by terrorists to reach their goals', that is, 'making subversion' and 'turning Turkey into a bloodbath'. For pro-Gezi interviewees, AKP attempted, through the redevelopment plans for Gezi Park, 'to erase the memory' of leftist, secular, and Republican movements associated with this public space (DİSK, IMC, and HYD interviewees). The DİSK interviewee emphasized the authoritarian Turkish state tradition, marked by martial law. Because of this, for pro-Gezi interviewees, being an activist in Turkey is much more dangerous than in the EU countries, so it is difficult to compare their situations: 'while EU LGBTI are fighting for equal marriage, we are fighting just to stay alive' (LGBTI interviewee); the Turkish 'government criminalizes our activities by labelling us as terrorists' (DİSK interviewee).

This difference also explains why attempts to transfer the EU 'civil society model' to Turkey do not work and why EU–Turkey transnational activist linkages are relatively weak (IMC and HYD interviewees). Similarly, EU efforts to promote social dialogue in Turkey cannot work since 'this requires equality between partners; Turkish business and the state have a lot more weight than us' (DİSK interviewee). This justifies why, during the Gezi protests, pro-EU 'advocacy groups were criticized' by Taksim Solidarity Platform leaders for being too compromising with the Turkish government and the EU. To some extent, Gezi 'marked, for pro-EU advocacy groups, the loss of their credit in the eyes of both Turkish society and government. The channels of dialogue were cut' (HYD interviewee).

Conclusion

This article has sought to analyse the extent to which Turkish civil society represented at Gezi protests reflected a Europeanization of the Turkish public sphere, using the indicators introduced in Table 1 as a guide.

The territorial scope of claim-making, simultaneously local and national, reveals the uniqueness and domestic nature of the protests, despite common features with simultaneous protests in EU countries and discourses against neoliberalism. This can be explained by Taksim as a site of national memory, Turkey's history of authoritarianism and the secular dimension of the Gezi protests.

Regarding the simultaneous claim-making and discourse convergence, the pro-Gezi interviewees frame their claims in a wider European and global context. They also share lifestyles and pluralistic values and norms with EU counterparts. There was also a degree of horizontal communication: Relatively low level in terms of activist linkage but very high level in terms of international media support, providing an international frame of solidarity that sparked reciprocity from Turkish pro-Gezi activists.

These findings reveal that there is a community of communication/discursive integration between Turkish pro-Gezi activists and their European counterparts. However, the level of integration and horizontal communication is differentiated. In this light, our findings highlight the heterogeneity of Turkish CSOs' degree of Europeanization, which depends on their history, ideology and multi-level relations with the EU and the Turkish state (individual, organizational, and national). Conversely, pro- and anti-Gezi CSOs converge on growing criticism of EU institutions.

The pro-Gezi interviewees stressed that Turkish state violence and the related securitarian mindset render Turkish activism, in terms of claims and activities, completely different from their EU counterparts', involving higher legal and physical risks. This is why pro-Gezi interviewees criticize the EU's attempt to transfer to Turkey a civil society model based on dialogue and advocacy that can have as a side effect the reinforcement of Turkey's authoritarian state culture. Additionally, some of our interviewees stressed that linkages with the EU can delegitimize their activities and goals due to a long-held suspicion in Turkey towards foreign countries and organizations. However, except for anti-Gezi interviewees, criticism of the EU does not necessarily mean that activists are returning to hegemonic nationalist discourses or that they distance themselves from their European counterparts. This can rather be seen as proof of pro-Gezi CSOs' inclusion in a European public sphere where EU institutions are the subject of contestation. This can also be attested by their favourable view of EU nationals at Gezi.

However, the Gezi protests also marked both the failure of Europeanization and the accelerated deterioration of EU–AKP relations. Discursive usage of EU leverage/linkage has become a liability for Turkish civil society, preventing the development of institutionalized expressions of transnational solidarity. This can be explained by many factors: First, the growing disconnection between EU negotiations and Turkey's democratization; second, the conflicts between social and market integration promoted by the EU; third, lack of grassroots membership of EU-funded Turkish CSOs; fourth, nationalist and anti-imperialist discourses shared by historical Turkish CSOs and to some extent by AKP; and fifth, the AKP's view that what happened at Gezi was a foreign-led project.

To some extent, the Gezi protests also marked an autonomization of Turkish citizens from all forms of pre-existing institutional representativeness, challenging both Turkish political parties and leftist trade unions, which failed to mobilize their grassroots during the Gezi protests, replaced to some extent by individual and direct political action. The Gezi protests also drew the line between anti- and pro-AKP camps, respectively pro- and anti-Gezi. The protests revealed a high degree of social polarization, a massive mobilization of formerly passive citizens and a reconfiguration from below of heterogeneous CSOs united against the AKP. However, this emergent counter-hegemony of Turkish civil society has been overshadowed by the arrests of Gezi's main leaders and HDP lawmakers (the party, created in October 2013, embodied the so-called 'Gezi spirit'), closures of pro-Gezi media and of pro-Kurdish associations, purges, and state infiltration of some pro-Gezi CSOs. In this sense, the state of emergency following the July 2016 failed coup marked the end of Gezi dynamics.

Notes

1. http://avrupa.info.tr/en/eu-and-civil-society/civil-society-development.html.

2. This expression refers to the obsession with the idea of Turkey becoming encircled by hostile foreign forces and the view that the state must survive. It refers to the abortive 1920 treaty with the same name and its draconian terms (loss of sovereignty and territory) imposed on the Ottoman Empire by the European victors of the First World War.
3. Following Şahin's (2015, pp. 441–442) definition, we use the term Green to denote the involvement of one of the organizations in electoral politics and its 'broader ideological framework that is not only environmentalist but also dedicated to grassroots democracy, non-violence and egalitarianism'.
4. A national resistance movement initiated in the 1990s by local farmers in the Aegean region against the first gold mine in the country.
5. For details on Turkish trade unions' integration in the EU, see Visier (2015).

Disclosure statement

No potential conflict of interest was reported by the authors.

ORCID

Isabel David http://orcid.org/0000-0003-1734-6457

References

Ahmad, F. (1993). *The making of modern Turkey*. London: Routledge.
Atak, K. (2014). Flap of the butterfly: Turkey's June uprisings. In Donatella della Porta & Manuela Caiani (Eds.), *Spreading protest. Social movements in times of crisis* (pp. 253–276). Colchester: ECPR Press.
Benhabib, S. (1992). *Situating the self. Gender, community and postmodernism in contemporary ethics*. Cambridge: Polity Press.
Bora, T. (2000). Professional chambers and non-voluntary organizations: The intersection of public, civil and national. In Stefanos Yerasimos, Günter Seufert, & Karin Vorhoff (Eds.), *Civil society in the grip of nationalism: Studies on political culture in contemporary Turkey* (pp. 99–142). Istanbul: Orient-Institut.
Börzel, T. A., & Risse, T. (2000). When Europe hits home: Europeanization and domestic change. *European Integration Online Papers (EioP)*, *4*(15).
Bourne, A. (2017). Social movements and the transnational transformation of public spheres. *Journal of Civil Society*, *13*(3), 231–246. doi:10.1080/17448689.2017.1354807.
Côrte-Real Pinto, G. A. (2015). Military domination by donations. In Marc Aymes, Benjamin Gourisse, & Elise Massicard (Eds.), *Order and compromise: Government practices in Turkey from the late Ottoman Empire to the early 21st century* (pp. 291–316). Leyden: Brill.
Dakowska, D. (2003). Usages et mesusages du concept de gouvernance appliqué à l'élargissement de l'Union Européenne. *Politique européenne*, *2*(10), 99–120.
David, I., & Toktamış, K. F. (2015). *'Everywhere Taksim': Sowing the seeds for a New Turkey at Gezi*. Amsterdam: Amsterdam University Press.
Della Porta, D., & Diani, M. (2006). *Social movements. An introduction*. Oxford: Wiley-Blackwell.
Della Porta, D., & Mattoni, A. (2014). *Spreading protest. Social movements in times of crisis*. Colchester: ECPR Press.
Díez Medrano, J., & Gray, E. (2010). Framing the European Union in national public spheres. In Ruud Koopmans & Paul Statham (Eds.), *The making of a European public sphere* (pp. 195–222). Cambridge: Cambridge University Press.
Diez, T., Agnantopoulos, A., & Kaliber, A. (2005). File: Turkey, Europeanization and civil society: Introduction. *South European Society and Politics*, *10*(1), 1–15.
Eder, K. (2006). The public sphere. *Theory, Culture & Society*, *23*(2–3), 607–611.

European Commission. (2002, December 11). *Communication from the Commission. Towards a reinforced culture of consultation and dialogue – General Principles and minimum standards for consultation of interested parties by the Commission*. COM(202) 704 final. Retrieved from http://eur-lex.europa.eu/LexUriServ/LexUriServ.do?uri=COM:2002:0704:FIN:EN:PDF#_Toc46744741

Featherstone, K. (2003). Introduction: In the name of 'Europe'. In Kevin Featherstone & Claudio M. Radaelli (Eds.), *The politics of Europeanization* (pp. 3–26). Oxford: Oxford University Press.

Flesher Fominaya, C. (2014). *Social movements and globalization. How protests, occupations and uprisings are changing the world*. Basingstoke: Palgrave Macmillan.

Foucault, M. (2004). *Naissance de la Biopolitique. Cours au Collège de France*. Paris: Gallimard.

Gramsci, A. (1977). *Gramsci dans le texte*. Paris: Éditions Sociales.

Gramsci, A. (1999). *Selections from the prison notebooks*. London: Electric Book.

Habermas, J. (1989). *The structural transformation of the public sphere. An inquiry into a category of Bourgeois society*. Cambridge: MIT Press.

Habermas, J. (1996). *Between facts and norms. Contributions to a discourse theory of law and democracy*. Cambridge: MIT Press.

İnsan Hakları Derneği. (2013). *Gezi Parkı Direnişi ve Sonrasında Yaşananlara İlişkin Değerlendirme Raporu*. Ankara: İnsan Hakları Derneği.

Ketola, M. (2013). *Europeanization and civil society. Turkish NGOs as instruments of change?* London: Palgrave.

KONDA. (2014, June 5). *Gezi report. Public perception of the 'Gezi protests'. Who were the people at Gezi Park?* Retrieved from http://konda.com.tr/en/raporlar/KONDA_Gezi_Report.pdf

Koopmans, R., & Statham, P. (2010). Theoretical framework, research design, and methods. In Ruud Koopmans & Paul Statham (Eds.), *The making of a European public sphere* (pp. 34–62). Cambridge: Cambridge University Press.

Kuzmanovic, D. (2012). *Refractions of civil society in Turkey*. New York: Palgrave.

March, J. J., & Olsen, J. P. (1989). *Rediscovering institutions: The organizational basis of politics* (Kindle ed.). New York: Free Press.

Michel, H. (2007). La "société civile" dans la "gouvernance européenne". *Actes de La Recherche en Sciences Sociales, 166–167*, 30–37.

Radaelli, C. (2004). Europeanisation: Solution or problem? *European Integration Online Papers (EIoP), 8*(16). Retrieved from http://eiop.or.at/eiop/texte/2004-016a.htm

Radaelli, C. M. (2003). The Europeanization of public policy. In Kevin Featherstone & Claudio M. Radaelli (Eds.), *The politics of Europeanization* (pp. 27–56). Oxford: Oxford University Press.

Risse, T. (2003, March 27–30). *An emerging European public sphere? Theoretical clarifications and empirical indicators*. Paper presented at the annual meeting of the European Union Studies Association (EUSA), Nashville, Tennessee.

Roos, J. E., & Oikonomakis, L. (2014). They don't represent us! The global resonance of the real democracy movement from the Indignados to occupy. In Donatella della Porta & Manuela Caiani (Eds.), *Spreading protest. Social movements in times of crisis* (pp. 117–136). Colchester: ECPR Press.

Rumelili, B., & Boşnak, B. (2015). Taking the stock of the Europeanization of civil society in Turkey: The case of NGOs. In Ali Tekin & Aylin Güney (Eds.), *The Europeanization of Turkey. Polity and politics* (pp. 127–144). London: Routledge.

Şahin, Ü. (2015). Intertwined and contested. Green politics and the environmental movement in Turkey. *Südosteuropa, 63*, 440–466.

Salvatore, A., Schmidtke, O., & Trenz, H.-J. (2013). Introduction: Rethinking the public sphere through transnationalizing processes: Europe and beyond. In Armando Salvatore, Oliver Schmidtke, & Hans-Jörg Trenz (Eds.), *Rethinking the public sphere through transnationalizing processes: Europe and beyond* (pp. 1–26). Basingstoke: Palgrave Macmillan.

Splichal, S. (2010). Eclipse of "the public". From the public to (transnational) public sphere. Conceptual shifts in the twentieth century. In Jostein Gripsrud & Hallvard Moe (Eds.), *The digital public sphere. Challenges for media policy* (pp. 23–40). Gothenburg: Nordicom.

Tuğal, C. (2013). "Resistance everywhere": The Gezi revolt in global perspective. *New Perspectives on Turkey, 49,* 157–172.
TÜSEV. (2006). *Civil society in Turkey: An era of transition.* Istanbul: Author.
Uysal, A. (2017). *Sokakta Siyaset.* Istanbul: Iletişim.
Visier, C. (2015). European policies to support "civil society": embodying a form of public action. In Marc Aymes, Benjamin Gourisse, & Elise Massicard (Eds.), *Order and compromise: Government practices in Turkey from the late Ottoman Empire to the early 21st century* (pp. 219–255). Leyden: Brill.
Zihnioğlu, Ö. (2013). *European Union civil society policy and Turkey. A bridge too far?* Basingstoke: Palgrave Macmillan.

European Counterpublics? DiEM25, Plan B and the Agonistic European Public Sphere

Óscar García Agustín

ABSTRACT
After the negotiations between the Syriza government and the European Union (EU), the European Left faced the dilemma of which kind of progressive Europe could be developed within the existing EU framework. Two initiatives were launched to foster an alternative Europe after the Greek crisis: 'A Plan B in Europe' (Plan B) and the Democracy in Europe Movement 2025 (DiEM25). These initiatives emerged to promote a new European project as a rejection of EU austerity policies and lack of democracy. The shaping of alternatives is understood within the framework of the public sphere and Europeanization from below. In this sense, both movements are considered counterpublics that introduce conflict within the European sphere and are capable of elaborating counterdiscourses and develop transnational connections. The article analyses the potentials and constraints of enhancing a transnational and agonistic public sphere from perspectives and experiences which, while sharing the need of internationalization, develop different strategies.

In an interview in 2013, Alexis Tsipras, leader of the political party Syriza and then candidate for Prime Minister of Greece, claimed that: 'I believe that Syriza can be the spark that set the fields alight. We are the tail end of existing neoliberal capitalism in Europe' (quoted in *The Guardian*, 2013). The influential intellectual Étienne Balibar maintained in May 2015 that: 'I think that Greece's future is in Europe, but in a Europe that still needs to be built, and not just any Europe' (quoted in Davidson, 2015). As is now well known, the expectations were not fulfilled. Tsipras accepted austerity measures imposed by the Troika (European Commission, European Central Bank and International Monetary Fund) and abandoned his intentions of renegotiating Greece's debt and building up an alternative against the neoliberal Europe, despite the fact that his politics were supported by the Greek population via the referendum. The possibility of re-founding the European Union (EU) through a progressive movement set up in Greece was suddenly blurred, and neoliberalism was thus reinforced as the dominant paradigm of the EU. The obstacles to changing EU institutions from a hypothetical wave of progressive governments stand in contrast to political and social movements, acting at the local and national levels and emphasizing that another Europe is possible. The need for re-imagining Europe within the existing institutional and economic constraints thus remains intact. Although progressive governments and political parties continue to be essential at the national level, the shaping of an alternative against neoliberal Europe, according to Prentoulis (2015), 'will only be possible through a European movement against austerity'.

In this context two initiatives were launched to foster an alternative Europe after the Greek crisis: 'A Plan B in Europe' (Plan B) and the Democracy in Europe Movement 2025 (DiEM25). Plan B was introduced in the summer of 2015 and the first summit took place on 23–24 January 2016 in Paris. A few months later, on the 9 February 2016, DiEM25 was launched in Berlin. These incipient initiatives have been led primarily by politicians, but they are open to collaboration with civil society and social movements in their search for a framework that is not constrained by the EU institutions.

The aim of this article is to analyse how Plan B and DiEM25 emerged, with their similarities and differences, to promote a new European project as a rejection of EU austerity policies and lack of democracy. I consider both movements to be counterpublics, promoting an Europeanization from below and introducing the conflict within the European sphere while being capable of elaborating counterdiscourses and developing transnational connections. The intention of the article is to assess the potentials and constraints of enhancing a transnational and agonistic public sphere from perspectives and experiences (Plan B and DiEM25) which, while sharing the need of internationalization, develop different strategies: forging a movement vs enhancing arenas; creating a discourse to reform the EU vs one to foster another Europe; and prioritizing the transnational dimension vs the national one.

The theoretical framework draws on a conception of the public sphere shaped by political parties and social movements which is agonistic – as defined by Mouffe (2005) – and transnational, as developed by Fraser (2008). The analysis is based on manifestoes, organizational documents, interviews, participant observation and videos from the meetings and conferences, as well as news on the events and summits. Whereas the document material and videos are used to gain insight into the emergence and dynamics of the two initiatives in order to be able to assess their similarities and differences in terms of aims and functioning, interviews and participant observation inform the analysis of strategies as well as potentials and constraints. This relates both to reflections on these matters as they are expressed in the interview material as well as the ways in which these are expressed implicitly or explicitly on-site and thus accessed through participant observation.

Europeanization, counterpublics and the agonistic public sphere

Debates about the European public sphere (EPS) are far from uncontroversial. Usually approached from Habermasian perspectives (emphasizing the importance of deliberative democracy) and related to the role of mass media (either connecting national ones or spurring the emergence of European media), the EPS is considered adequate to respond to the supranational and multi-level governance system of the EU (Siim & Mokre, 2013); to provide a solution to the lack of solidarity emerging from the lack of a common European identity; and to connect decision-making processes with broader publics. As an experimental arena of deliberative supranationalism (Eriksen & Neyer, 2003), there is a general conviction that the EPS has the potential to foster transnational democracy and to diminish the EU's democratic deficit (Nitoiu, 2013).

However, the theoretical framework proposed here differs from those approaches by emphasizing two other aspects to characterize the transnational public sphere: its agonistic or pluralistic nature, and the contribution of social movements and civil society to shaping processes from below. Such a conceptualization entails an identification of what is specific about being transnational and what it implies to be constituted from below (resulting in the formation of counterpublics) and to introduce the conflictual dimension (enhancing participation and plurality).

The transnational public sphere, as 'action at a distance' (Guidry, Kennedy, & Zald, 2000), allows for forms of collective actions to connect the global with the local (without ignoring the national) in a mutually constitutive way by elaborating discourses and practices beyond national boundaries. The shift to the transnational public sphere is, according to Fraser (2008), a question of legitimacy. There must be a discussion open to all with a stake in the outcome (inclusiveness condition) and with equal chances to express their opinions (parity condition). The dispute would no longer only refer to the 'how' but also to the 'who', since the subject does not coincide with the national citizenry, like in the Westphalian frame. Expanding the transnational public sphere through the inclusion of transnational counterpublics makes the questions of the 'how' and, even more so, the 'who' more complicated.

Europeanization from below shows how transnationalization by social movements works: It 'occurs when movements collaborate, or make horizontal communicative linkages with movements in other countries, contest authorities beyond the state, frame issues as European and claim a European identity' (Bourne & Chatzopoulou, 2015, p. 34). Therefore, Europeanization from below is contentious (Doerr, 2009) and places more focus on participatory democracy, not only deliberation. It is more open to non-institutionalized formations or, in more precise terms, to communication beyond institutions and is not only intended to become part of the decision-making processes. Rather than rejecting the supranational level of governance, a transnational approach from below criticizes the EU's democratic deficit, the decreasing emphasis on social policies (under the dominance of neoliberal policies), and the absence of transparency and accountability of the European institutions (Della Porta & Caiani, 2007).

However, an alternative is difficult to constitute due to the limitations of the institutional channels and the lack of an organized transnational European sphere, comparable to the national ones. Participation is indeed restricted in most of the cases to formal and well-established civil society organizations within mainstream politics (Ketola, 2012), which makes the inclusion of contentious actors difficult (Wimmer, 2005). This provokes a 'tension between the European public sphere and the counterpublics that are excluded, which raises the important question of how diversity and conflict are properly accommodated' (Ketola, 2012, p. 216). Therefore, Europeanization from below contests the exclusionary dimension of the public sphere (reducing European Public Spheres to the European Public Sphere) in order to introduce other discourses and practices. Thus, the approach adopted here aims to stress the role played by conflict and the questioning of the hegemonic formation.

To deepen the understanding of how plurality and conflict become essential to constituting the public sphere, it is relevant to remember the concept, introduced by Fraser

(1991), of 'subaltern counterpublics'. These 'are parallel discursive arenas where members of subordinated social groups invent and circulate counterdiscourses to formulate oppositional interpretations of their identities, interests and needs' (Fraser, 1991, p. 123). They are 'subaltern' because of the groups that produce the counterpublics; 'counter' because of their contestatory function; and 'publics' since these arenas have a publicist orientation and cannot be considered enclaves. Counterpublics entail the idea of conceiving the public sphere as a multiplicity (Asen, 2000) and as a site for political struggle and conflict (Karppinen, 2009). It is thus necessary to include the dynamic of countersphere as a way of challenging the existing public sphere. Mouffe (2005) proposes an 'agonistic public sphere' to stress the political importance of conflict and dissent as well as the significance of enhancing pluralistic institutions in which the debate can be developed in terms of political adversaries rather than within a friend/enemy dichotomy. In European terms, the shaping of an agonistic public sphere involves a dual challenge: the pressure from regionalist and tribalist movements, on the one hand, and from supranational powers (institutions and financial entities), on the other. Democratic forces should envision new forms of solidarity in order to organize a plurality of democratic spheres: on the one hand, avoiding the risks of nationalism, and, on the other, challenging the economic and political transnational powers that be.

In this framework, I consider Plan B and DiEM25 to be expressions of processes of Europeanization from below. Both movements emerged as a consequence of the 'failure' of Syriza in its negotiations with the EU and what is understood as the imposition of neoliberalism as the only economic model and the exclusion of progressive political projects. In the next sections I analyse how these movements contribute to fostering an agonistic European public sphere through some of the elements constitutive of counterpublics by responding to the following questions: (1) what kind of actors are emerging, if any; (2) what arenas are being used; (3) what types of counterdiscourses are being constituted and how do they position themselves against the hegemonic discourse; (4) how are multi-scales prioritized and used: locally, nationally and transnationally; and (5) how is conflict/exclusion understood, and how does it affect the establishment of agonism?

Initiatives: actors or arenas?

Plan B and DiEM25 emerged with a similar diagnosis of the reasons of the crisis of the EU. However, they developed as different kinds of European counterpublics due to how they foster Europeanization, based on their conception of Europe and on the need to create arenas for discussing the EU and the actors which must be involved in it.

Plan B was launched through a joint statement signed by well-known figures from the left: Oskar Lafontaine (former Die Linke leader in Germany), Stefano Fassina (Italian deputy and economist), Jean-Luc Mélenchon (leader of the French Left Front), Zoe Konstantopoulou (former deputy and parliamentary speaker in Greece), and Yanis Varoufakis (former Minister of Finance in Greece). From the foundational moment in 2015 two aspects became clear about the actors who should be involved and the type of political conflict: The initiative was led by politicians, at different levels from the European Parliament (EP) to local municipalities; and it was not supported by all the left-wing parties since it directly criticized the Syriza government (Flenady, 2015), a position that was not shared by all and created division within the European United Left/Nordic Green Left (GUE/NGL).

However, the initial intentions combined the political goals (renegotiation of the European Treaties, accountability for the Eurogroup, denouncement of the political interference of the European Central Bank) with the need to take part in the struggles of the European movements against the arbitrary uses of power by the EU. Thus Plan B emerges as a political initiative open to civil society participation in order to create a European counterpublic in which an alternative to the EU starts to be discussed and elaborated:

> Our Plan A for a democratic Europe, backed with a Plan B which shows the powers-that-be that they cannot terrorise us into submission, is inclusive and aims at appealing to the majority of Europeans. This demands a high level of preparation. Debate will strengthen its technical elements. (Plan B, 2015)

Without the intention of shaping a European movement, the counterpublics consist mostly of alternative arenas to the EP, open to other actors supporting a different kind of Europe and responding to the Plan B.

Since the definition of Plan B is not determined in advance, it is presented as open to the participation of citizens, organizations, and intellectuals. However, there is no intention (except for some nuances that will be presented later) to develop a common movement. Rather, Plan B favours the arenas in which politicians and civil society already meet to discuss and elaborate an alternative to the existing EU. For this reason, the summit or conference is selected as the proper way of enhancing spaces of debate and elaboration of alternatives. There have been three summits so far: France (January 2016), Spain (February 2016), and Denmark (November 2016) with their respective websites, but without any common website for the whole Plan B. The number of participants is far from massive, around 300 in Paris and Copenhagen, although in Madrid more than 1500 people were gathered.

Even if the three summits contribute to the Europeanization from below through proposals discussed by left-wing parties and progressive movements, the summits as arenas are also nationalized in the sense that they reflect the main points of the national agenda and the selection of civil society actors to participate. The summit in France was permeated by the role played by Mélenchon, while the one in Copenhagen fostered Euroscepticism in line with the organizers, the Swedish Left Party and the Danish Red-Green Alliance. The visibility of political parties was greater, and in Copenhagen the importance of Plan B as an 'arena of representation' was emphasized by referring to the considerable percentage of the European population who was represented by the participants, namely the left-wing parties. On the other hand, in Madrid there was a major confluence of political parties, activists, and social movements without any of them being attributed the organizational responsibility (Gil, 2016). The variety of topics, with more presence of the so-called 'refugee crisis', feminism, and democratization issues, was accompanied by the presence of different ideological positions. Whilst in France the euro-exit position was dominant and in Denmark European cooperation beyond the EU was strongly accepted, different positions on the euro, EU institutions, and similar topics coexisted at the summit in Spain. The summits therefore reflect the national agendas on EU politics but also the dynamics between political parties and social movements within the national contexts.

Although he participated in the Plan B in Madrid, former Greek Minister of Finance Varoufakis did not participate in Paris, as had been announced; instead he launched a new alternative, DiEM25, connecting with some of the points of Plan B but diverging on many others. In contrast with Plan B, DiEM25 was born with the intention of becoming a new actor and not only promoting public arenas for deliberation. In addition to the launch of DiEM25 in Berlin in February 2016, a manifesto was published and translated into 19 languages. The manifesto points directly to 'we, the peoples of Europe' as the actor who is going to bring change forward in Europe in an attempt to 'regain control over our Europe from unaccountable "technocrats", complicit politicians and shadowy institutions' (DiEM25, 2016). Since the subject of change is European, placed outside the institutional and political realm, and with the function of keeping the EU accountable, it is interesting to consider how DiEM25 concretizes the 'peoples' and which kind of counterpublic is forged through this initiative.

DiEM25 defines itself as a 'political movement', or simply a 'movement', but it is not a political party or a movement composed by politicians or parties. It cannot be considered a party, or a coalition of parties, but rather as a movement inspired by other social movements. Miguel Urbán, who participated in the inaugural coalition event in Berlin, explains, in this regard, that it cannot be a party since nobody is representing anybody (quoted in Rodríguez-Pina, 2016), that is, since there is no sense of representativeness. To overcome the party form, DiEM25 learns from European social movements, such as the Spanish 15M or the Greek indignados:

> At the moment, DiEM25 is not a party, nor an organisation or think tank. We consider the conventional model of political parties obsolete. Rather than build at a national level and then expand to Europe, we are turning that process upside down and starting a movement at an international level, but taking into consideration existing movements and grassroots at national, regional and local level. (Srećko Horvat, quoted in Oltermann, 2016)

DiEM25 is therefore conceived as a network to connect the movements in different countries and, as explained below, the initiative prioritizes the transnational level. However, as counterpublic, DiEM25 has a hybrid nature. It has the intention of becoming a movement and connecting local and national movements at the European level, but its actions include lobbying in order to improve democratic practices within the EU through the claim for full transparency in decision-making (live streaming of European Council, Ecofin and Eurogroup meetings, for instance) and for the redeployment of existing EU institutions to elaborate policies aimed to address major problems such as the crises of debt, poverty, and migration (Varoufakis, 2016b). In this regard, there is a combination of the need to promote a new kind of EU (an Europeanization from below as movement), the attempt to influence policy-making in concrete areas (as a weak public or lobby), and the achievement of advocacy (as a think tank).

The combination of functions remains clear in the variety of arenas promoted by DiEM25 or those within which it participates. Two tendencies become evident: the implementation of telematics tools and online-mediated communication, from streaming and showcasing to voting platforms; and the visibility and leading role assumed by Varoufakis as the most present, and sometimes the only, public face of DiEM25. Furthermore, there are several types of arenas in which DiEM25 is involved as organizer, co-organizer or supporter: conferences about key European issues (such as the assembly on the 'refugee crisis' in Vienna); meetings with progressive political parties (Italy's Five Star Movement); supporting campaigns (in favour of Julian Assange); or having national meetings to strengthen grassroots' cooperation (in Germany with 60 people attending, and in the U.K. with 400).

Due to its hybrid conformation as political movement, DiEM25 assumes different roles and is open to different arenas: adding its voice to the campaign and events against Brexit, supporting candidates for political office that favour the DiEM25 principles (Benoît Hamon in France, Nicola Fratoianni in Italy), and fostering grassroots activities. Despite refusing to participate in EU institutional arenas, DiEM25 is willing to enhance spaces of political and social cooperation. Its constitution as a movement responds to its interest in changing the EU institutions and in influencing policies, but from a radical perspective which will demand greater changes than the ones that can be achieved through the already established institutional means and arenas.

Counterdiscourse: EU or Europe?

It must be analysed whether the counterpublics are capable of generating counterdiscourses to formulate oppositional projects and identities; in this case, of articulating a different vision of Europe or of the EU. Although both projects, Plan B and DiEM25, emerged as responses to a sense of exclusion, provoked by the attempt of political closure and the lack of economic alternatives presented by the EU during the Greek negotiations, they do not share their understanding of what kind of agonistic European public sphere they could contribute to fostering. In other words, despite their opposition to the EU, their counterdiscourses regarding the character of a pluralistic Europe differ on substantial issues.

The heterogeneity of those who participate in the Plan B summits makes it difficult to articulate a coherent discourse about the EU. There are, however, some shared elements best articulated in the summit statements. There is no doubt about who the enemy is: the EU of austerity politics responsible for the 'financial coup' in Greece. I identify three features that characterize the Plan B counterdiscourse: the lack of satisfaction with the EU as political framework; the rejection of the economic model, particularly of the euro; and the defense of national sovereignty.

Plan B wants to enhance a European counterpublic which acts beyond the institutional EU fora and aims to forge a European sphere beyond the EU. The Euroscepticism present in the first summit in France and mitigated in Spain reflects the increasing mistrust from the Southern European countries towards austerity politics and inequality within the region. This is articulated through opposition to Germany and its leading role in the EU. The Southern Euroscepticism meets the one from the Nordic countries' summit, favourable to 'Eurexit', defended by the Swedish and Danish left-wing parties. Whilst the opposition to the EU elite has been continuous, the rejection of EU institutions has been more fluctuant, although it is becoming the dominant position. The first summit statement was formulated against the 'oligarchic Europe' causing impoverishment of the population and being responsible for the emergence of radical right-wing nationalism. There is an initial questioning of the possibility of enacting progressive policies within the constraints of 'this Europe'. Breaking with 'this Europe' is indeed 'the basic condition needed to rebuild cooperation between our peoples and our countries on a new basis' (Plan B, 2015). At the Madrid summit a month later, as a result of the plurality of participants, the opposition is clearly formulated to the neoliberal system, but there is an opening concerning the need for institutional reform. The Madrid summit statement proposes to break 'the EU wide system of austerity and to radically democratize the European institutions, putting them to work for the citizens' (Plan B, 2016a). The manifesto from the Copenhagen summit reinforces the initial rejection of the European institutions and deepens the idea of 'democratic and inclusive cooperation in Europe and beyond', meaning specifically, 'beyond the stifling confinements of the EU' (Plan B, 2016c). The EU is not considered as the space of change, but there is a shift to Europe, albeit more undefined, where the people can fulfil a 'real' alternative.

Nevertheless, there is no agreement among the participants about the possibility or necessity of exiting the European Monetary Union. In Copenhagen Plan B forged a major consensus among the speakers on the rapid euro exit (Patomäki, 2016b). Whilst the critique of the financial system, global corporate power, and debt is broadly accepted, the euro exit brings some problems about what kind of European project could possibly be developed. If the neoliberal EU is the enemy, and the European peoples the subject, national sovereignty and the return to the nation state become the alternative to the EU. This was already clear in Mélenchon's Euroscepticism and Lapavistas's proposal for a 'progressive exit' and 'progressive nationalism' before the France summit (Patomäki, 2016a). The tendency to return to national solutions is becoming dominant within Plan B as an alternative to the existing EU. Nonetheless, Plan B claims to be internationalist and in favour of international cooperation, as the appropriate response to neoliberalism as a global phenomenon, but this cooperation must not be built up on the basis of supranational powers. The Europeanization fostered by Plan B is consequently grounded in the shaping of alliances between countries, with the potential of achieving a progressive agenda within the national framework, and between people that should push the progressive agenda forward, particularly within the nation states.

The constitution of DiEM25 as a political movement, grounded in the foundational manifesto, makes it easier to articulate a common counterdiscourse on the EU and Europe. Also the fact that its discourse is often incarnated in mass media by Varoufakis contributes to strengthening its internal coherence. The manifesto, entitled 'The EU will be democratized. Or it will disintegrate', makes clear that the main goal is to change the EU towards a more democratic project without rejecting the ideal of Europe as the ground to build up an alternative EU. As mentioned above, the DiEM25 discourse constitutes an antagonistic relation between the EU as the powers that be ('We the Governments' and 'We the Technocrats') and the power of the people ('We, the peoples of Europe'). Substantial change would be impossible if it were limited to exclusively addressing policy-making processes. Indeed, DiEM25 does not believe in the efficiency of usual policy-making to reform the EU. The only 'real' option to 'save' the EU is to include the people as a political subject, integrating their demands and improving their material conditions. The understanding of democracy grounded in this antagonism (us/the people vs them/the establishment) indeed falls under the characterization of a populist discourse (Panayotu, 2017) which acquires a transnational dimension.

The acknowledgment of the alliance between technocrats and politicians is deployed to show how European peoples are the ones who are excluded from the EU project. The focus on 'peoples', embedded within the process of democratizing Europe, is presented as an alternative to the threats provoked by xenophobia and racism. DiEM25's contribution to pluralism, or in other words to an agonistic public sphere, is characterized by rejecting the retreat into nation states, contrary to Plan B. DiEM25 prefers to talk about 'the will of sovereign European peoples' instead of 'national sovereignty'. The 'Lexit', the left-wing arguing to leave the EU, is not a desirable option. The only way is to shape a pan-European movement, creating a European demos, against the EU elites. In the end, this would entail undoing the European discursive closure, upon which the political consensus is grounded, of the lack of alternatives to neoliberalism. Varoufakis refers to the euro-TINA, 'the reactionary dogma that there is no alternative to current policies besides the European Union's dismantlement' (2016c), as the worst enemy of European democracy.

Sharing with Plan B the unavoidable clash with the EU establishment, DiEM25 advocates for internationalism and, without neglecting the importance of the national level, aspires to a sort of transnational republic. The solution would consist of democracy from below (produced at the local, regional, and national levels) which must be complemented by a proper internationalist strategy. The alternative to the existing EU must be a pan-European coalition for democratizing Europe. Varoufakis points out several times how he understands the multi-level ways of action: 'the key to DiEM25's approach is that we refuse to prioritise the national over the transnational or pan-European level – just as we refuse to prioritise the national over the local' (Varoufakis, Barnett, Bechler, & Sakalis, 2016). Thus, the field of struggle to democratize the EU is mostly found in two dimensions: the transnational and the local without excluding the national as a necessary but insufficient level.

Compared with Plan B, whose internationalism is based on cooperation between nation states, DiEM25 proposes internationalism based on transnational democracy and on the antagonism between the EU establishment and the European people. This process of Europeanization from below implies that the EU must be redefined in order to be maintained. The agonism is apparently placed within the EU but, in reality, it would require radical institutional changes to create a public sphere capable of harbouring pluralism.

Multi-level sphere: transnational, national, or local?

The emergence of Plan B and DiEM25 entails the problem of how to develop a public sphere which is properly transnational. Since the 'who' is heterogeneous, disagreeing sometimes on the common discourse, the question of the 'how' becomes essential: How should a European movement be organized; should the existing movements and parties add the transnational dimension; or should it be developed as a movement at the transnational and local levels? Plan B and DiEM25 diverge on the question of the 'how' as well as on the 'who'.

In contrast to DiEM25, Plan B does not aim to create a European movement but instead a common space, collective reflections and agenda (Marsili & Urbán, 2016). The Podemos MEP, Urbán, advocates for a deliberative and pluralistic public where Europeanist discourses and nationalist ones can be confronted. However, this position is found mainly at the summit in Madrid where there was an openness to a 'movement turn'. The Spanish context offered the experiences accumulated by a vibrant civil society which was positioned as an alternative to the traditional political parties. By relying on the impetus of civil society, an agonist sphere is defined as conflictual against the elites and participatory in order to increase inclusion and plurality.

The only transformation from below would consist of using collective and participatory tools to foster heterogeneity and means of participation. In other terms, changing the 'how' (participation from below) would redefine the 'who' (major inclusion of actors). Since Plan B is composed of political parties or leaders and already existing social movements, the proposal launched in Madrid aimed to encourage the foundation of 'Plan B platforms'. The organizing group of the Spanish event considers Plan B to be 'a tool to organize an internationalist movement to dispute Europe, a project where there is room for everybody'. (Plan B, 2016b, own translation). This idea goes beyond confluence through summits and represents an effort to territorialize Plan B and take the European debate to the local level in cooperation with other political and civil society organizations. Europeanization is here understood as a process of 'localization' in order to introduce the European discussion into local agendas and to promote the diffusion of information and the creation of new channels of communication.

This was not the path eventually followed by Plan B, since the impact of the call to create local Plan B platforms was very limited, and because the organization is led by political parties which prioritize the national level and consider Plan B as an opportunity to discuss alternatives and explore possibilities for cooperation. The summit in Copenhagen was closed with an invitation to the next Plan B summit in Rome, which took place in March 2017 and reinforced the idea that cooperation among states is the only alternative to the EU. Thus, the idea of making the Plan B local becomes blurred, and the counter-public becomes mostly institutional-political, albeit open to dialogue with civil society, while the national level acquires a transnational dimension through the summits.

DiEM25 faces, however, a different challenge: How to organize transnationally and how to include the local level? The challenge is how to connect the existing local networks with a new transnational one, DiEM25, which has to relate to other existing transnational networks. Varoufakis explains that DiEM25's goal is to connect the existing movements with the 'silent majority', that is, those who so far have not done anything, but 'are now eager to be part of a movement that restores hope in a Europe that can become decent' (Varoufakis, 2016a). There are two implications: A transnational movement is constituted based on existing local struggles, rather than on existing transnational networks; and the existing struggles are not enough, hence an appeal to those who are not involved in such struggles must be carried out. Without aiming to replace other networks or fora, DiEM25 aspires to be organized transnationally too and to appeal to new actors.

The desire for putting the demos, the people, back into democracy is, as mentioned, inspired by the movements from 2011 and explains why DiEM25 prioritizes the local level as the core arena for democratic struggles. Referring to Gramsci, Varoufakis questions the predominance of the national level, since 'rebellion should happen everywhere – in towns, in regions, in nation state capitals, and in Brussels' (Varoufakis et al., 2016). This implies that the movement can become hegemonic in the different nation states if it is shaped as a pan-European network, whereas it would be very difficult to imagine hegemony fostered from one or more nation states. For this reason, sovereignty is applied not only to nation states but also to people and to city councils. Thus, the local represents a space of doing politics which can easily connect with a transnational movement without becoming embedded exclusively within the national framework. The purpose of 'localizing' the movement is, in this regard, quite different from that of Plan B.

Furthermore, DiEM25 establishes in its 'Organizational Principles' a transnational organizational structure, which makes it different from Plan B or the European Party of the Left. The main organs are transnational and do not respond to a national logic. The Coordinating Collective (CC), the main organizing committee, is composed of 12 members, elected through digital voting by the DiEM25 members, not following a country-based logic (one country, one representative). Similarly, the Validating Council (VC), which covers functions that exceed the CC, is comprised of 100 people who are selected by sortation, and any member has the possibility of putting her or his nomination forward via the website. The function of the remaining organs (the Advisory Panel and the spontaneous collectives) is to enhance public arenas to promote DiEM25's ideas, recruit new members, or participate in debates, meetings, and campaigns.

All in all, DiEM25 acts as a transnational counterpublic that aims to connect local movements, progressive parties, and European citizens, and, sometimes, it is organized as a transnational movement whose main organs avoid a national logic. Although DiEM25 has so far shown more capacity to be involved in other social struggles (such as Nuit Debout and a French anti-Brexit campaign) than to connect existing struggles, it is an explicit attempt at Europeanization from below without merely adapting to the existing EU institutions or rejecting any kind of participation. The responses offered by Plan B and DiEM25 to the questions of 'how' and 'who' are, in conclusion, quite different. The way in which transnationalization is developed at the local and national levels contributes as well to determining the actors who become involved and how they can contribute to building up an alternative Europe from below.

Conclusion

The obstacles encountered by the Greek government, led by Tsipras, to renegotiate the public debt and implement progressive politics without a hostile attitude from the EU have provoked different reactions about what kind of EU could be possible or desirable. Almost simultaneously, Plan B and DiEM25 start two different processes of Europeanization.

This article deployed an approach to examining the public sphere based on the importance of agonism (pluralism and conflict) and participation. The opposition to EU austerity policies (and to political closure) provokes the attempt to open up the European public sphere to more participation and inclusion of actors, that is, an attempt at Europeanization from below. It means that the public sphere must be transnational (by connecting different levels), conflictual (through the shaping of counterpublics), and agonistic (by fostering plurality and enhancing spaces for deliberation and discussion). Although both projects acknowledge that overcoming neoliberal policies can only be achieved through internationalization, I have identified three key points in which the disagreement between them is substantial: Being a movement (like DiEM25) or not; rejecting the EU as framework (Plan B) or not; and prioritizing the national (Plan B) or the transnational dimension (DiEM25). The application of the European public sphere model to both cases is summarized in Table 1.

DiEM25 and Plan B emerged with different intentions: Europeanization consisting in creating a transnational movement, and Europeanization aimed to preserve national sovereignty and cooperate to oppose the influence of the EU, respectively. Therefore

Table 1. DiEM25 and Plan B as European counterpublics.

	DiEM25	Plan B
Actors	'Political' movement	Cooperation between political parties and civil society
Arenas	Conferences, campaigns, rallies, etc.	Mostly summits
Counterdiscourse	Democratizing the EU, transnational republic, people's sovereignty	Democratic Europe against austerity, national sovereignty
Transnationalism	Connecting local and European struggles, transnational organizational structure, local spontaneous collectives	National cooperation, local platforms
Agonistic sphere	Within (and outside) the EU	Within (and outside) Europe

the two initiatives differ in the kind of agonistic public sphere that would be desirable: DiEM25 does not reject the EU framework but aspires to reform it by increasing people's participation and EU accountability; Plan B is mainly determined to abandon the euro and, with some disagreements, to leave the EU. In any case the conflict highlighted by Plan B is not between people and establishment, as in DiEM25, but between national sovereignty and EU interference. For this reason, Plan B aspires to contribute to an alternative Europe based on national cooperation.

Both initiatives aspire to strengthen cooperation between political parties and social movements and civil society. These initiatives are not confined to social movements, like the European Social Forum where the involvement of politicians was contemplated with suspicion. However, the constraints to forging such alliances are already evident. Plan B has a tendency to prioritize the work of political parties at the national level, and the celebration of summits is open to civil society but mostly as part of the political agenda. DiEM25 is succeeding more in being organized as a movement and connecting with grassroots, but the strategy of obtaining visibility and impact in the public sphere relies particularly on the figure of Varoufakis. Indeed, he is assuming the role as voice of the DiEM25 counterdiscourse, and the heterogeneity of the discourse somehow disappears.

Despite the sense of political exclusion and the imposition of neoliberal policies as the only possibility, the economic crisis together with the political crisis and the so-called 'refugee crisis' are enabling the appearance of new counterpublics demanding plurality and an alternative Europe. Plan B and DiEM25 are attempting different kinds of Europeanization from below. The potential of such counterpublics is remarkable and relies on the necessity to promote a more participatory, inclusive, plural, and democratic Europe. Plan B and DiEM25 respond to the questions of the 'who' and the 'how' by introducing new actors, with other discourses, into the European public sphere as well as new modes of understanding and acting within Europe. Looking at the agonistic public sphere, Plan B and DiEM25 share an important goal, with DiEM25 being more open to EU institutional change. The transnational dimension, however, shows how the initiatives differ in terms of the predominantly nationalized or transnationalized Europeanization options which are at stake. Both cases reflect the importance of introducing conflict and plurality (agonism) into the conceptualization of public sphere(s) in order to comprehend the dynamics established by different actors (political and social) in their attempts to improve the sense of democracy at the transnational level. In conclusion, the perspective of an agonistic and transnational public sphere enriches the understanding of emerging political and social dynamics aimed at participation and debate in order to oppose excluding forms of domination. Plan B and DiEM25 contribute to illustrating some of the potential and limitations of shaping European counterpublics from below.

Disclosure statement

No potential conflict of interest was reported by the author.

References

Asen, R. (2000). Seeking the 'counter' in counterpublics. *Communication Theory, 10*(4), 424–446.
Bourne, A., & Chatzopoulou, S. (2015). Europeanization and social movement mobilization during the European sovereign debt crisis: The cases of Spain and Greece. *Recerca, 2015*(17), 33–60.
Della Porta, D., & Caiani, M. (2007). Talking Europe in the Italian public sphere. *South European Society & Politics, 12*(1), 1–21.
DiEM25. (2016). *The European Union will be democratised. Or it will disintegrate!* Retrieved from https://diem25.org/wp-content/uploads/2016/02/diem25_english_long.pdf
Doerr, N. (2009). *How European transport transforms institutions of the public sphere*. Discourse and decision-making in the European social forum process, KFG Working Paper Series, Berlin.
Eriksen, E. O., & Neyer, J. (2003). Introduction: The forging of deliberative supranationalism in the EU? In E. O. Eriksen & J. Neyer (Eds.), *European governance, deliberation and the quest for democratisation* (pp. 1–22). Oslo: Arena.
Flenady, L. (2015). European left debates a 'Plan B' against austerity. *Green Left*, October 11. Retrieved from https://www.greenleft.org.au/content/european-left-debates-plan-b-against-austerity
Fraser, N. (1991). Rethinking the public sphere: A contribution to the critique of actually existing democracy. In C. Calhoun (Ed.), *Habermas and the public sphere* (pp. 109–142). Cambridge: MIT Press.
Fraser, N. (2008). *Scales of justice. Reimagining political space in a globalizing world*. Cambridge: Political Press.
Gil, A. (2016). El Plan B para Europa reúne en Madrid una cumbre social contra la austeridad. *Eldiario.es*, 18 February. Retrieved from http://www.eldiario.es/politica/Activistas-sociedad-conjuran-Madrid-austeridad-plan-b-Europa_0_485051792.html
Guidry, J. A., Kennedy, M. D., & Zald, M. N. (2000). Globalizations and social movements. In J. A. Guidry, M. D. Kennedy, & M. N. Zald (Eds.), *Globalizations and social movements: Culture, power, and the transnational public sphere* (pp. 1–32). Ann Arbor: University of Michigan Press.
Karppinen, K. (2009). European public sphere and the challenge of radical pluralism. In I. Salovaara-Moring (Ed.), *Manufacturing Europe: Spaces of democracy, diversity and communication* (pp. 53–67). Gothenburg: Nordicom.
Ketola, M. (2012). The everyday politics of the European public sphere: Moving beyond EU policy perspectives. *Journal of Civil Society, 8*(3), 213–228.
Marsili, L., & Urbán, M. (2016). Talk real voices. PlanB para Europa? *YouTube*, 17 February. Retrieved from https://www.youtube.com/watch?v=NNM2poo-WUM.
Mouffe, C. (2005). For an agonistic public sphere. In L. Tønder & L. Thomassen (Eds.), *Radical democracy: Politics between abundance and lack* (pp. 191–205). Manchester: University of Manchester Press.
Nitoiu, C. (2013). The European public sphere: Myth, reality or aspiration? *Political Studies Review, 11*(1), 26–38.
Oltermann, P. (2016). Yanis Varoufakis launches pan-European leftwing movement DiEM25. *The Guardian*, 10 February. Retrieved from https://www.theguardian.com/world/2016/feb/10/yanis-varoufakis-launches-pan-european-leftwing-movement-diem25
Panayotu, P. (2017). *Towards a transnational populism: A chance for European democracy (?) The case of DiEM25*, POPULISMUS Working Papers 5, Thessaloniki.

Patomäki, H. (2016a). *Preparing for Plan B in Paris*, 29 January. Retrieved from http://patomaki.fi/en/2016/01/preparing-for-plan-b-in-paris/

Patomäki, H. (2016b). *Plan B in Copenhagen in November 2016*, 26 November. Retrieved from http://patomaki.fi/en/2016/11/plan-b-in-copenhagen-in-november-2016/

Plan B. (2015). *A Plan B in Europe*. Retrieved from https://www.euro-planb.eu/?page_id=96&lang=en

Plan B. (2016a). *Plan B for Europe. Appeal to build a European area of work in order to end austerity and build a true democracy*. Retrieved from http://planbeuropa.es/manifesto/?lang=en

Plan B. (2016b). *Protocolo de Actos y Plataformas Plan B*. Retrieved from http://planbeuropa.es/wp-content/uploads/2016/03/PROTOCOLO-DE-ACTOS-Y-PLATAFORMAS-PLAN-B-2.pdf

Plan B. (2016c). *Statement for a standing Plan B in Europe*. Retrieved from http://euro-planb.dk/

Prentoulis, M. (2015). After Greece's defeat, we need European movement against austerity. *The Guardian*, 14 July. Retrieved from https://www.theguardian.com/commentisfree/2015/jul/14/greece-defeat-european-movement-austerity

Rodríguez-Pina, G. (2016). Qué es DiEM25, el movimiento con el que Varoufakis quiere devolver la democracia a Europa. *El Huffington Post*, 9 February. Retrieved from http://www.huffingtonpost.es/2016/02/09/varoufakis-diem25-movimiento-democracia_n_9195616.html

Siim, B., & Mokre, M. (2013). European public spheres and intersectionality. In B. Siim & M. Mokre (Eds.), *Negotiating gender and diversity in an emergent European public sphere* (pp. 22–40). London: Palgrave Macmillan.

Varoufakis, Y. (2016a). Diem and the movements. *ROAR*, 16 January. Retrieved from https://roarmag.org/2016/01/18/varoufakis-open-letter-diem-movements/

Varoufakis, Y. (2016b). The EU no longer serves the people – democracy demands a new beginning. *The Guardian*, 5 February. Retrieved from https://www.theguardian.com/commentisfree/2016/feb/05/eu-no-longer-serves-people-europe-diem25

Varoufakis, Y. (2016c). Europe's left after Brexit. *Open Democracy*, 9 September. Retrieved from https://www.opendemocracy.net/can-europe-make-it/yanis-varoufakis/europe-s-left-after-brexit-diem25-s-perspective

Varoufakis, Y., Barnett, A., Bechler, R., & Sakalis, A. (2016). Democratising Europe – a transnational project? *Open Democracy*, 13 September. Retrieved from https://www.opendemocracy.net/can-europe-make-it/yanis-varoufakis-rosemary-bechler-alex-sakalis-anthony-barnet/democratising-europ

Wimmer, J. (2005). Counter-Public spheres and the revival of the European public sphere. *The Public*, *12*(2), 93–110.

Essay: Rethinking Global Civil Society and the Public Sphere in the Age of Pro-democracy Movements

Ramón A. Feenstra

ABSTRACT

Pro-democracy movements have recently emerged in various places worldwide. The Pots and Pans Revolution (Iceland), Arab Spring, 15M and the Occupy movement, Yo Soy132, and the Gezi Park, Hong Kong, and Nuit Debout protests are all movements which, despite their differences, share a number of dynamics, links, frames, and repertoires. Paradoxically, in the academic field, we have witnessed a strong critical positioning against the concept 'global civil society'. The objective of this article is to reflect on the utility of this concept once again in light of recent developments and to respond to some sceptical positions. To meet this objective, a dialogue is established between civil society theories and progress made in the study of social movements. The public sphere notion (particularly its transnational dimension) becomes especially relevant for our discussion.

In recent years, a number of pro-democracy movements have emerged worldwide which have had considerable impact on political and academic domains and which are directly linked to theoretical discussion of the polysemous and much-discussed global civil society concept. The Pots and Pans Revolution in Iceland (2008), the Arab Spring, 15M and Occupy movement (2011), Yo Soy132 (2012), and the Gezi Park (2013), the Hong Kong Umbrella Revolution (2014) and Nuit Debout (2016) protests are just a few outstanding examples of citizen movements that have emerged.

Protests and manifestations have spread to different parts of the planet and have had a strong contagious effect and worldwide impact (Powell, 2015). Many studies have revealed the influence of Iceland and the Arab Spring on 15M (Flesher-Fominaya, 2014; Glasius & Pleyers, 2013; Tormey, 2015) and the impact of 15M on the later Occupy and Yo Soy132 movements (Kaldor & Selchow, 2013; Lawrence, 2013; Romanos, 2016). Neither can the Gezi Park, Hong Kong, and the more recent French Nuit Debout protests be analysed as isolated cases. No matter how many differences these movements have (which they undoubtedly do), certain repertoires, demands, and concerns are shared across these protest movements. This phenomenon has led theorists such as Glasius and Pleyers to discuss 'the global moment' (2013), Flesher-Fominaya to describe these protest forms as 'a global wave of protests' (2014), and Castells to stress the network characteristics of such transnational movements (2012). Many studies stemming from the field of social movement studies have examined the transnational and global aspects of these protests. However, it is pertinent to ask to what extent these movements and the studies that examine them may have a bearing on civil society theory, especially for the notion of global civil society and the sceptical positions that question it.

The intention of this article is to reflect theoretically on the concept of global civil society. Its objective is to closely examine and address, in light of recent developments, some of the criticisms regarding this notion in recent decades. To this end, the article re-examines a number of fundamental civil society studies and attempts to establish a dialogue with social movement theories. The public sphere notion (particularly its transnational dimension) becomes especially relevant for this discussion.

A brief introduction to civil society and the global civil society concept

Some authors in Western Europe stand out in the multifaceted, abundant reflection on the polysemic term civil society, after having reclaimed this term from progressive perspectives used in the last decades of the twentieth century (Feenstra, 2015; Kaldor, 2003). They used the concept to describe forms of political transformation in which citizens are politically active and capable and the state is the frame that guarantees rights. Such thinkers included Habermas, Keane, Barber, Kaldor, Alexander, Cohen, and Arato, who, despite defending different normative civil society models, shared some basic elements in terms of the possibilities and roles that were assigned to this sphere (Edwards, 2004). These proposals understood civil society as a social structure in which citizens were actively engaged.

Civil society is considered a place of participation in which citizens make claims and participate in common debate about established regulations and power relations. Habermas, one of the main theorists of visions thought to be neo-Tocquevillian (Ehrenberg, 1999), very graphically expresses civil society's corrective task when he characterizes it as having a 'siege-type' influence on the systemic (political-economic) world (Habermas, 1996, p. 360). Keane, another main theorist of civil society thought (Hall, 1995), talks of civil society as 'a thorn permanently in the political power's side' (Keane, 1988, p. 15) in which power relations are monitored (Keane, 2009). Finally, authors such as Barber trust in a civil society as a place capable of promoting the action of citizens responsible for, and committed to, the task of containing markets, civilizing society and democratizing governments (Barber, 1997).

The visions of civil society address various themes including discussions about the *actors* who make up civil society (e.g., do the family and economic actors form part of civil society?), the *principles* that define it (e.g., is civil society defined only by solidarity relations, or also by strategic action?), and the exact *functions* attributed to it (e.g., do they influence the political class, monitor it and/or influence the media/political agenda?). As a result of its polysemy, some theorists have argued that differences regarding the meaning of civil society are so profound that its theoretical and practical sense is lost (Wood, 1990).

However, several visions of civil society share meaningful similarities, especially those inspired by what is known as neo-Tocquevillian models (Ehrenberg, 1999). Civil society is understood as a structure that seeks to promote citizens' participation and political influence beyond the traditional electoral arena. Heterogeneous visions share the idea of civil society as a non-state domain that nevertheless requires that the state guarantee free press, the right to associate, etc. Despite differences regarding which actors are considered to form part of civil society, most conceptions undoubtedly include social movements, nongovernmental organizations (NGOs), and neighbour and consumer associations in this structure. In addition, non-violence is unanimously considered a key principle expected of civil society.

Still, the complexity of debate about civil society's role and function does not stop at this point. The increasing impact of globalization and increased interconnectivity through new communication tools have extended the term's polysemy to the concept that has become known as *global* civil society. The growing transnationalization of activism is considered evidence that global civil society is in the process of consolidation (Anheier, Glasius, & Kaldor, 2001; Kaldor, 2003). There is also talk of 'globalisation from below', presented as an alternative to the 'globalisation from above' process (Falk, 1998; Kaldor, Anheier, & Glasius, 2003). Keane defines the 'new' global civil society as 'a dynamic non-governmental system of interconnected socio-economic institutions that straddle the whole earth' (2003, p. 8), whose transnational attributes allow them to potentially 'pluralise power and problematise violence' anywhere on the planet (Keane, 2003, p. 8). In general terms, global civil society is conceived as a transnational arena of politics, interaction, and debate (Del Felice, 2011; Thörn, 2006) to which the pro-democracy movements seem to belong.

However, the global civil society concept has been criticized by sceptical theorists who believe that conceptualizing this space of participation and discussion (now global in nature) is even more diffuse, undefined and incomprehensible than the already disputed 'national' polysemous and confusing version of civil society (Bartelson, 2006). We now turn to review these criticisms.

Sceptics of global civil society

The meaning given to the global civil society concept is directly linked with its 'lesser' version of civil society confined to the nation-state. Nonetheless, an important nuance of the global version of this concept is precisely the 'loss' of its main reference point: the state. The original idea of civil society was defined as a space comprising different actors from the state political arena, who were capable of influencing the varied decision-making processes in each nation-state (Keane, 2009). Now the scope of such capacity of influence is transboundary, even global, in nature.

Not all have viewed the theorizing of civil society's global projection optimistically. Additionally, some perspectives point to imbalances that accompany civil society's globalization process, while others question whether a global civil society is feasible without a 'global state'. The critical literature outlines a number of considerations about global civil society that can be divided into two main blocks. On the one hand, there are those that stress the shortcomings or imbalances that affect the actors of global civil society, where works such as those of Anderson and Rieff (2005) and Chandhoke (2002; 2005) stand out. On the other hand, some considerations look closely at the problems that come with global civil society when there is no global governing system. For this, we look to the works of writers such as Brown (2000), Goodhart (2005), and Bartelson (2006).

The first block of criticism centres on possible shortcomings concerning the conceptualization of 'global actors', specifically a lack of transparency and representation as basic problems. Accordingly, it is seen as problematic that 'citizens do not vote for one type of civil society organisation or another as their representatives' and that 'NGOs exist to reflect on their own principles' (Anderson & Rieff, 2005, p. 29). Chandhoke also noted the unequal distribution of the world's resources and capacity to influence and that 'the majority of NGOs that are visible and influential in global civil society are based in the West' (Chandhoke, 2005, p. 361). This author suggests that the control of global civil society is in the hands of a handful of certain agents or groups. Chandhoke warns that the danger of imbalances and inequality between North and South may lead to gaps in the representativeness of global civil society. In turn, she questions the extent to which these actors manage to promote participation while 'people are disempowered rather than empowered' before 'highly specialised and professionalised civil society actors' (Chandhoke, 2002, p. 47). Similar critiques also point to serious problems in relation to transparency and accountability of civil society's global actors.

A second block of criticism centres on issues that arise from the absence of consolidated institutions of global governance, which makes transferring the close relation between nation-state and civil society to the global arena impossible (Goodhart, 2005). The problems encountered vary. For instance, Brown indicates that a basic guarantor of a global civil society frame is missing, which causes 'problems of a "law-and-order" type in the international system', and 'restricts global civil society's functioning' (2000, p. 16). This lack of a global governance structure also entails that global civil society actors play roles that do not correspond to them. It has been stated that 'global civil society's putative agents are obliged to become substitutes of a global state' (Brown, 2000, p. 17). The lack of a global political structure means that 'non-state actors are enrolled to perform governance functions by virtue of their technical expertise, advocacy, and capacity' (Sending & Neumann, 2006, p. 664). Thus, governance responsibilities are taken on by non-state actors that have not even been selected for those tasks, who are not-accountable and not always efficient in their work. This may lead to more problems than solutions in a situation in which there is no global political structure (Brown, 2000).

However, the most forceful criticism of sceptics lies in denial of even the possibility that a 'global' civil society actually exists. From statist political theory perspectives, this notion appears to be an oxymoron (Scholte, 2007). On this point, Bartelson states that 'if most accounts of global civil society assume this society to be distinct from governmental authority, where does this government authority then reside? Here theories of global civil society are silent' (Bartelson, 2006, p. 384). Sceptics argue that civil society theorists do not respond to the point about the absence of any global governmental authority (the state); paradoxically, the only thing that heterogeneous civil society models share (anchored to the national sphere) is their differentiation from the government. This silence leads sceptics to discuss the senselessness of the concept of global civil society and the impossibility of restricting what are or are not its possible functions. According to Goodhart, 'without global political institutions to translate the public will into law and policy, it is not clear what the political meaning of global deliberations is or should be' and thus 'it becomes unclear what exactly the democratic function of global opinion, discourse and deliberation might be' (Goodhart, 2005, p. 9). These criticisms deny the desirability, even the possibility, of global civil society's existence since 'its democratic functions cannot work outside the democratic state' (Goodhart, 2005, p. 10).

Given the state's centrality in the original consideration of civil society, especially in neo-Tocquevillian visions, it is not surprising that doubts and criticisms regarding its global vision arise. However, the examples included at the start of this text on pro-democracy movements suggest that, at least *a priori,* we face the very actors about whom authors such as Habermas, Keane and others have theorized in recent decades within the theoretical framework of civil society (now the global civil society). What can be learned from the experience of such movements, and from studies in the social movement field? Studies such as these may help us to re-think global civil society.

Social movements and the wave of global protests

The 'global moment' or the 'wave of global protests', consolidated since 2011, presents many complex characteristics. Indeed, movements in places such as Iceland, Spain, Mexico, Brazil, and France have varying internal actors and characteristics (and ideals). However, studies on such social movements have looked closely at common meaning structures and frames of movements, their transnational links, and their meaning for democracy theory. Glasius and Pleyers, for example, consider that 'the diffusion of slogans, repertoires of action and meanings from Sidi Bouzid (Tunisia) and Cairo to Athens, Madrid, New York and Moscow has been a major feature of the global wave of movements that started in 2011' (2013, p. 547). These authors stress the existence of common elements between the North–South or East–West divides as the most relevant factor. It is important to see how studies by Kaldor and Selchow (2013), Glasius and Pleyers (2013), Flesher-Fominaya (2014), Tormey (2015), and Gerbaudo (2017) on pro-democracy movements all appreciate the transboundary elements shared by civil society groups. Two key trends stand out in relation to rethinking global civil society: revitalizing domestic civil society and redefining the public sphere as global 'arenas'.

Revitalizing domestic civil society

Debate about the concept of global civil society includes, as mentioned, discussion about the 'real' level of transnationality acquired by both the actors that participate in it and their objectives. A dichotomy appears to be established between 'national' actors and 'global' actors. In the literature on global civil society, 'global actors' are conceived as groups simultaneously organized in different places around the world that debate shared concerns. However, it is not clear what it takes to be a global actor (a certain level of transnationality or a certain number of countries in which the actor is active). Different studies have identified some organizations as examples of such actors, for example, Greenpeace, Amnesty International, and Human Rights Watch (Keane, 2003), whose links go beyond those of a state and whose demands also stretch further than national frontiers. Nevertheless, recent studies on pro-democracy social movements provide useful information to help us reconsider this categorical dichotomy between national and global actors and examine the level of organization and the institutional arena at which they act.

The international study by Glasius and Pleyers on pro-democracy movements in place in 2011 points to a 'global generation' characterized as 'precarious'; capable of using a number of digital tools; and sharing slogans, concerns, repertoires of action and identities (Glasius & Pleyers, 2013, p. 549). At the same time, their work also concludes, in line with other contemporary studies in the social movements field:

> The national context ... is actually more important than a decade ago as more demands are made on local and national authorities. Moreover, within their own context, each of these movements— be it the Egyptian revolution, Spanish Indignados or Occupy Wall Street – is broad and heterogeneous, bringing together a wide range of activists, both in terms of generations and of activist cultures. (Glasius & Pleyers, 2013, p. 549)

Glasius and Pleyers's work shows that even if these pro-democracy movements share many similarities that transcend national borders, their key targets remain the governments of their respective nation states. A macro-study conducted in Europe by Kaldor and Selchow concludes that 'Europe is invisible' in activists' eyes. The authors specifically note that 'the question of Europe was almost never raised by our interviewees and only tended to be addressed in answer to direct questions' (Kaldor & Selchow, 2013, p. 19). A detailed analysis by Bourne and Chatzopoulou of recent movements in Greece and Spain also finds that 'social movement activity can be largely characterised as domestic in orientation. In both Spain and Greece, social movements targeted domestic actors in their protests' (2015, p. 54). In a study on Iceland, Tunisia, Egypt, Spain and U.S.A (Occupy), Flesher-Fominaya also concludes that the different 'global wave of protests' present national specificities and nationally rooted political demands linked to the lack of a 'transnational organisational infrastructure' (2014, p. 183). However, this author also highlights key transnational elements between given contexts that mark the essence of this 'global wave'. Flesher-Fominaya stresses that a specific transnational diffusion process occurs in various contexts, among which 'a global circulation of information, resources, ideas, practices, tactics and peoples' has been promoted (2014, p. 184).

These studies allow us to recognize the importance of the domestic or local issues in these movements, as well as their transnational links, solidarity, and influences. Since 2010, we have witnessed slogans that move around the world ('We are all Khaled Said', 'Real Democracy Now', 'We are the 99%', and 'Global Debout'), shared identities being consolidated ('*indignados*', 'anonymous'), the sudden appearance of common repertoires (occupations, technopolitics, etc.), and the use of new tools to share ideas and strategies. Similarly, all these movements share a concern to re-define and re-think democracy beyond its representative structure (Feenstra, Tormey, Casero-Ripollés, & Keane, 2017; Flesher-Fominaya, 2014; Keane, 2013; Tormey, 2015). In short, we face a trend in which a domestic civil society is not only revitalized but is also contributing to redefining the public sphere as global 'arenas', an aspect that is examined in greater depth elsewhere in this special issue by Bourne (2017) and García Agustín (2017).

Redefining the public sphere as global 'arenas'

Studies on pro-democracy movements stress not only the importance of domestic policy-making but also transnational trends, which are particularly relevant for defining the public sphere. A paradigmatic and illustrative example of this trend can be found in the political struggle of the Spanish PAH platform (Platform for People Affected by Mortgages), one of the best known activist groups within the 15M movement. PAH is an organization involved in the struggle against evictions of people who cannot pay their mortgages. This network has a decentralized structure and is present in more than 145 Spanish cities and towns (González-García, 2015). Over five years it has pressured the Spanish government to amend the Spanish law on mortgages. It is a civil society actor that has extended its pressure to multiple territorial levels. Locally, it has placed claims in town halls for them to declare their towns eviction-free. Nationally, it has proposed and lobbied through popular legislative initiatives for an alternative to the existing law on mortgages. In Europe, it has sought and found the support of the European Parliament and the EU Court of Justice in its demand that the Spanish government amend the Spanish law on mortgages. PAH coordinates with other European anti-eviction platforms from Italy, Germany, France, U.K., and elsewhere. Its actions, repertoires, slogans, and demands are reproduced in other contexts, with clear parallels in some places (Ordóñez, Feenstra, & Tormey, 2015). PAH promotes a network policy that blurs the divisions of what is local, national, and transnational. As it does so, it has a direct influence on public spheres where alternative discourses emerge. Civil society's pressure is exercised not only on a single focal point of governmental power but at many levels.

We can appreciate this complex multidimensional characterization, which particularly impacts on the contours of the public sphere, in relation to the 2016 French anti-austerity movement Nuit Debout where 15M activists offered their technical support and 'know-how'. This trend has been previously documented for earlier movements such as Occupy, which has been supported since 2011 by 15M activists who act as 'brokers' that facilitate the 'diffusion of particularly complex innovations related to the organisation of social movements and the development of collective action repertoires' (Romanos, 2016, p. 248). As 15M did in 2011, other movements have managed to introduce themes into the public and media-based agenda (e.g., eviction problems, the need to include new participation mechanisms, inefficiency of key state institutions, etc.). Nuit Debout has also introduced new themes in public (and media) discourse (e.g., labour reform, financial market power, meaning of political participation, etc.).

Citizen platforms such as PAH or the 'movements of the squares' such as *indignados* and Occupy Wall Street have become consolidated in different countries and have major transnational elements that contribute to their goal of influencing and defining the public sphere. Gerbaudo (2017) concludes that the achievement and real success of these movements lie in having reclaimed public space and involving the citizenry in public discussions about economic and political inequality and that this has facilitated a profound cultural change through public rituals. Different pro-democracy movements have consolidated counterpublics that offer alternative political discourses and re-think the set rules of the game in public debates. Accordingly, Kaldor and Selchow consider that these movements are 'projects of collective re-imagining of democracy' where practices and 'its relation to the everyday, to human lives' are re-thought (Kaldor & Selchow, 2013, p. 88). Pleyers concurs when noting that despite the national differences of these movements, they 'provide alternative meanings to the crisis and reclaim a more democratic society' (Pleyers, 2012, n.p.).

These movements certainly foster the consolidation of alternative discourses with high resonance (Tormey, 2015). It is worth noting, therefore, the conclusions drawn by Kaldor and Selchow when they state that 'unlike previous mobilisations and protests, they seem to have struck a chord in the mainstream; they generate a sense of public excitement wherever they happen' (2013, p. 79). Pro-democracy movements have repeatedly had the ability to influence the public sphere in a number of respects: Diffusing repertoires of protest manifest via many channels, including brokers, new media, mass media, etc. (Lawrence, 2013; Romanos, 2016); enhancing the relevance of new communication tools to alter classic political intermediation processes (Subirats, 2012; Tormey, 2015); influencing the mass media through media-based 'hacking'; organizing protests as if they were shows (Flesher-Fominaya, 2014; Micó & Casero-Ripollés, 2014); consolidating collective shared identities (Gerbaudo & Treré, 2015; Monterde, Calleja-López, Aguilera, Barandiaran, & Postill, 2015; Toret, 2013); and establishing occupations as places to practice in, to experiment in and for democratic 'incubators' (Gerbaudo, 2017; Postill, 2017). These are just some of the trends that define a transnational public sphere and as such it is plausible to consider that we are witnessing movements that form part of global civil society.

Rethinking global civil society in the pro-democracy movements era

Those sceptical about global civil society identify important criticisms that are worth considering. Problems such as lack of transparency and plurality, outlined by Chandhoke (2002, 2005) and Anderson and Rieff (2005), remind us of the critical nature of the civil society concept. As Chambers and Kopstein (2001) have examined in detail, civil society responds to a number of normative (ideal) principles that make it much more than merely non-state actors; terrorist or xenophobic groups would be included in this category, without distinguishing between bad and good civil society actors (see also García Marzá, 2008; Keane, 1998). Even though some recent studies draw different conclusions about Chandhoke's criticisms of the lack of transparency in relation to global civil society (Piewitt, Rodekamp, & Steffek, 2010), her work reminds us of the importance of civil society actors, in their institutional dimension, meeting certain minimum principles of transparency, openness, democracy, etc. that enable us to appreciate how civil society forms part of a social sphere that aims to closely examine and extend participation in democracy practice.

Nonetheless, criticisms that question the role, the desire for, and even the possibility of the existence of global civil society – essentially those which stress the problems of having no global political 'state' to accompany global civil society (Bartelson, 2006; Brown, 2000; Goodhart, 2005) – are more problematic. These criticisms, which question the central argument of those who have theorized civil society, are based on a limited understanding of the civil society theory. There are two basic responses to global civil society sceptics in this regard.

The growing 'glocalization' process

Many studies have examined the increasing relevance of actors that go beyond national frontiers to influence the political agenda, to consider alternative discourses or to propose political changes at different (local, national, or international) levels (Della Porta & Mattoni, 2014). Studies on civil society and international summits (Harrebye, 2011), the world's struggle against famine (Mati, 2009) or the transnational dimension of struggles against regimes such as apartheid (Thörn, 2006) highlight some examples of these transnational dynamics of civil society. To these, it is worth adding, as explained earlier, is the sudden appearance of a wave of protests and forms of political expression that can be classified as transnational or global. Undoubtedly, there are excellent reasons to argue that as a result of globalization and better connections, actors overcome separation imposed by national borders. Those sceptical about global civil society are aware of this trend, but they retain their criticism that there is no *alter ego* of global civil society, that is, there is no global state. We argue that these proposals stem from the perspective of statist political theory, which understands civil society and state as inseparable concepts (as well as global civil society and 'global state').

It is true that the absence of a global political state has its consequences and impacts civil society/societies, especially insofar as democracy is lacking. Moreover, it can be considered problematic when unelected civil society actors take up functions that are usually performed by governments. However, contrary to the sceptics' argument, global civil society has not arisen as a solution to the question (and current shortage) of global governance (of which global civil society only forms one part). Global civil society theories indicate an increasing blurring of civil society's spatial boundaries in terms of organization, networks and political objectives. Pro-democracy movements are yet another example of how pressure is applied at many levels: local, national and transnational. They may have the objective of redefining politics in their national democratic systems (where parliamentary decisions are made), but they do so in concert with other contexts and are influenced and inspired by other countries. These pressures also affect transnational political actors (e.g., EU or IMF institutions) and multinational companies as they are evident focal points of economic and political power. Just as the transnational character of organizations such as Amnesty International, Greenpeace, and Doctors Without Borders can be appreciated, the pro-democracy movements have also acquired a growing transboundary nature. For example, on 15 May 2016, which was the 5th anniversary of the Spanish 15M's emergence, the French Nuit Debout collaborated closely in organizing a Global Debout, which spread to 190 European cities, including Paris, Amsterdam, Barcelona, Madrid, and Berlin. In the international call, the slogan read 'The struggle for a better world is global and without borders; let us construct together a global spring of resistance!'[1]. As Kaldor, Selchow, Pleyers, Glasius, and others point out, these movements were not as massive in size as other former protests, such as those against the Iraq war, but they all (15M, Occupy, YoSoy132, and the like) had a strong impact and influence on defining themes within the public sphere. This leads us to the second key idea.

Civil society not as an alter ego of the state but as a global public sphere

Sceptical proposals generally consider that the only place where heterogeneous visions of civil society coincide is in relation to the state; a state upon which pressure is placed peacefully. Sceptics seem to take the view that 'national' civil society has the nation state as its inseparable partner, and global civil society must have a 'state' or 'political system' that is also 'global'. However, this is founded on an imprecise vision of civil society's role and meaning. Accordingly, global civil society sceptics disregard the relation between global civil society and the conception of the public sphere. Civil society is understood by authors such as Habermas, Keane, Cohen, Arato, and others as not only the complement or *alter ego* of the State but also as a place that influences and generates the formation of the public sphere. Habermas and Keane also define this quite clearly in relation to a democracy model, which is deliberative for the former (Habermas, 1996) and monitory for the latter (Keane, 2009; 2013).

Habermas defines the public sphere as 'a network of communication information and points of view; the streams of communication are, in the process, filtered and synthesized in such a way that they coalesce into bundles of topically specified *public* opinions' (Habermas, 1996, p. 306). The key to Habermas's deliberative model lies in the capacity of actors (civil society) to debate under ideal conditions of equality, plurality, and inclusion on themes of public interest; actors who are ultimately capable have an influence on 'administrative power' via the public sphere. Administrative power has control of binding decision making.

Defining the public sphere as a physical or media-based place where civil society questions and 'debunks power relations', Keane extends civil society's possibilities in several directions (Keane, 1998, p. 169; 2009). On the one hand, he attributes this not only to its role of influencing but also to the function of determining administrative power by monitoring and public scrutiny, especially when actors who hold power exercise this capacity arbitrarily and abusively. On the other hand, unlike Habermas, Keane extends civil society's pressure or 'siege' (through the public sphere) not only to political power but also to other powers, for example, economic ones. Both Keane and Habermas conclude that civil society is a key area in the definition and incorporation of new themes in public discussion.

The ever-increasing importance of new communication tools and the development of globalization have forced the public sphere to acquire a more complex and transboundary nature. Studies into pro-democracy movements allow us to appreciate just how civil society revitalizes the public sphere's role in many directions, and how it is not cloistered and only framed within the nation state. The analyses of pro-democracy movements allow us to appreciate how the concept of global civil society helps to introduce new themes into the public sphere, creating new frames and solidarities transnationally, and how it also promotes critical reflection within society itself. State institutions (either national or international) are not the only interlocutors of global civil society. Civil society itself makes sense in that it seeks to discuss and deliberate, through public sphere/s, about its own conceptions, values, ways of life, consumer habits, etc. It is important to stress global civil society's multidirectional nature, which addresses both state institutions and society (Cohen & Arato, 1992).

In the era of pro-democracy movements, global civil society offers us a valid and necessary theoretical framework to be able to understand the present revitalization of the domestic civil society, which is organized and addresses numerous levels (local, national, and global), and to re-think the ideal conditions that accompany (or must accompany) democracy and its basic pillars.

Note

1. #NuitDebout's International call
   https://nuitdebout.fr/globaldebout/en/globaldebout-mobilisation-may-15/
   https://spanishrevolution.wordpress.com/2016/04/16/llamada-internacional-de-nuit-debout/

Disclosure statement

No potential conflict of interest was reported by the author.

Funding

Ramón A. Feenstra is member of the research project UJI-A2016-04 funded by the Universitat Jaume I de Castellón, Castellón.

References

Anderson, K., & Rieff, D. (2005). Global civil society: A sceptical view. In H. Anheier & M. Glasius (Eds.), *Societies: Dilemmas of institutionalization* (pp. 211–238). London: Sage.
Anheier, H., Glasius, M., & Kaldor, M. (2001). Introducing global civil society. In G. Anheier & M. Kaldor (Eds.), *Global civil society 2001* (pp. 3–22). Oxford: Oxford University Press.
Barber, B. (1997). *Un lugar para todos*. Barcelona: Paidós.
Bartelson, J. (2006). Making sense of global civil society. *European Journal of International Relations, 12*(3), 371–395.
Bourne, A. (2017). Social movements and the transnational transformation of public spheres. *Journal of Civil Society, 13*(3), 231–246. doi:10.1080/17448689.2017.1354807.
Bourne, A., & Chatzopoulou, S. (2015). Europeanization and social movement movilization during the European sovereign crisis: The cases of Spain and Greece. *Recerca, 17*, 33–60.
Brown, C. (2000). Cosmopolitanism, world citizenship and global civil society. *Critical Review of International Social and Political Philosophy, 3*(1), 7–26.
Castells, M. (2012). *Networks of outrage and hope: Social movements in the Internet age*. Cambridge: Polity.
Chambers, S., & Kopstein, J. (2001). Bad civil society. *Political Theory, 29*(6), 837–865.
Chandhoke, N. (2002). The limits of global civil society. In M. Glasius, M. Kaldor, & H. Anheier (Eds.), *Global civil society 2002* (pp. 35–52). Oxford: Oxford University Press.
Chandhoke, N. (2005). How global is global civil society? *Journal of World-Systems Research, 11*(2), 355–371.
Cohen, J., & Arato, A. (1992). *Civil society and political theory*. Cambridge: MIT Press.
Del Felice, C. (2011). Transnational activism and free trade. Exploring the emancipatory potentials of global civil society. *Voluntas, 23*, 302–327.
Della Porta, D., & Mattoni, A. (2014). *Spreading protest. Social movements in the time of crisis*. Colchester: ECPR Press.
Edwards, M. (2004). *Civil society*. Cambridge: Polity Press.
Ehrenberg, J. (1999). *Civil society. The critical history of an idea*. New York: New York University Press.
Falk, R. (1998). Global civil society: Perspectives, initiatives, movements. *Oxford Development Studies, 26*(1), 99–110.
Feenstra, R. A. (2015). Activist and citizen political repertoire in Spain: A reflection based on civil society theory and different logics of political participation. *Journal of Civil Society, 11*(3), 242–258.
Feenstra, R. A., Tormey, S., Casero-Ripollés, A., & Keane, J. (2017). *Refiguring democracy: The Spanish political laboratory*. London: Routledge.
Flesher-Fominaya, C. (2014). *Social movements and globalizations. How portest, occupations and uprising are changing the world*. New York, NY: Palgrave.
García Agustín, O. (2017). European counterpublics? DiEM25, plan B and the agonistic European public sphere. *Journal of Civil Society, 13*(3), 323–336. doi:10.1080/17448689.2017.1360233.
García Marzá, D. (2008). Sociedad civil: Una concepción radical. *Recerca, 8*, 27–46.
Gerbaudo, P. (2017). *The mask and the flag: The rise of citizenism in global protest*. London: Hurst.
Gerbaudo, P., & Treré, E. (2015). In search of the 'we' of social media activism: Introduction to the special issue on social media and protest identities. *Information, Communication & Society, 18*(8), 865–871.
Glasius, M., & Pleyers, G. (2013). The global moment of 2011: Democracy, social justice and dignity. *Development and Change, 44*(3), 547–567.
González-García, R. G. (2015). El moviment per l'okupació i el moviment per l'habitatge: semblances, diferències i confluències en temps de crisi. *Recerca, 17*, 85–106.

Goodhart, M. (2005). Civil society and the problem of global democracy. *Democratization*, 12(1), 1–21.

Habermas, J. (1996). *Between facts and norms. Contributions to a discourse theory of law and democracy.* Cambridge: MIT Press.

Hall, J. A. (1995). *Civil society, theory, history, comparison.* Cambridge: Polity Press.

Harrebye, S. (2011). Global civil society and international summits: New labels for different types of activism at the COP15. *Journal of Civil Society*, 7(4), 407–426.

Kaldor, M. (2003). The idea of global civil society. *International Affairs*, 79(3), 583–593.

Kaldor, M., Anheier, H., & Glasius, M. (eds.) (2003). *Global civil society.* Oxford: Oxford University Press.

Kaldor, M., & Selchow, S. (2013). The 'bubbling up' of subterranean politics in Europe. *Journal of Civil Society*, 9(1), 78–99.

Keane, J. (1988). *Democracy and civil society.* London: Verso.

Keane, J. (1998). *Civil society: Old images, new visions.* Oxford: Polity Press.

Keane, J. (2003). *Global civil society?* Cambridge: Cambridge University Press.

Keane, J. (2009). *The life and death of democracy.* London: Simon & Schuster.

Keane, J. (2013). *Democracy and media decadence.* Cambridge: Cambridge University Press.

Lawrence, J. (2013). The international roots of the 99% and the 'politics of anyone'. *IC - Revista Científica de Información y Comunicación*, 10, 1–19.

Mati, J. M. (2009). A cartography of a global civil society advocacy alliance: The case of the global call to action against poverty. *Journal of Civil Society*, 5(1), 83–105.

Micó, J. L., & Casero-Ripollés, A. (2014). Political activism online: Organization and media relations in the case of 15M in Spain. *Information, Communication and Society*, 17(7), 858–871.

Monterde, A., Calleja-López, A., Aguilera, M., Barandiaran, X., & Postill, J. (2015). Multitudinous identities: A qualitative and network analysis of the 15M collective identity. *Information, Communication and Society*, 18(8), 930–950.

Ordóñez, V., Feenstra, R. A., & Tormey, S. (2015). Citizens against austerity: A comparative reflection on Plataforma de Afectados por la Hipoteca (PAH) and Bündnis Zwangsräumung Verhindern (BZV). *Araucaria*, 17(34), 133–153.

Piewitt, M., Rodekamp, M., & Steffek, J. (2010). Civil society in world politics: How accountable are transnational CSOs? *Journal of Civil Society*, 6(3), 237–258.

Pleyers, G. (2012). Beyond occupy: Progressive activists in Europe. *Open Democracy*, Retrieved from https://www.opendemocracy.net/geoffrey-pleyers/beyond-occupy-progressive-activists-in-europe

Postill, J. (2017). Field theory, media change and the new citizen movements: Spain's 'real democracy' turn as a series of fields and spaces. *Recerca. Revista de Pensament*, 21, 13–27.

Powell, F. (2015). The psych-politics of austerity: Democracy, sovereignty and civic protest. *Recerca. Revista de Pensament*, 17, 15–31.

Romanos, E. (2016). Immigrants as brokers: Dialogical diffusion from Spanish Indignados to occupy Wall Street. *Social Movement Studies*, 15(3), 247–262.

Sending, O. J., & Neumann, I. B. (2006). Governance to governmentality: Analyzing NGOs, states, and power. *International Studies Quarterly*, 50(3), 651–672.

Scholte, J. A. (2007). Civil society and the legitimation of global governance. *Journal of Civil Society*, 3(3), 305–326.

Subirats, J. (2012). Algunas ideas sobre política y políticas en el cambio de época: Retos asociados a la nueva sociedad y a los movimientos sociales emergentes. *Interface*, 4(1), 278–286.

Thörn, H. (2006). The emergence of a global civil society: The case of anti-apartheid. *Journal of Civil Society*, 2(3), 249–266.

Toret, J. (coord.) (2013). *Tecnopolítica: la potencia de las multitudes conectadas. El sistema red 15M, un nuevo paradigma de la política distribuida.* Barcelona: UOC.

Tormey, S. (2015). *The end of representative politics.* Cambridge: Polity.

Wood, E. M. (1990). The uses and abuses of civil society. *Socialist Register*, 26, 60–84.

Concluding Essay: Social Activism Against Austerity – The Conditions for Participatory and Deliberative Forms of Democracy

Thomas P. Boje

By concluding this special issue on social movements in the transnational public sphere, I want to focus on two core concepts for understanding social mobilization of citizens and the frame of reference in which they are active – citizenship and civic organizations. However, I start with a selective summary of some of the conclusions concerning democracy, participation, and emancipation, which I find most prominent in the articles published in the issue.

The first and probably most important conclusion to draw from the empirical analyses presented in this issue concerns the perception of democracy. The experiences and practices of the social movements and activists involved clearly demonstrate that representative democracy is insufficient. There is a strong demand for a participatory and deliberative culture of democracy with more inclusive forms of representation (García Agustín, 2017; Bourne, 2017; Feenstra, 2017): a democratic culture that empowers the citizens with rights as well as duties to be actively involved in decisions that directly affect their living conditions. A meaningful democratic system is a system involving all groups of citizens in a continuous debate and decision-making process concerning the economic, social, and cultural conditions for their living. Most important in this respect is it that the conditions for involving citizens are organized in a way that first of all makes it possible for all individuals to participate irrespective of differences in economic resources, ethnic background, gender, age, and education. Additionally, the claim for democracy also includes a demand for control of governing bodies at local, national, regional, and transnational level. There is a need for redefining politics in the national democratic system reflecting the decisions taken in other countries and transnational institutions (Feenstra, 2017). Here, modern communication technology has created completely new forms of publicity. The public sphere today is not limited to certain enclaves or forced to take place within a narrow geographical and organizational framework. It can easily be developed globally and thus disconnected from the local context and does not have to be tied to a particular public (David & Côrte-Real Pinto, 2017; Bourne, 2017).

Another and related conclusion to draw from the empirical studies is the declining confidence in the traditional channels of public decision-making through the representative democratic institutions and by collaborations between the political agencies (Baumgarten & Díez García, 2017; Dunphy, 2017). The activists and their demands do not reject democracy but want 'real democracy' and real involvement of 'the 99% of the population' instead of governing by a power elite representing a tiny proportion of the population. Therefore, the activist movements want to involve citizens directly beyond the traditional parties and interest organizations, an approach that is quite similar to populism.

It is here important to point out that populism in its different forms stems from the growing lack of democratic participation of citizens in the formulation of policy and in society's governance in general, as we have experienced globally since the late 1970s. Populism seems to be today's undemocratic and nationalist response to decades of undemocratic neoliberal politics. However, the approach to politics by the activist movements takes radically different forms, which are far from the traditional definition of populism and focus instead on political strategies combining social rights, cultural inclusiveness, and concerns with common goods embracing all citizens in a transnational or global perspective (David & Côrte-Real Pinto, 2017; Feenstra, 2017).

A third important conclusion to draw from the empirical studies concerns the format of anti-austerity protests, which have changed the perspective from democracy in formal organizational settings representing specific social groups to a 'democracy of the squares' with growing focus and attention to openness, transparency, and equality (Baumgarten & Díez García, 2017; Della Porta et al., 2016, p. 30). There is an emphasis on direct participation of citizens rather than mobilization through networks of associations. Against this background, social movements face a number of dilemmas in their struggle for democracy and emancipation, including:

- Embracing individuality within a collective community versus recognition of diversity and consensus building towards differentiation and majority representation
- Deliberative decision-making structures in horizontally structured organizations versus representative decision-making in organizations that are vertically structured.

Everyone's participation is fundamental for real democracy. Therefore, it must be based on diversity, deliberation, and decision-making in open, horizontal organizations. If we want to develop democracy with real content, it is necessary to start from the bottom – to get the individual citizen, local community, and civil society involved. Only through such an approach can we create governance at local as well as territorial and global level. In the struggle for democracy, self-organization, participation in decision-making, and the obligation to engage in the present and future community are key elements of an emancipatory democratic organization (Bourne, 2017). Such participatory democracy develops in a constant struggle, through conflicts and reconciliation. Without the insistence on equality of resources and a requirement to recognize diversity, it will not be possible to achieve real emancipation, which is necessary to ensure parity of participation (Fraser, 2005).

A fourth conclusion to be drawn from the articles relates to the scope of activism. Here the activist social movements have developed a cosmopolitan vision where they have combined calls for state interventions and inclusive citizenship with recognition of a need for global solutions to global problems. Two trends are important in this respect. On the one hand, transnational communication networks have facilitated global circulation of information, ideas, and people. On the other hand, the national governments have lost control over political and economic development due to the growing power of global corporations and international organizations. These simultaneous developments have forced the anti-austerity movements to go global in their activities. A focus on transnational solidarity and global justice by arguing that 'the struggle for a better world is global and without borders' (Nuit Debout 20016/04/16) is a general theme in all the contributions to the special issue.

About being an activist citizen – different types of citizenship

Citizenship has become a battlefield in the societies: a regulatory medium for sorting people based on nationality and simultaneously a political pledge with hopes of inclusion, social belonging, and democratic empowerment. When we discuss the potential impact of citizenship, it is important to remember the 'Janus face' of citizenship. On the one hand, it disciplines the citizens through regulation of citizenship rights – activation programmes, control of citizens receiving welfare benefits, enforcing social norms, etc. – and on the other hand, it emancipates the citizens by enacting citizenship rights by way of social protests, advocacy, political actions, etc. Citizens who have control over their lives and have a say in relation to their daily lives will have more confidence in the system's institutions and be more committed in relation to social activities, labour, network, etc. Defining citizenship and its conditions is highly related to struggles on economic, social, and political issues at local, national, and transnational level.

In the late-modern society, it is a major challenge for theories of citizenship to adopt a perception of citizenship that fits into the transformed conditions for governance and democratic representation in societies dominated by global economic transactions and transnational communication. This means that the theory needs to be revised in a way that it suits the changed conditions of citizenship – changing conditions for employment, diminishing importance of nation states, and growing diversity in the nation state's population. The task is to understand citizenship as an institution in transition constituted through the current social and political struggles about what it means to be a citizen. In this context, citizenship becomes a dynamic institution characterized by processes of domination and empowerment, which jointly determine who are the insiders, outsiders, or strangers and who is totally excluded from the community.

Here 'acts of citizenship' defines the acts through which political activists intervene in favour of groups excluded from the established citizenship norm:

> Thinking about citizenship through acts means to implicitly accept that to be a citizen is to make claims to justice: to break habitus and act in a way that disrupts already defined orders, practices and statuses. I provided a preliminary definition of citizenship as a dynamic institution of domination and empowerment that governs who citizens (insiders), subjects (strangers, outsiders) and abjects (aliens) are and how these actors are to govern themselves and each other in a given body politics. The emerging figure of the activist citizen calls into question the givenness of that body politic and opens its boundaries wide. (Isin, 2009, p. 384)

A condition for more equal participation in society must therefore be a combination of economic equality, social recognition, and equal political representation through a redistribution of power and more equal patterns of participation between individuals in the local community and in society as a whole as well as in transnational relations. Seen from this perspective, there is a need for an institutional frame that ensures a more active involvement of citizens on a transnational context enabling them to control the political and social organization of importance for their social protection on local, national, and transnational levels.

An important challenge in a future welfare society will be to create space for individual engagement in interpersonal relationships – socially and culturally – at the same time as society and the social community show solidarity towards weak groups wherever they live. The relationship between individual freedom and social and economic equality is central to this. Activist citizenship characterizes citizens who oppose everyday citizenship practices and fight for reformulating the economic, social, and political conditions that define the framework for social life. The activist citizen is a person fighting for rights and obligations and who through her actions demands inclusion of citizens who are not insiders – those who are outsiders or completely excluded.

Individual involvement in combination with social and political actions disrupts existing social structures and creates the necessary collective framework for social change. Through efficient forms of resistance, such as civil disobedience and refusal to cooperate, activist citizens accomplish social and economic reforms. Thereby, the citizen actively contributes to ensuring economic equality through redistribution of resources, recognition of differences based on gender, ethnicity, age, and sexual orientation as well as an equal representation of all social groups in the democratic institutions. This is exactly what Fraser (2013) argues for in her analysis of the conditions for democratic participation in the late-modern society – when she argues that redistribution and recognition have to be complemented with a third movement: emancipation. By adding emancipation through the public sphere of civil society, we ensure the empowerment of democratic institutions through citizens' participation in and control of the economic, social, and cultural organizations.

Civil society and the public sphere – to set the scene for activism

The core of civil society is the active involvement of citizens, critical dialogue, and free speech in the public sphere. However, it is important here to make clear what the starting point and terms of participation are. Over the past decade, we have seen increasing demands for citizen involvement and active participation in political decision-making combined with the emergence of grassroots political movements in different parts of the political system. Here the public sphere of the civil society became the core institution for deliberative and emancipatory actions among the citizens – in local, national, and transnational activities. Within civil society, citizens are able to exercise their active/activist citizenship more than in the nation state and the market. According to Alexander (2006), civil society is a solidarity sphere in which a universal community becomes culturally defined and institutionally supported through social networks. These organizations thus contribute to maintaining the solidarity community, which is represented by civility, critical attitudes, and mutual respect (Alexander, 2006; Boje 2015; Fraser, 2003).

The dynamics between justice, citizenship, and the institutional frame for participation in democratic processes have to reflect and counterbalance the restrictions in citizenship rights. The conditions for active participation among citizens differ radically between the European countries. Part of the explanations for these differences we might find in the structure and extension of civil society organizations. They may play an important role by including the less powerful social groups into the social fabric and giving them a political voice through their citizenship rights and responsibility. The civil society organizations are in this context perceived as an 'intermediate body', representing the ordinary citizens, giving voice to different social groups in society and revitalizing public participation in democratic institutions. Civil society represents the citizens' collective actions. It forms a kind of counterbalance to the prevailing individualism and represents a

> much-needed antidote against the cynicism that characterizes so much of modern politics ... while it establishes a balance in relation to the pervasive influence and control of state power as well as market forces. (Edwards, 2005, pp. 29–30)

This is, however, only the case if the civil society organizations are involving all the different groups of citizens relevant for the specific issue – not only the well off and those most connected. The civil society organizations must act on the principle of parity of participation (Fraser, 2005) and be able to include and empower all groups of citizens irrespective of their formal citizenship – they may be insiders, strangers, outsiders, and aliens. Participation and involvement of citizens in key issues on the political and institutional agenda become therefore fundamental for the legitimacy of the democratic process (Wright, 2010). The role of civil society is thus to advocate for social change and to raise public awareness concerning social inequality and injustice prevailing in society.

The organized civil society has as one of its most important tasks to create trust between the public institutions and the citizens by representing the marginalized and under-represented social groups and giving power to their voices. By doing this, civil society organizations have as one of their principal duties the responsibility to support and defend citizenship rights by emancipating the marginalized and vulnerable social groups and ensuring their representation in the public sphere at all levels. As discussed in several contributions in this issue, today the public sphere of civil society not only includes the national governance system but must also expand to counteract transnational or global governing institutions. The activists' demands are global. Therefore, the democratic responses must also be transnational/global despite weakness when it comes to organization and representability.

In discussing the advocacy role of civil society, it is important to distinguish between two different positions concerning involvement of civil society organizations. On the one hand, there is their role as actor in civic dialogues when the organizations take part in the political decision-making process. On the other hand, there is their role as watchdog outside the political decision-making system when the civil society organizations are defending the social rights of citizens (Janoski, 1998, 2010; Keane, 2006). While distinct, these two meanings are at the root of the resurgence of civil society activism and share an endeavour to broaden forms of political participation through 'participatory democracy' (Wright, 2010), 'social activism (Isin 2002)' or 'emancipation' (Fraser, 2003).

The possibility of civil society becoming a locus for democratic learning, political reflexivity and governance thus depends, on the one side, on its specific institutional mechanisms, and, on the other side, on the broader social and political institutional configurations of which civil society are part. Here it is important to understand in detail the feedback mechanisms between policy agencies, organized civil society, and civic action by citizens. Numerous studies of this relationship find that public policies and governmental programmes shape the constellation of civil society organizations. In short, if the involvement of civil society represents particularistic interests, and these are not counterbalanced by the universalistic approach taken by public institutions, then civil society intervention might be problematic and can lead to a reinforcement of already existing social, political and cultural cleavages in society – and to a lower level of citizens' involvement in decision-making generally.

Deliberative democracy through civic activism – emancipation for the minority?

Emancipation entails a number of opposing trends. Activist citizenship not only empowers citizens, but can also contribute to pressure placed on various forms of solidarity. Indeed emancipation might lead to inequality in resources and in access to social protection. The ambiguity is also evident because emancipation in recent decades has emerged as part of the political discourse dominated by a neoliberal ideology. The new capitalism characterized by flexibility, mobility, and transnational capital formation is part of the neoliberal discourse, but this discourse also includes the emancipatory critique of top-down regulation and bureaucratic organization of social institutions. Two social-political struggles are currently underway. The first is a struggle relating to the social security discourse: should social welfare be organized bureaucratically or in a participatory fashion, which is favourable or unfavourable in relation to diversity? The second is a struggle relating to the emancipation discourse: should it favour deregulation or regulation by controlling the market forces? In other words, how can emancipation serve the democratization of the social system and make it more accessible? In these struggles over political discourse, the principle of 'parity of participation' on equal terms – economically, politically, and socially – is essential to ensure equal conditions for all citizens.

The concept of 'participatory democracy' is generally associated with a strengthening of active citizenship expressed through civil society organizations and their involvement in the public sphere. It is in this context important to point out that democracy implies the existence of civil society organizations as components of an independent sector. An efficient and dynamic civil society is, however, also part of a pluralistic public sphere where citizens participate individually and actively. The understanding of 'parity in participation' implies thus that the traditional boundaries between politics and administration will be less important than the question of how cooperation between citizens, civil society organizations, and the public system works (or does not work). Civic participation constitutes one way of aggregating preferences that are perceived as an alternative to political parties. It may have a role in advancing democracy by assuring that citizens' interests are taken into account. From the perspective of deliberative democracy, the role of civil society organizations is to bring disaffected citizens back in touch with politics. Consequently, these organizations might become a crucial mediator between participatory democratic structures and policy-makers. Here it is again important to emphasize that this is only the case if the citizens participate directly in governing the civil society organizations.

However, numerous studies show that, while civil society organizations cultivate the image that they are inclusive and democratic, many are truly segregating and selective in the sense that they differentiate leadership and membership (and even beneficiaries) based on age, class, gender, race, and religion (Dekker, 2009; Eliasoph, 2014; Glasius & Ishkanian, 2017; Theiss-Morse & Hibbing, 2005). The discourse that dominates many of today's social movements/civil society states that they are democratic and inclusive in their design and that they practice participatory democracy. Though a few have truly open membership and inclusive criteria for the selection of board and committee representatives, the vast majority of social movements/civil society organizations do not have an inclusive approach to membership and representativeness. They tend to replicate rather than oppose the prevailing social and economic inequalities in society. Often the organizational work, which takes place in civil society organizations, reproduces or even amplifies the existing inequalities in terms of gender, age, class, and social experience (Glasius & Ishkanian, 2017).

Being a citizen in a participatory and equal democracy gives new meaning to having civic obligations. It commits the individual as well as the collective to actively participate and contribute to community development of public benefits to the 'common good'. Inclusion in democratic processes through participation and dialogue are prerequisites for well-functioning and socially justified democratic decision-making processes. However, it is important to point out that not all forms of participation and dialogue are democratic, tolerant, and solidarity-focused. Much of the communication that is currently taking place in the public sphere is limiting, exclusive, and selective. The starting point for the renewal of political culture through the creation of a real or participatory democratic system must rely on three key concepts:

- Everyone on equal terms has a voice that is not only listened to but also heard and included in the dialogue;
- Citizens' wishes, dreams, and ideas are included in the decision-making process and that all views are respected in the process of establishing consensus. Once this is achieved, however, it is also important that decisions are respected and implemented;
- All citizens assume the obligation to participate in the community's affairs. I am talking about creating a framework around the community that can ensure that the individual works with his or her own special wishes and dreams within the framework set by the collective: we must be able to live differently and at the same time be a collective (Glasius & Ishkanian, 2017).

Evaluating the different models of governance systems and the importance of activist citizenship and civil society organizations for civic participation, civility, and emancipation is the major task for future research. We need to combine activist citizenship, emancipation, and social protection in welfare policy – and to clarify the future role of the public sphere of civil society. How can participatory actors, procedures, and institutions influence public policies, political outcomes, and civic and political practices in different institutional settings? Activist citizenship has become a condition for social incorporation of citizens. How is it possible to ensure emancipation and participation for vulnerable social groups when we experience a growing risk of social polarization, poverty, and de-qualification for large groups of citizens? These groups are without the necessary economic and social resources to accomplish an inclusive citizenship and active participation in the economic, political, social, and cultural institutions of society. Therefore, we need policy strategies that are able to combine activist citizenship, emancipation, and social protection for all citizens.

Disclosure statement

No potential conflict of interest was reported by the author.

References

Alexander, J. C. (2006). *The civil sphere*. Oxford: Oxford University Press.

Baumgarten, B., & Díez García, R. (2017). More than a copy paste: The spread of Spanish frames and events to Portugal. *Journal of Civil Society*, *13*(3), 247–266. doi:10.1080/17448689.2017.1362127

Boje, T. P. (2015). Citizenship, democratic participation, and civil society. *CURSIV*, *15*, 27–44.

Bourne, A. (2017). Social movements and the transnational transformation of public spheres. *Journal of Civil Society*, *13*(3), 231–246. doi:10.1080/17448689.2017.1354807

David, I., & Côrte-Real Pinto, G. A. (2017). The Gezi protests and the Europeanization of the Turkish public sphere. *Journal of Civil Society*, *13*(3), 307–322. doi:10.1080/17448689.2017.1359887

Dekker, P. (2009). Civicness: From civil society to civic services. *VOLUNTAS: International Journal of Voluntary and Nonprofit Organizations*, *20*, 220–238.

Della Porta, D., et al. (2016). Late neoliberalism and its discontents: An introduction. In D. Della Porta, M. Andretta, T. Fernandes, F. O'Connor, E. Romanos, & M. Vogiatzoglou (Eds.), *Late neoliberalism and its discontent: Comparing crises and movements in the European periphery* (pp. 1–38). London: Palgrave.

Dunphy, R. (2017). Beyond nationalism? the anti-austerity social movement in Ireland: Between domestic constraints and lessons from abroad. *Journal of Civil Society*, *13*(3), 267–283. doi:10.1080/17448689.2017.1355031

Edwards, M. (2005). *Civil society*. Cambridge: Polity Press.

Eliasoph, N. (2014). Measuring the grassroots: Puzzles of cultivating the grassroots from the top down. *The Sociological Quarterly*, *55*, 467–492.

Feenstra, R. A. (2017). Essay: Rethinking global civil society and the public sphere in the age of pro-democracy movements. *Journal of Civil Society*, *13*(3), 337–348. doi:10.1080/17448689.2017.1359886

Fraser, N. (2003). *Social justice in globalization: Redistribution, recognition, and participation*. EUROZINC.

Fraser, N. (2005, November–December). Re-framing justice in a globalizing world. *New Left Review*, *36*, 69–88.

Fraser, N. (2013, May–June). A triple movement? Parsing the politics of crisis after Polanyi. *New Left Review*, *81*.

García Agustín, Ó. (2017). European counterpublics? DiEM25, Plan B and the agonistic European public sphere. *Journal of Civil Society*, *13*(3), 323–336. doi:10.1080/17448689.2017.1360233

Glasius, M., & Ishkanian, A. (2017). What does Democracy mean? Activist views and practices in Athens, Cairo, London and Moscow. *Democratization*, *24*, 1006–1024.

Isin, E. (2002) *Being political. Genealogies of citizenship*. Minneapolis: University of Minnesota Press.

Isin, E. (2009). Citizenship in flux: The figure of the activist citizen. *Subjectivity*, *29*, 367–388.

Janoski, T. (1998). *Citizenship and civil society: A framework of rights and obligations in liberal, traditional and social democratic regimes*. Cambridge: Cambridge University Press.

Janoski, T. (2010). The dynamic processes of volunteering in civil society: A group and multi-level approach. *Journal of Civil Society*, *6*(2), 99–118.

Keane, J. (2006). *Civil society: Berlin perspectives*. New York, NY: Berghahn Books.

Theiss-Morse, E., & Hibbing, J. R. (2005). Citizenship and civic engagement. *Annual Review of Political Science*, *8*, 227–249.

Wright, E. O. (2010). *Envisioning real utopias*. London: Verso.

Index

Note: **Boldface** page numbers refer to tables and *italic* page numbers refer to figures. Page numbers followed by 'n' denote endnotes.

AAA *see* Anti-Austerity Alliance
Acampada Salamanca 37
active participation 6, 130, 133
activism: anti-austerity 49, 51, 56, 59, 59n3; community 47, 58; Irish social movements 4; in Lisbon 39; scene for 130–2; scope of 128; transnationalization of 117
activist citizenship 3, 6, 130, 132, 133
activist movements 128
'acts of citizenship' 129
'agonistic public sphere' 104
AKP *see* Justice and Development Party
AKP Istanbul Youth board 91, 96
Alexander, J. C. 130
alter-globalization movement 26, 30
Anderson, K. 117, 122
Anti-Austerity Alliance (AAA) 49
anti-austerity movement 3, 121, 128; after 2011 50–2; Ireland's trade unions 49; Irish political elite to 49; mass movement of 48; poster child for 49; transnational view on 26–7; in 2008-2011 48–50; water charge payments, boycott of 52
anti-water charges movement 52
AoR *see* attributions of responsibility
'A Plan B in Europe' (Plan B) 102; 'arena of representation' 105; in Copenhagen 108, 110; counterdiscourse 107; DiEM25 vs. 109; emergence of 104–5, 109; as European counterpublics 111–13, **112**; in Madrid 105, 109–10; summits 105
Arab Spring 25, 26
attributions of responsibility (AoR) 65, 70

Balibar, Étienne 101
banking crisis 63
Blockupy 9, 10, 14, 17–19
Boje, Thomas P. 6

Böll, Heinrich 92
Bourne, A. 120
Brown, C. 118
Bush, George W. 48

CAHWT *see* Campaign Against Home and Water Taxes
Campaign Against Home and Water Taxes (CAHWT) 50
Carnation Revolution 36
Catalonia independence 14
Celtic Tiger economic 45, 48
Centre of Sociological Research (CIS) 27
Chambers, S. 122
Chandhoke, N. 117, 118, 122
Chatzopoulou, S. 120
CIS *see* Centre of Sociological Research
citizenship 129–31
civil disobedience, acts of 51
civil society 86, 90, **91**, 116–17; Barber trust 116; core of 130; domestic 119–20; globalization process 117; and international summits 122; intervention 131–2; organized 130–1; original idea of 117; post-national 92; pressure 121; pro-Kurdish institutions 94; public sphere of 6; role and function 117, 131; as social movement 3; theoretical framework of 116, 119, 122; TMMOB and DİSK 94; visions of 116 *see also* global civil society
collective identification 15
Collins, Joan 55, 58
'community activists' 47
'community of communication' 19
contemporary social movements 6
'Coordinadora 25-S' 29, 40n9
Coordinating Collective (CC) 111
Copenhagen summit 108, 110
Coppinger, Ruth 49
Côrte-Real Pinto, G. A. 5
counterpublics, notion of 104
Cowen, Brian 48

135

INDEX

Cox, Laurence 47
'criteria of relevance' 14–15, 18, 56
Customs Union 89

DAAA *see* discursive actor attribution analysis
Daly, Clare 48, 55, 57
David, I. 5
'debunks power relations' 124
deliberative culture, of democracy 127
deliberative democracy 132–3
Democracia Real Ya! (DRY) 18, 28
Democracia Verdadeira Já 31
Democracy in Europe Movement 2025 (DiEM25) 5, 102; arenas 106–7; challenges 110; emergence of 106, 109; as European counterpublics 111–13, **112**; hybrid nature 106; 'organizational principles' 111; as political movement 106, 108; as transnational counterpublic 111; vs. Plan B 109
democracy theory 119
'democratic centralist' model 58
democratic culture 127
democratic political systems 30, 127
Denmark summit (November 2016) 105
DiEM25 *see* Democracy in Europe Movement 2025
diffusion processes 4, 25, 27
digital communication technologies 27
discourse convergence 15, 18
discursive actor attribution analysis (DAAA) 69–70
discursive Europeanization 67, 76–8, *77*
discursive integration 15, 20
domestic civil society 6, 119–20, 124
Donnay, Sirio Canos 57
DRY *see* Democracia Real Ya!
Dunphy, R. 4

ECB *see* European Central Bank
Economic Adjustment Programme 48, 51
EFSF *see* European Financial Stability Facility
EPS *see* European public sphere
ESM *see* European Stability Mechanism
Euro-Pact protests 29, 37
European Central Bank (ECB) 17, 63
European Financial Stability Facility (EFSF) 63, 66
Europeanization 86–7, 103
European media system 66
European parliament elections 54
European public sphere (EPS) 66–7, 86–9, 102; Europeanization 66, 86–9; horizontal Europeanization 87–8; mass media systems 66; social movements 67–9; supranational 87; transnationalization 66; vertical Europeanization 87

European Social Forum 112
European Stability Mechanism (ESM) 63
European Trade Union Confederation 94
European Union (EU): anti-austerity demands 14; austerity policies 102, 107, 111; Catalonia independence 14; civil society centres 86; 'civil society model' 96; civil society organizations 88, 90, 92; counterparts 93, 96, 97; democratic deficit 103; democratic politics in 11; European Financial Stability Facility 63; Europeanization of public spheres 66; European Stability Mechanism 63; leverage and linkage 86, 94, 97; member states 92; politicization of 12, 16, 68; project culture 90; scholarship 90; transnationalization 21; Troika policies 68; Turkish civil society 89, 94
Euroscepticism 107
euro-TINA 109

Fassina, Stefano 104
Feenstra, R. 5
FF party 48, 49
15M activists 29, 121
Flesher-Fominaya, C. 120
France summit (January 2016) 105, 107
Fraser, Nancy 9, 130
'Free Otegi, Free Them All' campaign 18, 19

García Agustín, O. 120
García, Rubén Díez 5
'general European public' 11, 16
General Secretariat for Research and Technology (GSRT) 70
Geração à Rasca protests 26, 31
Gerbaudo, P. 121
Germany: addressees of attributions 71, **74**; Blockupy 17, 77; domestic senders in 72, **72**; European crisis 4, 64; Europeanization of public spheres 64; Europeanized attributions **76**; protest events 71; public budget 64
Gezi Park protests: AKP Istanbul Youth board 91, 96, 97; autonomization of Turkish citizens 97; Böll, Heinrich 92; civil society 86, 88, 90, **91**, 92–3; 1982 Constitution 89; democracy 88, 97; environmental protest 85; Europeanization 86–7, 97; European public sphere 86–9; Justice and Development Party 85; Marxist organizations 93, 94; Mazlumder 91, 95; neoliberalism 96; non-governmental organizations 88, 90; Özal, Turgut 89; police brutality 85; political violence 96; pro-Gezi activists 90–2, 96–7; pro-Kurdish institutions 94; social polarization 89, 97; TMMOB and DİSK organizations 94; Turkish civil society 89–90; Turkish public sphere 92–6; violence 89

INDEX

GJM *see* Global Justice Movement
Glasius, M. 120
global 'arenas,' public sphere as 120–2
global civil society 116–17; *alter ego* of 123–4; concept of 116, 119, 124; control of 118; Keane, J. 116; notion of 116; in pro-democracy movements era 122–4; reconceptualization of 5; rethinking 119; sceptics of 117–19, 123
global governing system 117
Global Justice Movement (GJM) 68
GlobalMay manifesto 40n12
'global moment' 119–22
'Global Spring' event 31, 36, 37
'glocalization' process 122–3
Goodhart, M. 118
'Grândola' 31, 41n16
grass roots-led movements 56
Great Recession 63
Greece: addressees of attributions 73; domestic senders 72, **72**; European crisis 64; Europeanized attributions **75**; policy measures 64; public budget 64
Greeks, the Germans and the Crisis (GGCRISI) 70

Habermasian perspectives 102
Habermas, J. 1, 116, 119, 124
'Habita' 36
Higgins, Joe 48
horizontal communication 14, 19
horizontal Europeanization 13, 64, 66–7, 71–6, 78, 87–8

Iceland Revolution 40n2
IMF *see* International Monetary Fund
Independents4Change group 53, 58
Indignados 32, 38, 121
Information Age 27
International Monetary Fund (IMF) 1, 13, 63, 101
international resonance 26, 29
Iraq war 15, 48, 123
Ireland: anti-austerity movement in 48–53; anti-bin changes movement in 48; anti-system parties 46; anti-war charges movement 52; civic activism 47; 'dysfunctional' nature of 56; Economic Adjustment Programme in 48, 51; economic inequality 48; first-past-the-post electoral system 46; gay and lesbian liberation movement 47; general election 50, 53; 'health check' of 47; Labour Party 45, 49, 50; left-vs.-right realignment in 50; neo-liberal policies 48; new political formation 53–9; parliament 46; political culture 46; political landscape in 47; politicians 46; public sector, austerity programme of 48; radical mass movement in 55; social movements in 47–8; social partnership agreements 55; trade unions 55; unemployment 48; Water in 2013 51
Irish Socialist Network 48
Irish Water's admission 52
Irish Women's Liberation Movement 47

'Janus face' of citizenship 129
Juntos Podemos 35
Justice and Development Party (AKP) 85

Kaldor, M. 120, 121
Kanellopoulous, K. 4
Keane, J. 116, 117, 119, 124
Konstantopoulou, Zoe 104
Kopstein, J. 122

Lafontaine, Oskar 104
'Largo do Carmo' 32

Madrid: escraches in 41n16; Geração à Rasca 31; Plan B in 105, 109–10; summit 107–8
Marcha Popular Indignada 29
Marchas de la Dignidad 29
Marches of Dignity 30
'Mareas' 29
Mareas Ciudadanas 29
Marés– Spanish Mareas 35
Marxist-Leninist vanguard party 56
Marxist organizations 93, 94
MAS *see* Movement for a Socialist Alternative
mass media systems 27, 66
Maude Barlow's Blue Planet Project 56
Mazlumder 91, 95
McDaid, Shaun 50
Mélenchon, Jean-Luc 104
monitoring governance 15, 19
Movement for a Socialist Alternative (MAS) 41n19
'movements of the squares' 121

NAMA National Asset Management Agency
national anti-austerity protests in European crisis 62; attribution of responsibility 65, 70; diagnostic framing 65; discursive actor attribution analysis 69–70; discursive Europeanization 67, 76–8, **77**; European public sphere 66–7; Germany 64; Global Justice Movement 68; Greece 64; horizontal Europeanization 67, 70, 71–6; mass media systems 66; national institutions 63; national public spheres 66, 67; prognostic framing 65; protest events 71–3; social movements 63, 67–9; transnational institutions 63; vertical Europeanization 67, 70, 71–6

INDEX

National Asset Management Agency (NAMA) 48
national democratic system 127
National Economic and Social Council (NESC) 55
NATO *see* North Atlantic Treaty Organization
neo-Tocquevillian models 116, 119
NESC *see* National Economic and Social Council
new social movements (NSM) 46
NGOs *see* non-governmental organizations
non-governmental organizations (NGOs) 88, 90
North Atlantic Treaty Organization (NATO) 14
NSM *see* new social movements

Occupy movement 1, 3, 9, 56, 115
Occupy Wall Street 121
Ogle, Brendan 49, 51, 52
'oligarchic Europe' 107
Özal, Turgut 89

PAH *see* Plataforma de Afectados por la Hipoteca
pan-European movements 14
'parity of participation' 6
participatory democracy 128, 132
'partitocracy' 28
People Before Profit Alliance (PBPA) 49, 55
Plan B *see* 'A Plan B in Europe'
Plan B for Europe (Plan B) 5
Plataforma de Afectados por la Hipoteca (PAH) 17, 29, 120, 121
Pleyers, G. 120
Podemos 4, 25, 31, 35, 52, 54–9, 59n3, 109
political communication 13
political decision-making system 131
Portugal: Carnation Revolution 1974 25; political groups 32; third-wave democracies 25
Portuguese anti-austerity movements 3, 25
Portuguese case: action forms and activist groups 32–3; diffusion, overview of **33–4**; exchanging ideas, channels of 37; framing 33–7; Geração à Rasca 31; international demonstrations 36; otherness, construction of 37–8; Spanish 'Indignados' movement 31–8
Portuguese framing 36
Portuguese government's austerity program 31
Portuguese movements 3–4
Pots and Pans Revolution 115
Pringle, Thomas 58
pro-democracy social movements 119–22; era of 124; global civil society in 122–4
professionalization 90
pro-Gezi activists 90–2, 96–7
progressive Irish government, policy principles for 54
pro-Kurdish institutions 94

public sphere(s) 1–2, 123–4, 127, 130–2; of civil society 6; conception of 2; Europeanization 4; 'general European public' 11, 16; Habermas' conception of 10; 'segmented publics' 11, 16; 'strong public' 11; supranational 14; transformation of 12–13 *see also* transnationalization of public spheres
Puerta del Sol Square 28, 31

Que se lixe a troika (QSLT) 31, 35, 37

'real democracy' 127
real/participatory democratic system 133
representative democracy 127
rethinking global civil society 5, 119; 'glocalization' process 122–3
Rieff, D. 117, 122
Right2Change 56, 57, 59
Right2Debt Justice 54
Right2Democratic Reform 54
Right2Education 54
Right2Health 54
Right2Housing 54
Right2Jobs and decent work 54
Right2-Water and Right2Change movements 4
Right2Water campaign 51
'Rios to Carmo' 41n17
Risse, T.: 'criteria of relevance' 14–15, 18; 'simultaneous claim-making' indicator 18; 'transnational' European sphere 14
Roose, J. 4

scholarship 90
'segmented publics' 11, 16
Selchow, S. 120, 121
SF *see* Sinn Féin
'simultaneous claim-making' 18
Single Transferable Vote (STV) 46
Sinn Féin (SF) 49
Socialist Workers' Party 49
social learning 13
social media 9, 21, 70, 94, 95
social movements 16–17, **17,** 21; activism 26; as civil society 3; community of communication 19; criteria of relevance 18; discourse convergence 18; discursive integration 20; dissemination and advocacy 3; European public sphere 63, 67–9, 78; monitoring governance 19; public sphere transformation 16; simultaneous claim-making 18; strong horizontal communication 19; as 'subaltern counterpublics' 16; territorial scope of claim-making 17, 18; transnationalization by 103; weak horizontal communication 19
social polarization 89

INDEX

social-political struggles 132
socio-economic situation 36
Sol's Proposal Commission 28
Sommer, M. 4
Southern Euroscepticism 107
sovereign parliaments 3
SP *see* Trotskyist Socialist Party
Spain: 15M movement in 31; third-wave democracies 25
Spain summit (February 2016) 105
Spanish case: diffusion, overview of **33–4**; formal democracy 21–38; Indignados movement 28–31; 15M's mobilization frames 28; 'partitocracy' 28; political claims 28; Portuguese case 21–38; pre-15M activists 29
Spanish democracy 30
Spanish frames 36
Spanish Indignados movement 25, 26
Spanish 15M movements 3–4
Spanish movement 26, 28, 35, 38
Spanish PAH platform 120
'state'/'political system' 123
'strong horizontal communication' 19
'strong publics' 3, 11
Structural Transformation of the Public Sphere, The (Habermas) 1, 10
STV *see* Single Transferable Vote
'subaltern counterpublics' 2, 9, 16, 104
supranational European public sphere 87
supranational public spheres 14
Syriza 101; capitalist system 56; political formation 52, 57; radicalism 59n3; Tsipras, Alexis 101; water charges protest movement 56

territorial scope of claim-making 17, 18
'transnational collective action' 1
transnational diffusion 27
transnational institutions 63, 127
transnationalization of public spheres 103; collective identification 15; 'criteria of relevance' 14–15; discourse convergence 15; discursive integration 15; emergence of 14; horizontal communication 14; monitoring governance 15; political communication 13; Risse's approach 14
Troika loan 48
Trotskyist parties 52, 55
Trotskyist Socialist Party (SP) 48
Tsipras, Alexis 101, 111
Turkish civil society 89–90
Turkish public sphere 92–6

United Nations (UN) 14
Universal Declaration of Human Rights 30
Urbán, Miguel 106, 109

Validating Council (VC) 111
Varoufakis, Yanis 104, 105, 109, 110
vertical Europeanization 67, 70, 71–4, 87
violence 89, 117; police 94, 96; political 96; against women 92, 93

'wave of contention' 1
'wave of global protests' 119–22
'weak horizontal communication' 19
West European parliaments 46
'Westphalian political imaginary' 2, 10